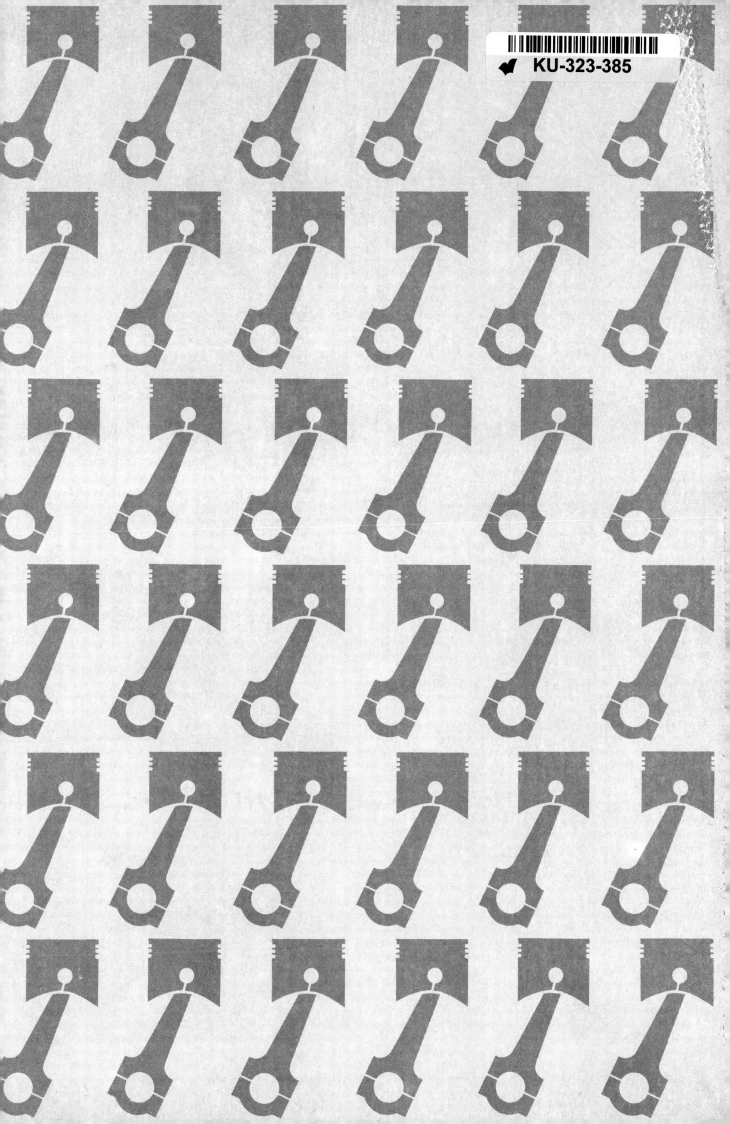

THE TOTAL BOOK OF
CAR REPAIRS
& MAINTENANCE

THE (TOTAL) BOOK OF
CAR REPAIRS & MAINTENANCE

Marshall Cavendish
London & Sydney

Consultant: Doug Mitchell
Editor: Eden Phillips
Art Editor: Graham Beehag
Designers: Jonathan Alden
            Jane Turton

Printed in Great Britain

Published by
Marshall Cavendish Books Limited
58 Old Compton Street,
London W1V 5PA

First published: 1980

Some of the material in this book was first
published by Marshall Cavendish Limited in the
partwork *On The Road*

ISBN 0 85685 763 7

Introduction

The modern motorist is faced with so many unavoidable costs – tax, insurance, fuel – that it makes sense to save money wherever economies can be made. By doing your own *Car Repairs and Maintenance* you can save on garage bills, breakdown emergencies and petrol wastage and keep motoring costs to a minimum. While the book does not pretend you will never need the services of a garage, it does aim to help keep your car running smoothly and show what to do when troubles occur.

There are chapters on the upkeep and repair of the bodywork, engine, electrics and running gear, describing how the parts of the car work and explaining procedures for servicing them. Information on topics such as rust prevention and cure, the carburettor, clutch and brakes is clearly set out, together with solutions to problems like what to do when the starter motor jams, how to cope with an over-heating engine, and how to understand a wiring diagram. Passing the Department of Transport roadworthiness test (or 'M.O.T.') is dealt with in detail, and this serves as a comprehensive check on the safety of the car. Each chapter is illustrated by a series of step-by-step photographs which explain the job in hand.

The section on emergency repairs describes measures to get you home in the event of a breakdown. The causes of likely problems and their remedies are carefully set out, and there are cross-references to the main text for subsequent, more thorough repairs. The book also contains the 'Automotive A-Z' – a comprehensive glossary of technical terms – and a detailed index to help you find the information you need as quickly as possible.

This is a book to keep in the car for safe, economical day-to-day maintenance, and to turn to if and when emergencies arise.

Foreword

I have a love-hate relationship with my car. I love it when it is going well and hate it when it lets me down. But to be honest, if it does let me down it is basically my own fault. In theory at least, a well-maintained car should never fail its owner, although 'teething troubles' direct from the factory are all too common. Once these are ironed out however, and you start doing your own car servicing, major repairs and garage jobs need be only a last resort.

Apart from making sure that all the important components are in good order and doing their jobs properly, regular servicing allows you to spot things which might otherwise go unseen. For example, if you inspect the condition of the brake linings periodically, you might find that a wheel cylinder has begun to weep fluid. Neglected, this will not only cause fluid loss from the reservoir, but the brake linings are almost certain to become contaminated and lose efficiency. If this happens they will have to be replaced however much 'meat' they have left – an unnecessary expense which can be avoided with a little basic know-how.

This book is designed to provide that know-how, with information on both prevention and cure, as well as delaying the inevitable wear and tear on a car. For instance, progressive corrosion in the bodywork can be arrested by regular cleaning, especially after driving on snow-covered, salt-treated roads. Nevertheless, rusting cannot be eliminated completely, and despite all precautions the bodywork will eventually begin to resemble the classic 'banger', with door sills of rusty fretwork. Do not despair, however, we show you how to repair rust damage, and although this is not an all-time cure it will keep the rust at bay for quite a long time.

Few motorists, however careful and expert they may be, can drive through the hurly-burly of town motoring without at some time becoming involved in a shunt, scrape or scratch. There is nothing more infuriating than for your car to be parked tidily outside the house and yet suffer a dent inflicted by some wretched incompetent who disappears into the night before you can get his number. Take heart, cosmetic treatments for the bodywork are also described.

If you use the car as anything more than a runabout it is wise to carry a few tools and spare parts. I remember an occasion when travelling as a passenger – for a change – to the Motor Show in Birmingham, an almost new Cortina suddenly showed the red ignition light burning brightly. The driver, not a inexperienced motorist, made a couple of appropriate comments on fan belts in general and his in particular, and pulled on to the hard shoulder of the M6. A quick look under the bonnet confirmed his diagnosis: a broken fan belt, and this only days after the car had been serviced by a garage.

Not having the benefit of a young lady companion willing to sacrifice her tights so we could make a temporary repair (this celebrated method is described, appropriately, under 'emergency procedures'), we had to wait for one of the motoring organisation's patrol vans to rescue us. Had we carried a spare fan belt, we could have been on our way within minutes, albeit with dirty hands, instead of having to wait impatiently for the van to arrive.

In the emergencies chapter of this book there are some ingenious ways to get you out of roadside bother, most of which derive from 'necessity is the mother of invention' thinking. When you are stuck on a silent moor, miles from any hope of succour, it is remarkable how the brain cells get to work on a problem.

To illustrate: I once received a letter from a reader of a magazine I was then editing telling an extraordinary story. He had been driving his Morris 1000 across a desert, and at one point, miles from anywhere, the engine refused to go further. It just spluttered and then petered out. The ignition was working properly and because of the conditions – dust blowing up everywhere as he drove along – he decided the problem was some sort of blockage in the carburation.

The first thing he looked at was the air filter, on the reasonable assumption that it had become clogged. It had. He shook sand free from the paper element, replaced the filter, and tried to start the engine. Nothing. Being of a logical mind, he then turned his attention to the carburettor. He checked there was petrol in the float chamber and since it was full, he decided that either the jet or the needle was at fault. So, off with the dashpot and out with the air piston and needle.

As he lifted the piston he thought he felt slight resistance, and guessed that the needle was sticking, which can happen if it is not properly centred in the jet. He examined the jet and the short flexible pipe which goes to the float chamber from the bottom of the jet, and found dirt. Consequently, he blew the jet and pipe clear of obstructions, and having done this, decided to centre the needle in the jet.

Disaster struck. As he loosened the needle it fell out of the piston into the engine compartment. He searched every inch of the compartment without success. He then rolled the car back and raked through the sand diligently. No needle. After half an hour he gave up searching and sat in the car thinking.

The nearest outpost of civilization was over fifty miles away. The road was little used and even if another driver came along he would be unlikely to have a spare needle. The alternatives seemed to be to hope for a tow – and if a vehicle did pass by would it have a tow rope? – or to abandon the car and search for a garage.

As he sat dolefully contemplating his plight, he noticed that the scrub on either side of the road consisted largely of tough thorn bushes. Ingenuity came to his rescue. He cut off one long thin thorn, whittled down its thicker end to fit the hole in the piston, and installed it where the needle should have been. He reassembled the carburettor, crossed his fingers and switched on. The electric pump dutifully clicked away, filling the float chamber. He tried the starter. Unbelievably, the engine fired first time.

With his heart somewhere near his tonsils, he drove on and reached civilization without further incident. Alas, his troubles were not yet over. Neither of the garages in the town where he found himself had any needles, and there were no old carburettors which could have been cannibalized. Nothing daunted, our ingenious traveller decided that luck was finally on his side, and drove to his destination – another 200 miles – without the engine missing a beat.

An unlikely story you might think, and at first I thought the same, but on reflection I came to the conclusion that it was so outlandish it had to be true. In any event, this story does illustrate the principle that in dire need ingenuity can get you out of what might at first appear to be an impossible predicament. The secret is, of course, not to get into a predicament in the first place, by looking after your car properly. Here is a book that aims to help you do just that. The emergency section should be a last resort. I hope you never need to use it.

Doug Mitchell

Contents

Preventing breakdowns

Even if you are the type of motorist who dreads ever having to look under the bonnet, you will still build up an awareness of how your car is running. The longer you drive a particular vehicle the more sensitive you become to signs of potential trouble. An unfamiliar rattle, a component vibrating or the engine misfiring – although not necessarily preludes to disaster – may be indications of poor performance. Working on the basis that prevention is better – and certainly cheaper – than cure, it is as well to open the bonnet regularly and make some simple checks. It will take only a short time and may save many hours of frustration. The cost of a breakdown can be very high, particularly if you are not a member of a recovery service.

Topping up the various fluid levels is one of the most straightforward, but important jobs on your car. For example, should the radiator lose all its water, or the battery not be checked frequently, the results could be disastrous – and expensive. So it pays to check the levels in the sump, radiator, hydraulic reservoirs and battery, and the windscreen washer bottle on a regular basis – ideally once or twice a week, and certainly before a long trip. Sustained cruising at fairly high speeds will inevitably place a different kind of stress on the components from normal day-to-day motoring.

There are two reasons for regularly checking levels. The obvious one is to make up for any loss of fluid in a particular component, but just as important is spotting a sudden decrease in a level—a pointer, perhaps, to a major fault.

Checking the oil level in the sump
Checking the oil level in the sump is easy. With the car on a flat surface and the engine switched off – for fifteen or twenty minutes – pull out the dipstick (see fig. 1). Wipe the end of the dipstick and then replace it in its holder. Now pull the dipstick out again and note the reading (fig. 2). If necessary, add oil to the engine until the oil level reaches the 'full' mark on the dipstick.

If the engine appears to be continuously losing oil, first look to see if you can see any obvious oil leaks. Check especially the drain plug at the bottom of the sump, the oil filter housing and the rocker cover gasket. If you cannot see any oil leaks then the engine may be burning oil, which is often the result of a worn engine (that is, wear in the piston rings, the cylinder bores or valve guides) and is much more serious.

Checking the cooling system
In the radiator, only a token amount of water – less than half a litre (a pint or so)—should be needed to bring the level up to the indicated point. That is, above the tops of the tubes in the header tank but below the overflow opening (figs. 3 and 4).

If you overfill the radiator it doesn't matter: the excess will eventually spill out through the overflow. But take care if there is anti-freeze in the system, as the spillage could lower the dilution rate of the anti-freeze with a consequent loss of protection against freezing.

Should the cooling system need consistent topping-up, check for leaks in the hoses (including the heater hoses), water pump, the thermostat area of the top radiator hose, the core plugs in the cylinder head and the joint between

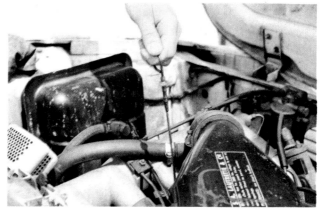

1 To check the level of the engine oil, place your car on a flat surface and switch off the engine. Then pull out the dipstick

2 Wipe the end of the dipstick with a rag and replace it in its holder. Now pull the dipstick out again and note its oil level

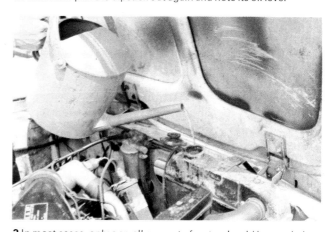

3 In most cases, only a small amount of water should be needed to top up the radiator. A watering can is ideal for this job

Nelson Hargreaves

4 Never fill your radiator up higher than this. The level should be above the header tank tubes but below the overflow opening

5 It is important to check the level of the hydraulic reservoirs on a regular basis. Keep the fluid away from the car's paintwork

6 You can make yourself a simple but effective battery filler at home with an empty washing up liquid bottle and some thin tubing

7 Having filled up the bottle with distilled water, you can now use your new filler to carefully top up each cell as necessary

8 Many modern batteries have this trough arrangement for topping up. Note the one-piece plastic snap-on lid on top of the battery

9 With some types of battery, it is possible to see the level of the electrolyte in each cell by looking through the casing

10 This heavily-sulphated battery terminal will almost certainly hinder any flow of current. Corrosion like this is due to neglect

the cylinder head and cylinder block. Check also the neck and the core of the radiator. A leak is usually easy to see by the stains of anti-freeze and rust, but it is possible for a concealed leak to occur in an area such as the heater matrix where the water will dribble away unseen. If the site of the leak cannot be found, a garage can conduct a pressure test of the cooling system quite cheaply.

Overheating is another cause of water loss. It immediately results in a high reading of the temperature gauge. Common causes of overheating include a slack fanbelt (which will also result in a low rate of battery charge), partial blocking at the radiator (including dirt clogging the honeycomb), a failing water pump or a partially blocked system which includes the cylinder block as well as the radiator. Additionally, a thermostat which is not opening fully or even a bottom hose that has become 'soggy' will restrict the flow of water and so cause the engine to overheat.

Topping up the hydraulic fluids
The amount of fluid needed to top up the hydraulic brake and clutch systems, via the small reservoirs in the engine compartment, should be minimal. If, during the course of your regular check, you find that either level has fallen to a marked extent you should immediately examine the entire hydraulic system for leaks.

Pipe unions will sometimes leak, and metal pipes can corrode over a period. Flexible pipes that rub against a suspension unit will rapidly wear away, while a concealed leak (inside a brake drum, for example) will often show up through stains on the brake back plate. To help you locate a brake hydraulic fluid leak, it is a good idea to have a friend sit in the car and press the brake pedal hard to set up pressure in the system.

When checking and topping-up the brake and clutch reservoirs (sometimes they are combined), it is essential to thoroughly clean the areas around the inspection caps—before you remove them—as this will help prevent dirt falling inside. Make sure also that each cap is clean and that the air holes are free from dirt.

Although it is generally recommended that you use a universal Girling fluid for a Girling system or a universal Lockheed fluid for a Lockheed system, any fluid that conforms to BS SAE J 1703 E will be safe in your car, unless it is a Citroen. (Some Citroens use a different hydraulic fluid and normal hydraulic fluid should *not* be used.)

Hydraulic fluids have an affinity for moisture, so the reservoirs and containers of the fluids should not be left open for longer than necessary. It is equally important that the fluids are not contaminated by petrol, mineral oil or any other material. They will attack and ruin any paint work and so care must be taken to avoid spilling; rags used for mopping up odd drips of hydraulic fluid should be thrown away to avoid any chance of their being used to wipe the bodywork of the car.

Servicing the battery

You may well need to top-up the battery each week as the level of the fluid—the electrolyte—falls through evaporation. Just how much evaporation takes place depends on whether the battery is situated in the engine compartment or not. The electrolyte of a battery housed in the boot, for example, may well evaporate less. The rate of evaporation will be higher in hot weather than in cold weather; also, too high a charging rate will cause excessive evaporation (to check the charging system, see pages 118-122) and an old battery will need more topping-up than a newer one.

The electrolyte in the battery is of sulphuric acid diluted by the addition of de-ionized water, more commonly known as distilled water. Distilled water is chemically pure and inert and it is the only liquid that can be used for maintaining the levels of the cells. Ordinary tap water should not be used in a battery because of the impurities it may contain. The lime content found in much tap water can, over a time, leave a deposit over the plates which will reduce the efficiency of the battery.

Ideally, you should check the levels in the battery when the car has been standing idle for some hours—overnight if possible. This is because the action of the charging system warms the battery to an extent, resulting in the electrolyte expanding slightly and giving you a false reading. Before starting the check, brush the top of the battery clean to avoid the chance of dirt falling into the cells.

Some 12-volt batteries have six separate covers on their tops and others have a one-piece snap-on lid. In the latter case, the battery may have an automatic-filling arrangement whereby the distilled water is dribbled into a trough. Plastic level-finders allow just the correct amount of water to enter each cell and then close. All that needs to be done is to wipe away excess water and replace the lid.

With other types of battery, simply add distilled water until the tops of the plates are just—and only just—covered. If too much distilled water is added, the expanding electrolyte forces an acid mist out through the breather holes in the filler caps or through any splits in the battery casing. The result is a soft, white powder-like substance, iron sulphate, which can attack the battery clamp assembly and the battery terminals. If you allow the level of the electrolyte to fall, lead sulphate forms and can do irreparable

damage to the battery, because it gradually covers the plates—and soon it is impossible to charge the battery because the current cannot reach the plates.

The best way to remove any iron sulphate that you spot on the battery clamp is to take the clamp away from the car and pour hot water over it (to deal with the battery terminals, see below). The iron sulphate will immediately dissolve. When replacing the clamp, make sure it holds the battery firmly in place for, if the battery is allowed to move about, the cells and plates may be damaged. Sulphation inside the battery can also be cured sometimes (see panel).

New batteries that have six separate covers on their tops are rare. The vast majority of modern car batteries have just the one piece lid on top (some Ford batteries are sealed for life and require no maintenance). You can make yourself a simple battery filler with an empty washing up liquid bottle and a length of windscreen washer tube (fig. 6). Fill up the bottle with distilled water and carefully top up each cell as necessary (fig. 7).

If one cell regularly consumes more distilled water than the others, premature failure of the cell or a small crack in the battery case could be the cause. If all the cells consistently use more than about 10 cc of water a week in hot weather, it may be due to overcharging or the battery itself may be failing. As long as the consumption of distilled water is equally low among the cells and the starter motor turns the engine over briskly, then the battery is performing well. In fact, given regular maintenance, a battery will last for at least three years and possibly as long as six.

Checking the battery terminals

The condition of the battery terminals is important because, if they have corroded or become loose, they may prevent your car even starting (see pages 38-39). To clean the terminals, use a screwdriver and then hot water (figs. 11 and 12) to remove any sulphation, dirt or rust. Then smear each terminal with a protector such as No Crode. Finally, make sure that the battery leads are in good condition and that the terminals are secure.

Using a hydrometer

The best d-i-y way to check the condition of the battery is by the use of a hydrometer, which measures the specific gravity of the electrolytes in each cell. The hydrometer works by taking a sample of the electrolyte and reading its

Curing sulphation

Sulphation in a battery can result from a number of causes: running the battery down by over-enthusiastic use of the starter, failing to keep the fluid level topped up, and using tap water rather than distilled water for topping up.

Provided it has not reached an advanced stage, it is sometimes possible to cure sulphation by continuously discharging and recharging the battery. You connect a flasher bulb across the battery to run it down, then trickle-charge it at about 1.5 amps, then discharge through the bulb again . . . and so on.

This treatment needs to be carried out for at least a week, which means of course that a spare battery will be needed. At the end of that time, a discharge-meter test will show if the sulphation has been eliminated.

specific gravity through marks on the instrument itself or by the position of a coloured float inside it.

To get a reliable reading, top up the cells and give the car a short run of about 5 km. Then insert the nozzle of the hydrometer into each cell in turn, squeezing the bulb on top to induce the electrolyte into it (fig. 16). Hold the instrument vertical and check its reading.

A reading of 1.280 shows a fully-charged cell, 1.200 is the sign of a half-charged cell, while 1.150 means the cell is completely discharged. In another design of hydrometer, the red portion of the float rising to the surface of the electrolyte means that the cell is discharged; the yellow section at the surface means a half-charge and the blue portion is a sign of a full charge (fig. 17).

All the cells should record about the same reading (either a full or nearly-full charge). If one cell shows a different reading from the others, it is a sign of fairly imminent failure; if all the cells give out a half-charge reading, the charging system could well be at fault, or the condition may be due to several short runs or heavy use of the starter. The battery can be charged either by a daylight run of 30 km or by the use of a trickle charger (fig. 18).

When the hydrometer shows a high state of charge in each cell, but there is a heavy loss of fluid, it is likely that the charging system is set at too high a rate. This fault can rarely be corrected at home and must usually be left to a garage to cure. Overcharging is a serious fault because the plates in the battery could distort or an internal short-circuit could arise. It is also possible that the battery is nearing the end of its life and, because of this, is drawing heavily on the full output of the generator.

An even more exact check on the condition of a particular cell in a battery can be carried out by a garage with a

13 The sulphation will now dissolve, but it will soon return if the terminals are not protected. So undo the battery post clamp

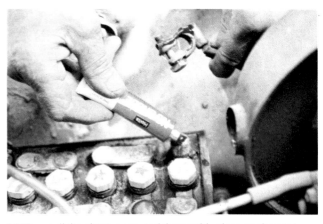

14 Then pull the clamp away and thoroughly clean up the post. Give both the post and the clamp a generous coating of No Crode

11 All battery sulphation must be removed. To do this, first use a screwdriver to scrape away as much of the corrosion as you can

15 Return the clamp to its post and tighten the clamp firmly. Do not forget to treat the other battery terminal in the same way

Nelson Hargreaves

12 Next, carefully pour some hot water over the terminal. Take care you do not soak any of the other electrical components

16 To test the condition of a cell in a battery simply place the nozzle of a hydrometer into the cell and squeeze the bulb on top

17 This will draw the electrolyte into the hydrometer. You can now check its reading. This particular cell is only half-charged

18 A trickle charger can be used to charge up a flat battery at home. It is best to remove the battery from the car to do this

19 A crack in the battery casing can occasionally be repaired. First use a sharp knife to cut a clear path for the repair paste

21 When the repair is dry, the cell will have to be filled with dilute sulphuric acid. An auto electrician may have to do this

20 When the walls of the repair are as dry as possible, work in the repair paste—this example is Batrepair—with your knife

22 You can remove much of the traffic film that accumulates on the windscreen with an additive in your windscreen washer fluid

high-rate discharge tester. This machine throws a massive load on each cell for about 10 seconds. A good cell will maintain a reading of 1.5-1.8 volts during the test period, and one that cannot manage this is failing. If you find that one cell has failed, you must replace the battery, as it is not possible to make repairs.

Repairing cracks in the battery casing

A crack in the battery casing can sometimes be repaired, but there is no guarantee that the repair will be successful for any length of time. This is because the walls of the crack will absorb any acid leaking out, so it is difficult to make any repair 'stick'. On the other hand, there is little to lose and a great deal to gain in attempting to repair a crack especially in view of the prices of new batteries.

First remove the battery from the car and stand it on a plastic surface. Carefully clean it with detergent and a nail brush to remove all traces of dirt, oil and grease. Next, carefully widen out the crack with the blade of a small knife (fig. 19) and make the repair with a battery-case cement (a typical example is Batrepair, available from motor accessory stores). Push the filler firmly into the crack, leaving a fairly generous overlap (fig. 20).

When the repair is complete, the cell will have to be filled with dilute sulphuric acid at a specific gravity of 1.280 due to the loss of the electrolyte. To do this, it may be necessary to take the battery to an auto electrician for filling.

Topping up the windscreen washer bottle

Windscreen washer bottles need filling up at intervals (in Britain, for example, it is illegal to allow a washer bottle to run dry) but ordinary water may not be able to cope with the oily content of the atmosphere, especially in areas of high-traffic density.

A small amount of washing-up liquid added to the washer water will help remove traffic film and haze from the windscreen. Alternatively, products such as Decosol All-Seasons Screen Clean—available from motor accessory stores—do the same job and, in addition, prevent the washer fluid from freezing in winter.

Topping up the dashpot
A check-point often overlooked is the dashpot of variable jet carburettors. A metal or plastic cap on the top of the carburettor has to be unscrewed and the fluid brought up to the level mark. Fresh engine oil is usually suitable for this, or a special dashpot oil can be obtained from accessory stores. If the dashpot is allowed to run dry, the idling mixture tends to become lean and acceleration may become jerky.

Cleaning the crankcase breather valve
When the engine is running, it is essential that the crankcase is adequately ventilated; there must be a flow of clean air through the engine to prevent a build-up of pressure in the crankcase (caused mainly by gases leaking past the pistons on the compression and firing strokes). The clean air also reduces any contamination of the oil with by-products from the combustion chamber, and helps to remove any fuel or water which would dilute the crankcase oil. If these gases, water and unburnt fuel are not removed from the crankcase, then sludge and acids could soon cause the lubrication system of the engine to clog up and the engine bearings to be starved of oil and fail.

Although crankcase ventilation systems vary in layout and

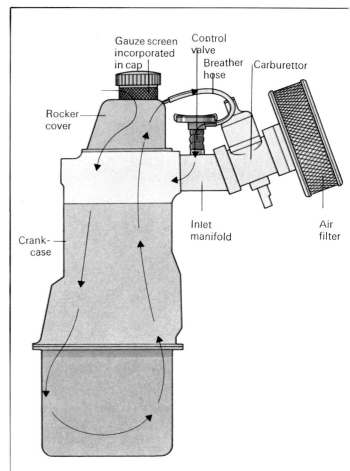

25 This type of regulator valve is found on the Triumph 2500

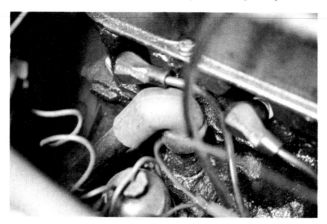

23 An elementary type of crankcase ventilation. The fumes from the crankcase are drawn out of this pipe and into the atmosphere

Nelson Hargreaves

24 Any fumes inside the rocker box are transferred via the pipe to the air cleaner where they re-enter the engine and are burnt

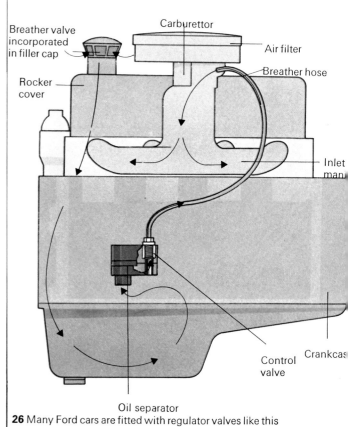

26 Many Ford cars are fitted with regulator valves like this

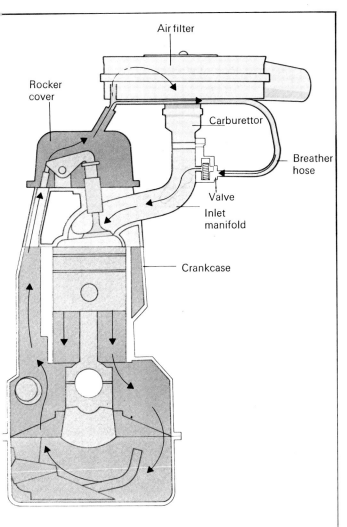

27 Some Fiats have a regulator valve fitted in the carburettor

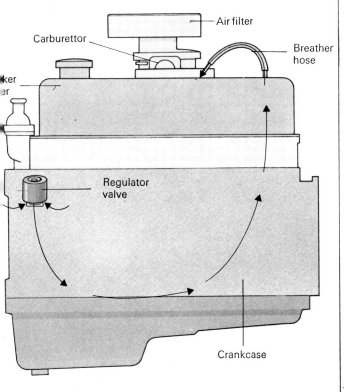

28 Several Leyland cars have a regulator valve on the crankcase

design (for example, not every system has a breather-valve you can clean out), their purpose is the same—to remove unwanted gases from the crankcase. The engines in the majority of cars built before the mid-1960s were ventilated by means of a simple open-ended pipe to the atmosphere. The pipe, fitted from the crankcase, projects below the bottom of the engine (fig. 23). The motion of the car and the rotation of the crankshaft helps the build-up of fumes in the crankcase to be drawn out of the pipe and into the atmosphere, while clean air can enter only when the engine is stopped.

A breather of this type needs little maintenance beyond occasionally checking that the pipe has not become clogged. In most cases, the pipe is a press-fit into the crankcase and is held in place by a small bracket.

In later versions, a wire-mesh filter is sometimes built into the engine end of the pipe. Its main purpose is to trap oil which would otherwise drip out of the pipe. The filter is liable to become clogged by sludge and periodic cleaning is necessary. The mesh can usually be prised out of the pipe for washing in paraffin (kerosene), or the whole pipe can be removed and immersed in paraffin and swilled around until it is clean.

Newer than the 'open' ventilation arrangement is a flexible rubber or plastic pipe running from the rocker-box cover to the air filter housing (fig. 24). The induction effect of the carburation removes the fumes and pressure from the rocker-box back into the engine. The heavier oil fractions in the fumes collect on the air filter and the remainder goes back into the engine to be consumed by the normal action of combustion.

The main thing to look for in this system is a blockage of the breather pipe, as a considerable amount of sludge can collect inside the pipe to restrict its internal diameter and, in some cases, block it completely. Check also that the pipe has no cracks and that its retaining clips are tight. In this, and other crankcase ventilation systems, a wire mesh gauze filter is often incorporated in the oil filler assembly—usually in the cap itself. Again, simply remove the filter and clean it in paraffin.

When the laws governing air pollution became stricter, a new emission control system for car engines was necessary. Now filtered air is drawn into the crankcase through the oil filter or a separate filter on the side of the engine and the fumes are directed from the crankcase to either the carburettor or (in the majority of cases) the inlet manifold to be burnt with a fresh supply of fuel/air mixture. But if too much air were allowed to flow into the inlet manifold while the engine was idling, the carburation would be affected. To compensate for this, a regulator valve is fitted to control the amount of air. This valve is usually to be found either on the inlet manifold (fig. 25) or in series with the pipe running from the crankcase to the inlet manifold (fig. 26). Occasionally it is fitted in the carburettor (some Fiats, fig. 27, use this system) or to the outside of the crankcase fig. 28, where air enters.

The valve should be checked and cleaned out if necessary as part of the servicing routine. To do this, carefully dismantle the regulator valve and, having noted their correct location, clean all the components in petrol. If the valve is or looks faulty the only answer is to replace it with a new one. A damaged regulator valve will certainly result in the engine performing badly—running-on and stalling in particular. It is also often the cause of blue smoke coming from the exhaust pipe, especially on overrun. Most manufacturers recommend that both valve and filter are replaced at 20,000 km (12,000 miles).

Nigel Osbourne

17

Easy bodywork repairs

Repairing and repainting their cars' bodywork is a job from which some d-i-y- mechanics shy away. Yet the work involved is not difficult, calling for care and patience rather than a high degree of skill or experience.

The most important things are to take time over your preparation work and to choose your aerosol paints carefully. That done, you will find that the results you can achieve can be thoroughly professional.

A flying stone hitting the front of the car can crack the paint film and allow water—and often salt—to seep in and get to work on the metal beneath. After a couple of months the surrounding paintwork will begin to lift and blister and the entire damaged area will have to be removed.

To do this, take a small penknife and lift off all the damaged paint, which will flake away without effort. Keep chipping away at the paint film in a circular pattern until shiny, untarnished metal is revealed all round. Still using the penknife, scrape away any flaking, rusty metal exposed underneath and blow away the dust.

To remove the final traces of rust and stop it spreading underneath your new paint coat, use a rust killer. Some proprietary brands can be painted on with a small paint brush or, if the rust has really got a hold, worked in with a wire brush. The rust killer should be left for a time (see the instructions on the bottle or tin), and then wiped off.

Sanding down

Smoothness is essential in respraying, so the next step is to sand down the affected areas. Use wet-and-dry sanding paper in two grades—a fairly coarse one such as 180 grade, and a fine one such as 360.

With the coarser paper, begin dry sanding from the centre of the rust spot backwards and forwards right over the exposed metal area and slightly overlapping the good paintwork around its edges. By running your finger lightly over the affected area you will feel all the little bumps and lumps—not least where the edge of the good paint layer stands proud. All these irregularities must be removed.

Then, with a wet piece of fine-grade paper, begin wet-flatting, using less pressure. Keep flatting until you begin to 'peel' back the top coat to expose the layers of undercoat and primer underneath—each will be a different colour. Keeping the area of exposed metal as small as possible, but large enough to ensure that all the rust-affected metal has been removed, go on flatting until the whole area is absolutely smooth to the touch.

Repairing small dents

Small dents—too obvious to be just touched in with paint, but not big enough to warrant panelbeating or filling in with glass fibre—can ruin the appearance of an otherwise spotless vehicle. These are filled in with body filler.

The filler will need a surface to grip on that is rough, but not loose and flaking. So first chip away all the loose paint and rusting metal and treat the area with rust killer. Then rough up, with a sheet of ordinary coarse sandpaper, the remaining paint surface all over the area you are going to fill. Go slightly beyond the limit of the repair so that every bit of filler can get a firm grip.

Now for the filler. A trip to your car accessory shop

1 Rust spots usually fan out beneath the surrounding paintwork. So chip off all the flaking paint with the blade of a penknife

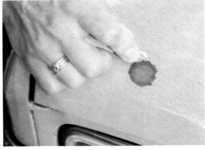

2 Keep chipping away until all the loose paint and rust has gone, and bare metal emerges in a roughly circular area

3 Using a fairly coarse wet-and-dry (about 180 grade) dry sand the patch area, working from the middle towards the edges

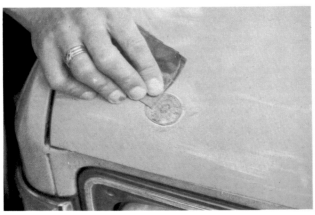

4 With a fine grade paper, extend the sanded area until it just overlaps the adjoining paintwork and the whole is perfectly smooth

5 To prevent rust from spreading under your new paintwork, use a rust killer. Paint it on or wire-brush it into the metal

will reveal a variety of makes. A particularly good one is Plastic Padding, which is to some degree elastic. Its flexibility is an asset on an area where there is a lot of vibration, jolting or jarring. (It has been known for an entire wadge of filler to jump right out as the car goes over a bump in the road.) Another good brand is Isopon.

These fillers are of the two-pack variety; in one packet is the resin containing the filler material, and in the other is the hardener. Kept apart they have a life of two to four years, but mixed together they go off in just ten minutes or so. They are resistant to petrol, oil, water and many acids and, unlike household plasters, do not shrink or crack.

Because of the chemicals they contain, undue skin contact should be avoided with fillers of this type. Hands and tools can be cleaned with cellulose thinners.

Immediately before filling, degrease the whole area to which the filler is to be applied—this is vital for proper adhesion. Use paraffin (kerosene) or turps. substitute to remove the car polish, then detergent and water, and finally clean warm water for this job.

Once the area is bone dry, mix the filler thoroughly, following the maker's instructions. Use a piece of card, or a plastic spreader, to build up the filler a thin layer at a time, working from the centre of the dent outwards. Keep filling until the filler stands slightly proud of the surrounding surface.

If the filler tends to 'sag' out of the hole, it is because your layers are too thick. Scrape back the surface, press the remaining filler well in, leave it to harden, and then mix and add another layer.

The two-pack fillers harden by chemical reaction, so they harden right through at the same rate and can be sanded after about 30 minutes. When sanding, use a coarse sandpaper to obtain the approximate contours of the repair. Then finish off with a fine-grade wet-and-

dry to ensure a perfectly smooth finish that merges into the surrounding bodywork. Do not use a flat sanding block except on a perfectly flat surface; a flexible rubber or plastic block will better follow the contours.

Wipe every speck of dust off the surface with a lint-free rag and clean water before painting.

Matching colours

Manufacturers of vehicle refinishing paints for the trade have formulations for thousands of different colours from car manufacturers all over the world. In some cases they even have several variations on the same colour, compounded in different ways.

The range available in d-i-y aerosols is smaller, but your chances of matching your car's original colour are quite high. In Britain, for example, the Duplicolor range includes 350 of the most popular shades.

You can tell as you rub down what colour of primer was used for the original job, and whether a different finishing colour has been applied at any stage. Buy a primer to match the original one, if possible, since the colour of the primer can affect the colour of the top coat. The standard primer colours are grey and red oxide, but some of the more exotic finishing colours are used over special primers.

A small metal plate fixed on every car—most often under the bonnet—will tell you the manufacturer's code for the original finish colour. Your motor accessory dealer should be able to match this colour from stock, or by buying it in for you. Failing this, try a main agent for your make of car; the big importers carry extensive stocks of aerosols in their more popular colours.

If your car has already been resprayed, you will have to experiment on a sheet of scrap material until you find an aerosol that matches.

And if you find it impossible to match either the

6 To fill the tiny irregularities in the metal, squeeze out small quantities of filler and hardener on a sheet of cardboard

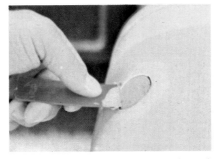

7 Using the spreader supplied, or a piece of card, apply a thin layer of filler over the metal and leave it to dry hard

8 Next, smooth off the filler with a fine grade wet-and-dry. Use your fingertips to check that it is perfectly smooth

9 Using newspaper and masking tape, mask off the surrounding area. Press the tape down firmly to prevent paint 'creeping'

10 After wiping the whole area clean, apply the first coat of primer — a light coat to cover the patch and adjacent paintwork

Richard Thomas

19

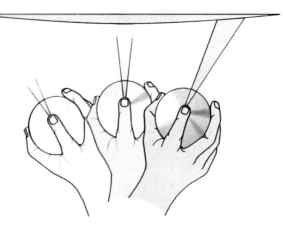

11 The wrong way (above) and the right way (below) to spray. Keep the wrist flexible and spray in a straight line for an even coat

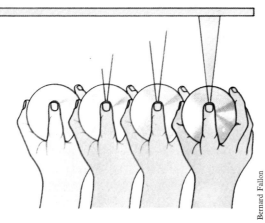

Bernard Fallon

original primer or top coat, your only recourse is to mix your own colours and use a spray gun instead of an aerosol.

One small problem remains: the paint from your aerosol may end up brighter than the car's original colour if the latter has faded and weathered. This can be dealt with either by using cutting paste as described below, or by using a clear spray (which has a slightly yellowish tinge) over both the new paint and the original. Again, a trial run using a piece of scrap material will be worthwhile.

Making sure paint is compatible

The aerosol you buy will almost certainly contain a cellulose paint; the vast majority do. This can be used over any original factory finish. It can also be used over a resprayed finish—provided the refinishing firm used a cellulose or acrylic, and not a synthetic, paint.

Most professional refinishers do use cellulose paints. But if your car has been resprayed with a synthetic paint, and you try to use cellulose over the top, crinkling of the new paint surface will result and the finish will be quite unacceptable.

So if you are certain that your car's paint is the original finish, you can go ahead with confidence. Alternatively, if it has been resprayed and you know which firm did the job, you can ask them what kind of paint they used. If they used a synthetic, the only way out is to apply a coat of 'isolater'—unfortunately not available in d-i-y aerosols—between the old paint and the new.

If in doubt, test with your aerosol a small area that is hidden from view; inside the boot lid is a good place.

Masking

An aerosol will, by its very nature, spray some paint over a far wider area than you want to cover. So masking off those parts that you do not want to spray is essential, and the car should stand well clear of anything else— another car, for example—that 'stray' paint would disfigure. Even a light breeze will carry paint a long way.

Do not mask too close to the patch. Instead, allow room for the primer and new top coat to overlap the existing paintwork by 2.5-5 cm (an inch or two). Lay newspaper down over the area you do not want to paint, and secure its edges with masking tape to ensure that no

12 When the first coat of primer is dry (about 15-20 minutes) apply the second. This time it can be applied more thickly

13 Once the primer is dry, well-flat it with a fine grade paper, such as 600 grade, to smooth it in with the original paint

14 Carefully remove the masking tape and move it back a few centimetres so that the top coat entirely covers the primer

15 A further, light wet-flatting at this stage removes any stray particles of primer that have landed around the edges

16 Next, wipe the entire area with a damp cloth and leave it to dry. Be sure to remove any traces of masking tape

Richard Thomas

17 As you begin topcoating, fully depress the aerosol button — and make sure that the sprayed area begins on the masking material

When colours fail to match

New paint on a small repair job cannot always be matched with the original paintwork, especially if this has faded.

But professional finishers try to avoid having an obvious join where the new paint meets the old. One trick is to lay the new paint over the old in a series of steps, so that the change in colour from one step to the next is barely visible.

On the actual repair area (represented by A in the illustration at left below), they spray pure colour. On a larger area (A and B) they dilute the colour slightly with clear paint so that the old paint shows through slightly. On a still larger area (A, B and C) they dilute even further so that the old paint shows through distinctly.

This makes the change from new to old gradual, not sudden.

The technique cannot be used with aerosol paints, since mixing is impractible.

But the 'next best thing' is shown in the illustration at right below. After the repair area has been given its two or three coats, clear paint (not thinners) is sprayed over the repair area and a surrounding area.

This produces three visual 'steps'—old paint; old paint plus clear; new paint plus clear—and helps blur the edges of the colours.

Try to keep the colour joins where they will be least noticeable—for example, along a ridge in the car's sheet metal work, or where the narrow window surround meets a larger panel below.

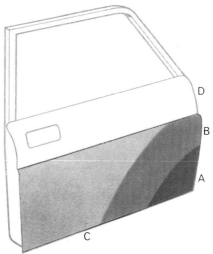

18 The 'professional' way to disguise non-matching paint

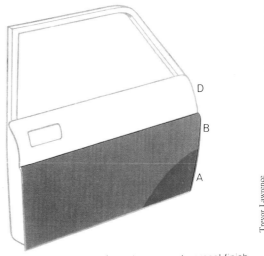

19 An amateur alternative, using a transparent aerosol finish

Trevor Lawrence

loose spray can reach the paintwork below. Seal any joints in the newspaper with masking tape, and use tape to cover any trim such as mirrors or door handles. Press all the tape down firmly.

When spraying inside a garage, open a window to ensure good ventilation. The solvents which evaporate into the air will not harm you in the small quantities contained in an aerosol, but prolonged work in a confined space should be avoided. When working in the open air choose a day that is dry, with little wind, and try to avoid dust falling on to newly-sprayed surfaces.

Priming
Before you apply the top coat you will need to put on a primer. The primer has a number of functions. First, it is a rather coarse material which helps to fill the minor surface irregularities that the filler—however carefully you have flatted down—is almost certain to contain. Second, it adheres strongly to metal to protect it. And finally, it also adheres strongly to the top coat which follows.

Applying the primer is quite easy, and in fact provides good practice for the more tricky task of spraying the top coat. But if you have a large area to spray and you are not confident of your ability to spray evenly it is worth using some paint on a 'trial run'. A large sheet of metal panelling is best for this. Alternatives are the garage wall

(though this will absorb oversprayed paint and will not tell you if your work will run) or the shiny side of a sheet of hardboard.

The can should be held upright—or, for horizontal surfaces such as a roof or bonnet, as near upright as possible—and about 25-30 cm (10in.-12in.) from the surface to be sprayed. (Read the instructions on the can for extra guidance.)

Just before the swing of your arm makes the can reach the surface you want to paint, press the aerosol head fully down. (Partially depressing the button will result in too little paint being expelled.) This way, paint will be sprayed on the paper and masking tape—but by the time the spray hits the car it will have achieved its correct pattern and will give good coverage. Continue spraying fractionally on to the masking material at the end of each sweep to ensure coverage at the other end too.

Fully release the spray head after each sweep and, starting from the top and working down, ensure that each sweep overlaps the one above by about 2.5 cm (1in.). This is to avoid 'striping'—alternate bands of thick and thin paint which can be particularly noticeable on large areas, such as a full door panel.

With the first coat, aim to cover the entire area with just enough primer to conceal all the bare metal or filler. Do not try to spray on too much primer at one go—it will only run and sag. Instead, build up the paint in layers,

20 While each coat is drying, use thinners (or, if necessary, cutting paste) to remove any over-spray from nearby paintwork

21 Small dents in which rust has not yet begun showing through can be treated in much the same way as rust-affected areas

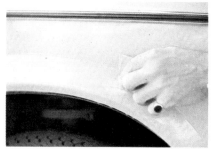

22 First, rough up the surface with a coarse sandpaper. Then fill, sand, prime and topcoat as described above

allowing each thin coat to dry (normally, this takes about 15 minutes) before applying the next.

If you do get a sag or run, leave the paint to dry thoroughly, then wet-flat it down with a fine-grade wet-and-dry (360-400), leave it to dry and start again.

After two or more coats of primer have been applied and left to dry thoroughly, peel off the masking tape and leave for at least two hours before wet-flatting down.

Top coating

First, remask the area, leaving a fairly generous amount of the original paintwork exposed to ensure that the new paint completely covers the patched area. Next, shake the can of finish paint thoroughly, and test it on a piece of scrap material to make sure you have the colour you want (it is not unknown for cans to be wrongly labelled).

The same spraying technique that you used for the primer is correct for the top coat. Extra care is needed this time, though, to see that the spray head is held at exactly the right distance from the car surface. Too close, and you may get runs or sagging; too far away, and you may get a rough surface finish, due to some tiny paint particles starting to dry out before they hit.

It is always better to under-spray than over-spray. Although under-spraying may reduce the glossiness of the final finish, this is preferable to using so much paint that the whole lot runs and you have to sand it off and start again.

Two coats will probably be enough to give a satisfactory finish, but a third coat will do no harm (provided the first two have dried!) and may enhance the finish. Leave the paint to dry with the masking materials in place for at least two hours, and see that no rain or dust gets on the finish until it dries hard (about 12 hours).

Remove the masking tape carefully. If the new finish does not blend in satisfactorily with the old, use a cutting paste—sparingly!—on both the new paint and the surrounding area. Then polish thoroughly.

23 The finished job

Richard Thomas

Rustproofing

Rust is the biggest single cause of a car's deteriorating. It attacks two main areas—the lower parts of the body, which are subject to the impact of stones and grit, and the inner skins of the structural box-sections, into which water finds its way through tiny joints not fully closed in manufacturing. In addition, any rust which has settled on a sheet of steel in the factory will keep on spreading until its progress is stopped.

A rust-prevention treatment is ideally suited to a new car where, hopefully, rust has not had a chance to get far. Older cars can also be treated, but only formation of further rust can be prevented. Rustproofing will not clear up existing rust damage.

Rustproofing involves scraping all the mud and dirt that has collected on the underside of the car, brushing off any flaking rust and applying one or more coats of an under-body protection material. The process also includes spraying inside the sills and box sections (fig. 2) with a rust-preventive fluid.

This is a long and messy job. Its main benefit is that the rust will be virtually banished for years. It is also likely that noise inside the car will be less, and that the car will fetch a higher trade-in-price.

Removing the mud
The easy way of removing the dirt from underneath is to take the car to a specialist garage with a steam-cleaning service. High-pressure steam blasts all the mud from the underside of the car and also removes any oil and grease.

To clean the underneath of the car yourself, you will need some scrapers and a wire brush. You will also need a hose and some old clothes, preferably a set of overalls. Wearing a balaclava helmet and a face mask is a good idea.

In order to make a thorough job, the car will have to be jacked up fairly high. So for safety's sake it will be worthwhile to hire a trolley jack and axle stands. (A trolley jack in particular can be expensive to buy.)

With the car jacked up and the axle stands in position, remove the road wheels. This makes it easier to reach the wheel arches. To ensure that the brakes are not contaminated by the rust preventative, tie a polythene bag over the brake assembly and steering joints.

Dry dirt can easily be removed, but the lack of water will produce clouds of dust. So thoroughly wet the underside of the car so that all the dirt is sodden and can be prodded away with a scraper. Most of the dirt will fall away fairly easily, but a wire brush will probably be needed to shift mud away from odd crevices. Every bit of dirt should be removed, or the action of the rust preventative will be spoilt.

Patches of oil and grease will call for special attention with a detergent or degreaser, and any flakes of peeling paint or rust must be wire-brushed away. Do not use an electric drill with a wire-brush attachment; apart from being too harsh, it tends to shower you with dirt.

Heavily-rusted areas should be thoroughly scraped and then a rust killer (for example, Jenolite) applied.

Brush-applied sealant
One type of d-i-y underside sealant (a good one is available from Holts) takes the form of a 'paint' which is applied with a brush. Such paints usually have a bitumen/rubber base which withstands physical impacts from stones and grit as well as providing a water-repellent layer.

Sprayed-on sealant
The alternative to the paint is a wax-based spray such as Rustex. Good kits of this type include a special hand-operated spray gun, a gallon of sealant for inside the doors and box sections, a gallon of underbody protector, a spray gun, various lances and an instruction manual. There are also plugs to block up the holes through which the material is sprayed.

The process is much the same as with a brush-on sealant, except that the job is usually a little easier because it is possible to work a short distance away from the area of metal being covered, thus avoiding the chance of the protective material falling on to one's face.

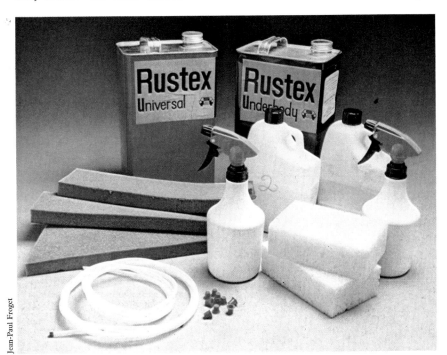

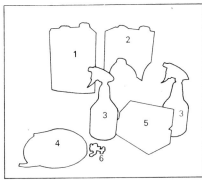

1 This d-i-y rustproofing kit includes (1) a gallon of sealer for inside the car's box sections (2) a gallon of underbody spray (3) two spray guns (4) three plastic probes of various lengths (5) two sponges and (6) plastic plugs for stopping the holes that you drill in box sections. These sections, although sealed, are prone to rust that creeps in via the hairline joints left in manufacturing. A good d-i-y rustproofing system lets you deal with this rust. Not all commercial treatments are so thorough.

Jean-Paul Froget

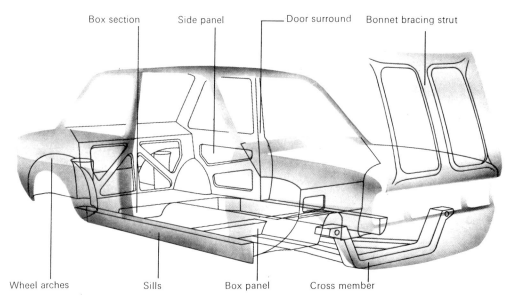

Box section   Side panel   Door surround   Bonnet bracing strut

Wheel arches   Sills   Box panel   Cross member

Antonio Toma

2 A modern unitary-construction car contains many box sections, all of which need to be found and treated in a thorough rustproofing job

Using the sealant

The material—spray or brush—is best applied in a fairly thin coat followed by a second, and even a third, coat when the first has dried. As a fairly thin coat dries out quite quickly, the first half of the car is usually ready for the second coat by the time the other half has been completed.

When applying the material, avoid the handbrake cables, adjuster points, grease nipples and other items that demand periodic attention. The best method of protection is to tape them securely with masking tape. Metal brake pipes can safely be treated, but keep the material away from the propeller shaft.

Pay special attention to the jacking points and sub-frames bolted to the main bodywork. Work the brush or spray along these joints with plenty of compound, but try not to block up any drain holes.

'Mud trap' areas—under the front wings and other places—will have become obvious when the car was

being cleaned. Wheel arches, where abrasion is a problem, can benefit from extra layers of the material. When the job is completed, it is a good idea to use in these places any sealant left over.

Some cars may have deflector plates fitted to keep the worst of the mud away. If these plates can be easily removed, do so and work behind them. Otherwise, treat the plates themselves and work the rust-preventative behind them.

Treating the exhaust is a waste of time since the compound rapidly burns off. Similarly, electrical connections should not be treated in case the material works between the connections to form an insulating barrier. But on old cars whose battery carrier is underneath, it is well worth treating the carrier thoroughly, as it is subjected to attacks from road-borne contaminations as well as any leakages of acid from the battery.

Keep the material away from leaf springs and moving parts of the suspension. Avoid also the breather holes around the back axle.

Where the bodywork is concealed by the bumpers, the material can be extended slightly up the outside of the car on top of the paint, to offer protection against stones and grit. A strip of masking tape along the sills will allow the sealant to be applied to the outside of the

3 (below) Commercial steam cleaning thoroughly removes the dirt from under the car. Water and a wire brush is cheaper—but harder

4 When the underside of the car is dry, apply one or two coats of the sealer. Wheel arches need especially thorough treatment

5 When the bottom edges of paintwork are out of sight, they too can be sprayed. Use masking tape to give a clean finishing edge

car along its lower edges, where it cannot be easily seen. This extra work is well worthwhile because it is the lowest parts of the car that are most prone to corrosion.

The materials used for underbody protection are safe enough to use, but care should be taken to avoid inhaling any fumes. Keep the material away from naked lights. Odd drips of the material finding their way on to the paintwork can be removed, while they are still damp, with a rag dipped in turps. substitute or whatever other solvent is suggested on the container.

Inside the box panels
The box panels call for more specialized treatment. The idea is to put two or three layers of rust preventative material all round the insides of box panels in order to provide a barrier against moisture. In some cases, new cars may have had their sills already treated by the manufacturers, but no harm is done by adding further protection.

Start with the inner sills. In many cases, removing the carpets will reveal holes suitable for inserting the nozzle of the probe supplied. If there are no such holes, a 6 mm ($\frac{1}{4}$ in.) drill will make a row of openings, say, two or three per sill.

Feed the probe into the sill until it can be felt to have reached the end. Pump the spray gun to start the liquid flowing and as the pumping continues, bring the probe slowly back towards the hole. The liquid will flow all around the sill interior and find its own way into odd corners. By the time the second sill has been treated, the first will be ready for a second application.

The outer sills may have drain holes in them already. If this is the case check that the drain holes are free and not choked with mud. Apply the material in the same manner as before.

Cross-members supporting the steering and rear suspension assemblies can easily be reached from inside the car by drilling through the floor. Drill a hole

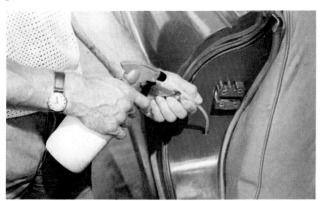

6 Side panels often have existing holes through which a probe can be inserted while you spray their interiors

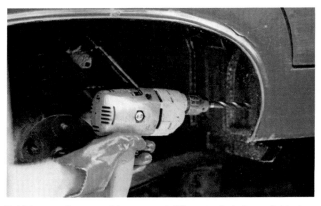

7 All box sections must be sprayed. Where no hole is available for the probe, drill one and fill it later with the pvc plug supplied

8 Door surrounds need a thorough coating. With this kit, a range of probes is supplied so that you can reach the farthest recesses

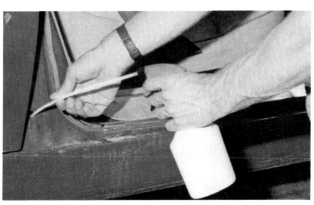

9 The bottom parts of door surrounds are treated in the same way. Wipe any 'dribbles' off the paintwork with turps. substitute

Jean-Paul Froget

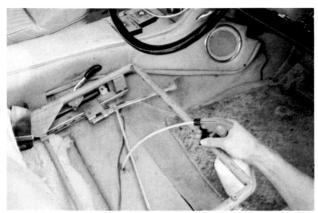

10 Lifting the seats or removing the carpets will give easy access to most box panels in the floor. Welding marks help to locate them

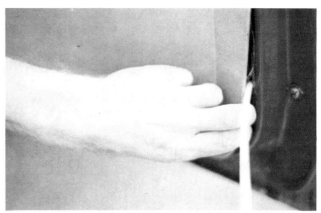

11 Pull the trim aside to reach the bottoms of the doors. Make sure the windows are closed so you do not splash spray on the glass

in each section to insert the probe and follow the same routine.

Structural sections that brace the floor can be found by looking for twin rows of weld marks, which show up as small dents in the floor. A hole can be drilled anywhere between a pair of such lines to allow the probe to enter. If the location of the sections cannot be found from inside the car, it will be necessary to go underneath and drill through the sections themselves.

The bottom parts of doors tend not to be as vulnerable as they were a few years ago, but nevertheless they should still be treated. Drain holes are usually found under the doors and these holes (cleared of mud if necessary) make good probe-holes. Otherwise a 6 mm ($\frac{1}{4}$in.) hole will be needed.

12 Alternatively, you can reach the bottoms of the doors without touching the glass by using the longest probe — in this case, 1 m

Slide the probe upwards until it is balked by the window winder gear; this is high enough to protect the interior of the door. It may be necessary to treat the doors from both front and rear edges to make sure the entire area is covered. This is especially true of two-door cars, where the doors are larger than those on four-door models.

While you are working in the door area, the door surrounds ought to be treated. Courtesy light switches can usually be pulled out to allow entry to the surrounds; otherwise a hole can be drilled at any convenient spot.

The areas in front of and behind the front wheels are established 'rust-traps' calling for treatment.

Access to the panel between the windscreen and back of the front wheels is gained from underneath the carpets inside the car. Here it is a good idea to lay on three or four coats of rust preventative.

Many cars show signs of serious corrosion around bracing struts supporting the bonnet and boot lids. With the bonnet and boot raised, drill holes at the top of the bracing struts, push the probe down to the bottom and apply the sealer in the usual way. If traces of liquid appear from under the braces, they can safely be left as they will harden off in a short time. Alternatively, they can be removed easily with a rag moistened with white spirits.

By the time the box sections have been treated, the underside of the car will be dry. Odd traces of fluid from both operations may appear at first, but again they can be removed with white spirits and a rag.

There may be some slight smells from the car as any sealer that has fallen on the exhaust is burned off. This will pass within a day or less.

The underside of the car should be checked once a year in case any parts of the sealer have worked loose.

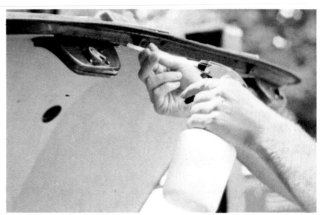

13 In many cars, the areas around the boot and bonnet are prone to corrosion. Give them two good coats of the sealer

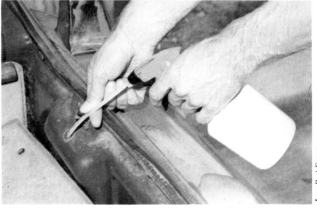

14 Usually you can find an inconspicuous place to drill a hole in a box section. Here, a panel below the boot lid is being treated

Jean-Paul Froget

Wheel arches and front panels

It is worthwhile paying particular attention to the wheel arches, front and rear, since they are more prone to damage from road gravel than other parts of the bodywork. Moreover, if there is any suspicion of paint bubbling on the upper surface, it is worth digging away some of the bitumastic (sealant with a bitumen/rubber base) to see if there is moisture trapped between it and the underside of the metal.

If this has happened, the only thing to do is to cut back the sealant until you find it is adhering solidly to the metal. You must then de-rust the affected area by rubbing down to bare metal and applying a rust 'killer', and then re-sealing the area.

The front panels, around headlamps and below the bumper, are particularly vulnerable to chipping from flying stones, and any sign of the paint skin being fractured should be dealt with before rust can start eating away at the metal. Stone chip marks are usually very small at first and you may be able to make good the damage simply by touching in with a small brush without having to rub down the area with wet-and-dry paper. If the paint you have is in an aerosol, squirt some of it into the protective cap and use a small water colourists brush to apply it.

Fitting accessories

It may be that after your car has been underbody sealed with a bitumastic preparation, you fit a radio. In most cases this will entail boring a hole in the front wing to mount the aerial. During the process of making the hole you will, obviously, cut through the sealant and unless you seal this section after the aerial has been fixed, water thrown up from the road will seep in under the bitumastic skin and set up rusting.

The same holds good for wing mirrors or any other accessory which involves cutting through the existing anti-rust skin. So, having installed the aerial, wing mirror or other accessory, re-seal around the component with fresh bitumastic.

Washing and polishing

Nowadays, when acrylic paints are much favoured as finishing coats, manufacturers often claim it is unnecessary to polish a car and only a regular wash is required to keep the paintwork in good condition. Although this is largely true, a thorough polishing every three months does keep rust at bay if a good quality wax polish is used.

The body must first be given a good wash with a proprietary brand of shampoo. Do not use ordinary household detergents as many of them contain additives which could harm the paint, good as they may be for domestic purposes. Pay particular attention to places where mud may lodge, since the mud retains moisture which will start up corrosion.

If you have access to a garden hose, a useful device can be made up for treating the underside of the car. Take a three foot length of $\frac{1}{2}$ in. copper tube – the type used by plumbers – and block off one end by flattening it with a hammer and folding it back on itself. Next bore $\frac{1}{16}$ in. holes at two inch intervals along its length. When attached to the hose with the water at full pressure, the spray will cover the underside adequately. This treatment is especially useful after driving over salt-treated roads in winter. Much the same effect can be obtained by using a lawn sprinkler if there is room for it beneath the car.

When the car has been washed thoroughly, dry off with a leather, allowing it to dry by itself is not a good idea. When applying the polish, work it well into any seams where it can form a protective coating. If you are really dedicated, you can polish under the wings as well.

Despite what manufacturers may say, a well polished car does retain its appearance and keep rust at bay far better than one which is only washed.

15 Holes cut with a round file will need to be re-sealed

16 Make sure the component is tight against the body

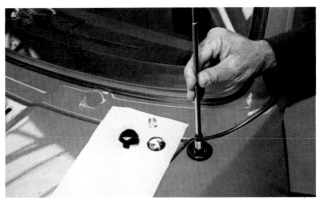

17 Aerial holes are a typical danger point

18 A finishing cap will exclude rainwater penetration

Rust-damage repairs

Holes in the bodywork, isolated from other more extensive damage, are unlikely to result from an accident. Rust will almost certainly be the cause.

Rust which starts on the outside of the paintwork is normally spotted quite early and should be dealt with quickly before it spreads (see pages 18-22). The dangerous rust is likely to be that which starts on the underside of the body, gets a good hold because it cannot be seen and then eats its way right through.

Rust damage

The first signs for the owner are usually bubbles in the paintwork. It is only when you start sanding down the area with a view to repainting it that the true extent of the damage is revealed. Be warned: if there is a line of bubbles the rust has almost certainly worked its way through the metal from underneath and there will be holes, possibly quite large ones, all the way through.

Repairing this type of damage is not technically dif-
ficult but the work must be done meticulously and, even then, it is as well to realize that eventually the rust will start up again. It is possible only to delay its progress—you will never cure it entirely.

How the repairs are tackled will depend on the extent and size of the holes and where they are on the car. One point must be emphasized, however. Never use glass fibre and body filler to repair damage in a load-bearing part of the body or chassis. Cleverly done and disguised afterwards, it might deceive a tester who checks the car but there is (literally) little future in driving a car that is about to fall apart. Selling a car with this sort of repairs and not disclosing them at the time of the sale might also result in legal action being taken—something else to be avoided.

Repairing a rust hole

Start by scuffing off the paint in the area, using a coarse 120-grit disc in a drill-powered disc sander. Take all the paint off right back to bare metal and extend this cleaned area to some 25 to 50 mm (1in. to 2in.) clear all around the

1 Rust holes like this one on a car wing can be easily repaired by using either a glass fibre mat or a piece of zinc mesh

2 An electric drill with a sanding disc is especially useful for bodywork repairs. Remove all the paint—right back to bare metal

4 One way of supporting the filler is to use a sheet of zinc mesh, which is available either separately or as part of a kit

5 Use a pair of scissors to cut the mesh slightly larger than the hole and then check that it fits into position correctly

Ray Duns

damage. If you do not have a sanding disc for your drill, it is worth buying one, since they are not expensive—and the alternative is to use coarse emery cloth and a sanding block, which is a laborious and time-consuming method.

If the area to be worked on is close to another panel which is not affected by rust, it is as well to use adhesive masking tape to protect it, as a disc sander is effective but can be a bit clumsy to use.

You will now be able to see the extent of the damage. If the hole is a tiny one, or if there is a series of holes not much larger than pin holes, it is possible to effect the repair using only body filler, as described on page 18.

If the hole or series of holes is larger and the whole area is weakened, one way of bridging the holes and strengthening the surrounding metal is to apply a patch of glass mat. Buy one of the three-part proprietary body repair kits—the type with an inert filler powder, pre-accelerated resin (binding agent) and a paste-type catalyst (hardener). A good one is David's Isopon. This type of kit usually includes some glass mat, probably in two forms—a chopped strand mat and a staple fibre mat. The former is a very coarse mat consisting of random chopped short fibre strands and is normally used for larger repairs. The

3 To make sure the surface is free from any grease or dirt, next rub down the area with a coarse and then a fine grade sandpaper

6 Pull out the mesh and then use a metal putty knife or spatula to mix up some glass fibre repair paste—such as David's P.40

latter is also a random fibre material but very much finer and of a semi-transparent, cobweb-like appearance. The staple fibre mat is best for tackling fairly small holes or a single small hole.

A substitute for staple fibre mat is a compound such as David's P.40, whose glass fibre strands are already mixed in the repair paste and only the hardener has to be added, as in figs. 6 and 7.

Preparing the surface

Use a small hammer or a hammer and a small cold chisel to knock out any wafer-thin metal or loose flaking areas from the centre of the rusty area. Then carry on tapping gently until the area around the hole or holes is slightly recessed compared with the surrounding contours. This is to take the repair material. It is important, if additional strength is needed and more than one layer of mat is to be used, that this initial hammering of the area is sufficient to accommodate the extra materials.

Adhesion of glass fibre patches can be assisted further by scouring the metal surrounding the damage with a piece of coarse grade sandpaper. An even better method is to drill a series of small holes (a series of 6 mm or $\frac{1}{4}$in. holes would be ideal) to enable the resin to flow into them to provide a really firm fixing.

Before mixing the hardener and resin, prepare the glass fibre patch. Use scissors to cut a piece of the staple fibre mat to shape about 25 mm (1in.) larger all round than the area to be treated.

Mixing the hardener and resin

Follow the instructions for mixing supplied with the kit, but blend only resin and hardener. Do not add the filler powder. Use an old bowl or saucer for the mixing, in which a typical operation would entail tipping a measured quantity of resin into it and adding hardener paste from a tube. Proportions (again of a typical kit) are 25 mm (1in.) of hardener squeezed from the tube to a tablespoonful of resin.

Setting action starts quickly, particularly in hot weather, so do not mix any more material than you need or can conveniently handle. When mixed, use a cheap paint brush to apply the mix to the entire area of the hole where the glass fibre patch is to go, stippling it well into the pits and dents and around the edge of the hole itself.

Next, place the pre-cut piece of glass mat into position, using the brush to jab it and stipple it well on to the surface. Immediately apply more resin and hardener mix on top, brushing, jabbing and stippling until it is well soaked in the resin and the mat takes on a transparent look.

If additional strength is required, the whole process can be repeated and a second or even a third layer of glass mat applied. Make sure, though, that each mat is thoroughly soaked in resin and hardener.

Allow the resin and mat to set hard. This should take about 20 minutes but it might take longer if the weather is cold.

The final stage is to use a filler such as David's P.38 to smooth the surface ready for painting. Details are on pages 18 and 19, and in figs. 8 to 11 on page 30.

Patching on the underside

A slightly different technique can be used, still employing the glass mat, when the rear of the panel is accessible.

The work starts in the same way by scuffing the area of damage clean with a disc sander. Then repeat this operation on the underside of the metal. Exactly the same procedure

7 When the repair paste and hardener are thoroughly mixed, apply the P.40 to the surface of the mesh and press it into position

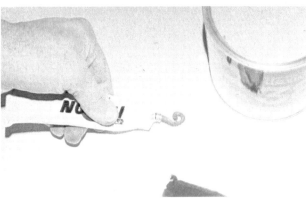

8 The next step is to mix up some filler paste and then apply it to the top surface of the repair. This paste is David's P.38

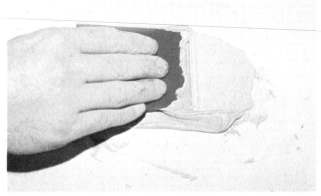

9 Follow the manufacturer's instructions closely when mixing the P.38 as too much hardener could impair the hardening process

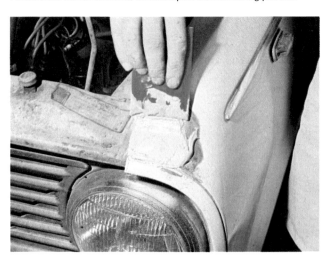

10 Using the spatula, apply the filler paste to the repair in thin layers until it just stands proud of the original bodywork

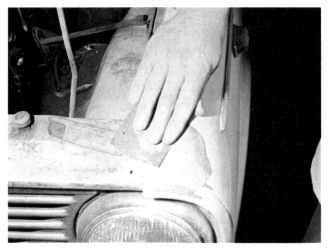

11 When the filler has dried, rub it down with coarse, followed by wet-and-dry, paper. Make sure the surface is perfectly smooth

is then followed to apply one or more glass fibre patches, but this time on the underside of the panel. Adhesion can be helped in the same way as before by scouring the edges of the area before applying the patch. Finish off the repair by applying filler from the front side and sanding smooth.

A good way to support the mat firmly and accurately during the fixing of the patches to the underside is to use a cardboard 'former' on the front side of the repair. When the metal is sanded and clean on both sides, cut a piece of card to suit the size and shape of the repair. Cover this with a sheet of polythene or alternatively coat one side of it with wax polish. (This is to stop the resin and hardener adhering to it.) Then fix the card on the front side of the repair, holding it in position with cellulose tape or masking tape. Ensure it goes on polythene or wax side downwards. When all the glass mat has been laid up on the underside and has set hard, the cardboard can be lifted off and all traces of wax and so on removed from the glass fibre before applying the final filler to the front of the repair.

Using zinc mesh

A popular alternative material used to support the filler when repairing holes is a sheet of perforated metal (usually zinc) or mesh.

Where access to the rear of the damaged area is available, the technique is once again to clean back to bare metal to a few centimetres all round the damage on both sides of the panel. Again, it would help also if holes were drilled through the metal around the hole to help key the filler. A piece of mesh or perforated zinc is cut and shaped slightly larger than the hole. If the material is that supplied with the kit, use an old pair of scissors to cut the material—it is quite soft. The next step is to mix up some filler.

When fixing a repair using mesh instead of a glass fibre mat, it is best to use a simple two-part paste filler. There are a number of these on the market. A typical proprietary brand is supplied in two tubes (for example, Holts Cataloy), or in a tin with a tube of hardener (for example, David's P.40). The larger of the Holts tubes and the tin in the David's kit contain the bulk paste (equivalent to the resin and the powder mixed). The mixing instructions are basically the same for both types. The paste and the hardener are mixed together on a non-absorbent surface using a plastic spatula and then applied straight to the work.

Spread a layer of filler all around the mesh and then immediately press the mesh into position. Add more filler to the rear side of the mesh to ensure it is firmly fixed in place. The final filling job can be done from the front.

'No access' holes

Where a hole is being filled in some part of the car where access to the other side of the panel is impossible, a slightly different technique will be needed. Cut the piece of mesh in the same way as before and then attach a couple of pieces of wire to it. Then, to make sure the mesh is the correct size, try to 'fiddle' it through the hole. This, depending on the shape of the hole, may be possible to do with the mesh in one piece or, alternatively, the mesh may have to be cut into two and each piece inserted separately. When you are satisfied, pull the mesh back through the hole again.

You can now either spread the filler around the mesh and then 'fiddle' the mesh back through the hole or, alternatively, spread the filler paste around the edge of the hole at the rear and then push the mesh through the hole. Then pull the wires hard into the layer of paste and hold them tightly until the paste sets firm. Filling is then completed in the usual way from the front.

Methods of supporting repair material

Crude but sometimes effective methods of supporting glass fibre are possible in order to bridge a larger hole in a sill or a section of bodywork where the underside is inaccessible. In some cases, after the area of the hole has been cleaned up and slightly recessed, it is possible to push wire netting or any non-absorbent filler into the cavity until the level is right to support a glass mat soaked in resin. This will adhere to the front side of the metal and, once again, a few drilled holes and some deep scouring of the metal will aid adhesion.

Using foam support

A modern alternative now available is to fill the cavity or part of the cavity with foam and to use this to support the repair materials. Isovoss is one such foam and all you need to do is simply mix the two liquids together and shake them. The result is instant polyurethane foam which expands very rapidly and then sets hard.

Clean up the area of the rust hole to be filled as before, slightly indenting the surround metal. If the inaccessible cavity underneath the rust hole is a very large one, it is a good idea, if possible, to restrict it so as not to use vast quantities of the foam. In a sill, for instance, non-absorbent material can be pushed inside and positioned each side of the hole to act as a filler.

When using the foam, the next step will depend a little on which type is used. In general, however, it is a matter of mixing the two liquids in recommended proportions and

13 Using the correct proportions supplied with this glass fibre kit, pour the resin into the container. Then mix in the hardener

14 Next, having cut the glass fibre mat to shape, stipple and jab the resin and hardener mix into it with an old paintbrush

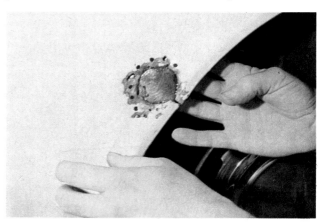

15 Then carefully press the mat into position. If additional support is needed a second or third layer of mat may be used

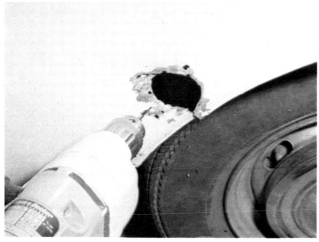

12 In order to assist the adhesion of glass fibre patches, it is a good idea to drill several small holes around the repair

16 Once the resin and mat have set hard—around 20 minutes—mix up some filler to finish off the repair as in figs. 8 to 11

17 To repair a large gap like this, one way is to use Isovoss. First place a piece of card in the gap to localize the Isovoss

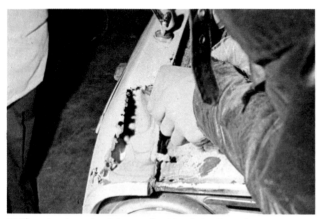

18 Next, having mixed the two liquids, shake them vigorously in the container supplied and then inject the mixture into the gap

19 The mixture will now expand rapidly and will soon overflow the cavity. When it has set, use a sharp knife to trim the foam

then shaking or stirring them. Directly the mixture shows signs of taking on a creamy consistency, it must be tipped or injected into the cavity to be filled. It will immediately expand into a large golden mass, filling the cavity and overflowing. Trim off the bulk of the overflow as soon as it begins to set and later, when it is hard, trim off the excess with a sharp knife until the foam is level with the metal. Finally, complete the repair with filler paste.

Aluminium repair tape
One of the simplest rust hole repair methods is to use an aluminium body repair tape. Like the other procedures, start off by cleaning up the metal around the rust damage, getting right back to bright metal and removing all signs of loose and flaking rust. Then use a hammer to recess the area to slightly below the surrounding metal.

The tape is supplied in a roll, usually 50 mm (2in.) wide with a backing cover. First, offer it up to the repair area and then cut it into the required lengths. Peel off the backing tape and lay each strip into position over the rust holes so that it just meets the surrounding body metal. The tape sets quickly after the backing is removed. So make sure you know exactly where it is going, so it can be applied quickly. Once set, it blends in with the metal and becomes very hard. The final stage is the application of filler.

Impregnated glass fibre cloth
Another self-setting repair material is glass fibre cloth, such as Bondalight, which is impregnated with resin that hardens when exposed to sunlight or an ultraviolet light source. The patch material is pliable while protected by its backing and is self-adhesive.

To use it, clean the damaged area back to bright metal by sanding. Then use a pair of scissors or a knife to cut the Bondalight to size and shape. Next, pull off the green backing, then stick it, tacky side down, over the damaged area. What you need now is sunshine, although Bondalight can be applied to a damp surface. On a good bright day with plenty of sunshine, it will take a couple of hours to harden. If the weather is overcast and there is a temperature of 10°C, hardening could take up to 24 hours. In really cold weather, below 5°C, it is not recommended that Bondalight should be used outdoors. Use your garage, if you have one, and train a high intensity mercury vapour lamp or an ordinary sunlamp on the repair and it will harden in 10 to 15 minutes.

When it has hardened, the clear film which covers the patch material can be removed. Filling, sanding and painting can then follow in the normal way.

Ray Duns

20 One or two layers of glass fibre mat are now applied—although in less complicated body repairs this is not always necessary

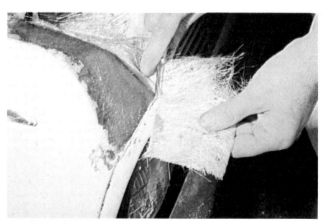

21 Trim off the excess mat with a sharp knife once the mat and resin have set. Finally, complete the repair with filler paste

Blind holes

A useful method of repairing a 'blind' hole – one where you cannot get at the back – is to make a contour patch. As before, the damaged area must be sanded back to bare metal making sure that all loose paint is removed. It is likely that the edges of the hole will be ragged. If so, file or cut the metal so as to get a fairly uniform shape.

With a ball-ended hammer, tap down the edges of the hole all round to a distance of about two inches, and about 3mm (0.125in) deep, so that when the glass fibre patch is applied it will be slightly below the level of the surrounding panel. Score the bare metal area with criss-cross lines using the pointed end of a file or any other sharp tool, to give a good key for the patch.

Box sections

When you are treating a true box section, as distinct from a door skin, it is a good idea to inject rust 'killer' through the hole before making the repair. There are aerosols on the market which come with a long thin probe so you can get through quite small holes (see pages 25-26).

The next step is to make sure the area is free of grease, oil, or other contamination by cleaning the sanded area with methylated spirits or paint thinners, using a clean non-linting cloth.

For repairing the prepared hole you will need glass fibre matting, resin and hardener, and a piece of release paper. The release paper can be thick polythene, acrylic sheet, or even waxed paper.

Cut a piece of glass fibre mat to fit the hole, a second piece about one inch larger all round, and then a third piece about one inch larger all round than the second. Lay the large piece of mat on the release paper, followed by the second and, finally, the piece which fits the hole. Make sure

you arrange the pieces of mat as concentrically as possible, so that when the patch is applied the two larger pieces will overlap the edges of the hole by a good margin.

Make up a mixture of resin and hardener and apply it to the glass fibre matting so all three layers become saturated, but avoid using excessive resin. Carefully apply the patch to the hole with the release paper so the smallest patch fits into the gap, and tape the release paper in place. Masking tape is best for this but you can use cellulose tape, although this sometimes leaves a deposit behind.

When the patch has thoroughly set, peel away the release paper with care. You can now use filler paste to bring the patch up level with the surrounding area and slightly proud of it, so when it is rubbed down the repair will be a smooth continuation of the panel.

Trim strips

A favourite place for rust to appear is behind body trim strips and badges. The first sign is a little rust showing at the edges of the trim. To deal with this rust, the trim will have to be removed.

Strips may be held in place by spring clips, plastic studs, or in some cases studs and nuts. Feel behind the panel to find out which type you have. If there are plastic studs, the strip can be slid off lengthwise. With clips, start at one end and use a chisel pointed piece of wood gently to lever the strip free. Work along the strip from clip to clip. Badges may be bolted in place or be held by plastic studs. Use the same methods to get them off.

When the rust is exposed, treat it as described on pages 28-29. Metal body strips are likely to have corroded at the back too. Clean away the rust and paint them before replacing.

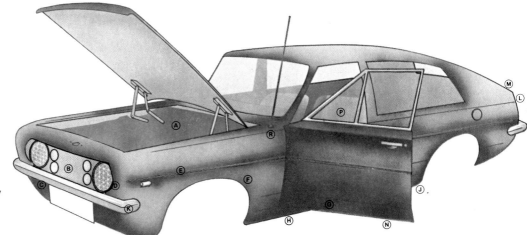

22 Common rust areas on the car's bodywork. Bad repairs will not last long so check very carefully.

A Engine Compartment
General signs of rust around side panels, on the bulkhead and near the battery.

B Badges and Grills
chrome areas and mounting points.

C Bumper and panel below
chrome areas. Paintwork may have become chipped due to stones and gravel. Also number plate and bumper mountings.

D Headlamps
around rims where water may become trapped.

E Trim
decorative trim, and badge/name mountings may trap water and encourage rust.

F Wings
check for signs of rust eating through the wings

G Doors
water can become trapped,

particularly at the bottom of door panels. Look also at adjacent bodywork.

H Sills and jacking points
small holes and paint blisters indicate rust working its way through from below, rusty jacking

J Underbody panels
check for chipped areas and general rust.

K Bumper
rust on chrome areas.

L Rear lights
water under sealing rubbers can encourage rust.

M Boot lid
check for rust around edges.

N Drainage channels
poor drainage can lead to rusting.

P Floor panels
lift carpets to check for rust.

R External accessories
mounting for wing/door mirrors and car aerials are possible rust spots.

The nuts and bolts

Just not being able to undo an important nut or bolt is one of the most frustrating experiences of the kerbside mechanic. But a few simple techniques can rapidly overcome the effects of rust, dirt and age—and save a great deal of time, which, to the d-i-y man as much as anyone else, is money.

Removing any sort of fixings demands the right tools. Badly fitting tools will rapidly burr an obstinate screw or bolt. They are also liable to slip or gouge—harming both the workpiece and the mechanic's temper. For this reason, adjustable spanners should be used only in an emergency.

Spanners and screwdrivers of the correct size—a good firm fit on the nut or screw-head—will help preserve the fixings and allow them to be used again.

For removing bolts, ring spanners are the best tools, as they grip right round the nut. A socket spanner is an excellent second best.

Open-ended spanners have one jaw that is slightly longer than the other. This is designed to reach round behind the nut and secure a better grip. To take advantage of this, place the spanner so that the longer jaw follows the shorter in the direction of rotation (fig. 1).

Whatever spanner you are using, always push it with the palm of the hand (fig. 2) and not with your fingers wrapped round the end. If the spanner slips, as it is likely to do, you will have a better chance of avoiding cut and bruised knuckles.

If a conventional spanner cannot cope, Mole grips or Stillson wrench will provide extra leverage.

Cleaning
The mud, sludge and rust which accumulate around bolts and screws help to hold them in position. So the first step in loosening a stiff fixing is to clean it thoroughly.

With bolts, remove the worst of the mud or oily sludge by scraping with a screwdriver. Then use an old paint brush soaked in paraffin to remove the rest, making sure that the threads at the end are thoroughly clean. If the sludge is still persistent, clean it off with a wire brush.

Treat screws in the same way, making sure that the slot and the edge of the screw-head are thoroughly clean.

To remove dirt that has accumulated down in the thread of a nut, run a little penetrating oil on to the top of the nut and allow it to soak for an hour or so. Then try to undo the fixing.

Jarring
Screws and bolts that have been in position for a long time often need to be jarred before they can be undone. This loosens the grip of the threads.

With bolts, the flats of the nuts should be tapped three or four times with a hammer. Do not do more than tap; anything more forceful risks damaging the threads (fig. 3).

If the nut cannot be reached easily with a hammer, hold the blade of an old screwdriver against the flats and hit the handle with a hammer.

With screws, place the screwdriver upright in the slot and hit it four or five times (fig. 4).

Removing stiff bolts
If you find that after being soaked in penetrating oil and being jarred the nut can be moved slightly, tighten it up

1 Open-ended spanners grip best if the long jaw is placed behind the nut. In this case the longer jaw is nearest the camera

2 If the spanner slips off the nut, holding it like this will be much less painful than having your fingers wrapped round the end

3 When jarring nuts with a hammer, be extremely careful to avoid hitting the thread. This will make removal even more difficult

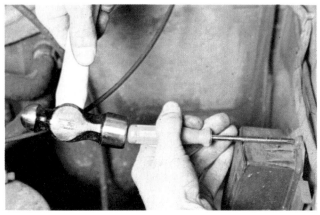

4 Jarring screws should, ideally, be done only with a wooden handled screwdriver. Use a plastic one only on small screws

and loosen it again. Continue this back-and-forth motion so that any clinging traces of dirt are forced up the thread, and remove these before completely undoing the nut.

If it still will not move, the most likely reason will be that it has been over-tightened.

This can be overcome by momentarily springing the threads apart. To do this, apply normal unscrewing pressure with a spanner and at the same time give the end of the bolt a sharp blow with a hammer. You will need, however, to protect the thread—it is all too easy to distort the last half turn or so of thread with a careless hammer blow.

The best way to protect the thread is to screw an extra nut on to the end of the bolt. But this works only if there is enough thread for the second nut to go on for at least one full turn—any less and all the force of the hammer will fall on to the same small area of thread that you are trying to protect.

If you have neither a second nut nor sufficient thread to screw it on to, there are two alternative means of protecting the end of the bolt, both requiring the help of an assistant:

1: Place a buffer of softer material between the bolt and the hammer. A block of copper, brass or any other metal softer than the bolt can be used (fig. 5).

2: Take another bolt, steel drift or nail punch with a diameter fractionally less than that of the bolt being treated, rest it squarely on the end of the bolt and tap it sharply while your helper applies pressure to the spanner (fig. 6).

If the bolt still refuses to budge, try loosening the nut by heating it with a blowlamp and squirting oil on it; this will cause the nut to expand and so ease the threads. Before you begin, make sure that the bolt is well away from fuel lines, fuel tank or carburettor and that any other flammable material in the car—such as plastic insulation or rubber—is removed or pushed as far away as possible. Alternatively, protect it with a temporary metal shield cut, for example, from an empty oil can (fig. 8).

Ensure that the blowlamp flame is directed only on to the nut and heat it slowly. (It does not need to be very hot, but just beyond the point where you can still touch it.) Squirt liberal amounts of oil on to the threads and leave the nut to cool. Repeat the process and allow the nut to cool again, and it should turn with a spanner.

If this fails, all that is left is to break the nut off the bolt. A nut-splitter is the best tool for this job. It can be a fairly simple mechanical device or a hydraulic version, but both kinds work in the same way: a stout metal collar encloses the nut while the tip of a cold chisel comes through one side of the collar to split the nut (fig. 10).

An ordinary cold chisel will do the same job. Rest it

6 A punch will do the same job. Try to keep the punch directly in line with the bolt as this will maximize the jarring effect

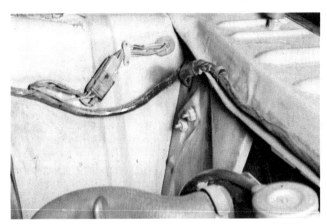

7 When a nut needs to be heated, nearby wiring—such as that in the middle of the picture—needs to be protected by a shield

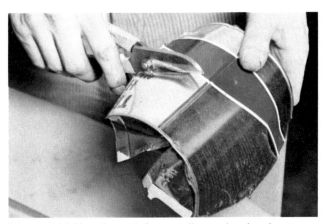

8 A metal shield can be made from an oilcan, using tin snips and a hammer to get it to the right shape. Beware of sharp edges

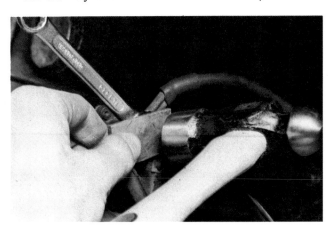

5 Using a small piece of brass to protect the thread. A helper should apply firm pressure to the spanner as you use the hammer

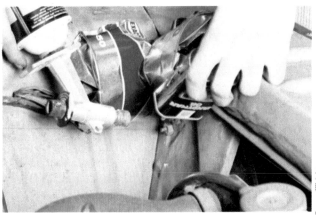

9 Heat the nut steadily and have the oil can ready. Keep an eye on any wiring ; if it starts to smoke remove the torch immediately

George Wright

against the most convenient flat of the nut and hit the end with a hammer (fig. 11). Do not hit the chisel too hard; you might bend the bolt.

If the nut turns but does not come undone, you will probably find that the bolt is turning with the nut. Try one spanner on the head of the bolt and another on the nut. If you do not have another spanner of the correct size, use one which is slightly too large, with the blade of a screwdriver wedged in to make it tight (fig. 12).

Once the nut has come off, you may have difficulty in getting the bolt out. If you have to hammer it out, protect the threads as described above (and see fig. 6).

Loosening jammed screws

A screw is often more difficult to remove than a nut or bolt because it is not possible to apply the same degree of leverage as with a spanner. If jarring has no effect, try to tighten the screw a fraction before attempting to undo it again. Some screwdrivers have a pair of 'flats' on their stems, and extra leverage can be applied by tightening a pair of Mole grips or Stillsons so that the jaws grip the flats and give a side handle to the screwdriver (fig. 13).

In a cruciform or cross-head screw, the slots offer a better purchase to the tip of the screwdriver, but even here the correct sized tool must be used. A large screwdriver will engage in the cross of a small screw, but only the tips of the blade will enter and there is the likelihood of the screwdriver rising out of the slots and burring them.

Where self-tapping screws pierce right through the metal and out the other side, use a hacksaw or file to slice off the end of the screw before punching it out with a small drift or punch. Alternatively, file off the head and punch the shank through from the front.

When a self-tapping screw has finally been removed, see if a bolt can be used in its place. A smear of grease on the bolt will largely prevent rust and facilitate future removal.

If the screw is blind—that is, does not go right through the metal—the remedy is slightly more time-consuming. The screw-head must be filed or sawn right off, a hole drilled into the shank, and a screw extractor used to twist it free. (A screw extractor looks rather like a large woodscrew, the major difference being the fact that it has a left hand thread.)

Freeing jammed split-pins

Nuts are often locked on to their bolts or studs by a split-pin passing through a hole drilled in the bolt; the split-pin

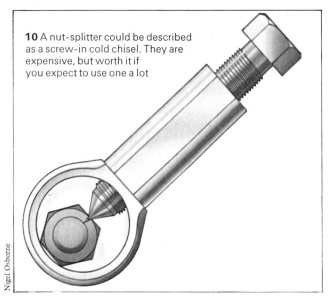

10 A nut-splitter could be described as a screw-in cold chisel. They are expensive, but worth it if you expect to use one a lot

Nigel Osborne

11 Before using a cold chisel to cut off a nut, drill a small hole in the flat you intend to cut. This will weaken the nut

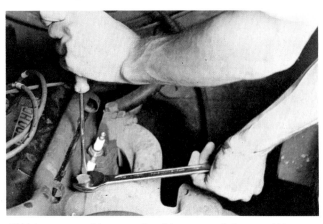

12 Using a screwdriver to make a big spanner fit is a good idea if the right size spanner is in use on the other end of the bolt

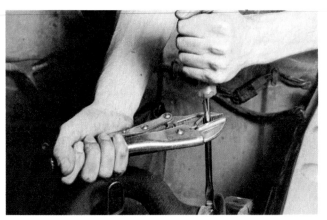

13 A great deal of extra leverage can be obtained by clamping a pair of Mole grips on to the shaft of the screwdriver

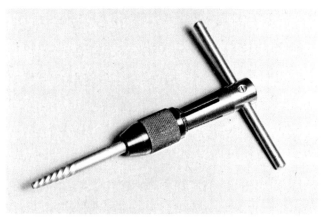

14 Before buying a screw extractor, measure the diameter of the screw concerned, as it is essential that it is of the correct size

has to be removed before the nut can be unscrewed (fig. 15). Sometimes, though, the complete pin may not come out, leaving a short length trapped in the hole with just enough poking through to lock the nut.

If you cannot see whether the hole is clear, as sometimes happens with castellated nuts, probe the hole with a piece of wire. If it is blocked, tighten the nut a fraction so that it does not cover the edge of the hole, push a nail into the hole and tap it to remove the split-pin remnant.

A more sophisticated version of the split-pin is an insert, usually white in colour, in the nut itself (fig. 16). The insert grips the threads tightly to prevent vibration from shaking the nut loose. All that is needed in this case is extra leverage on the spanner to break the lock.

Once the lock has been broken in such a nut it must not be used for locking again. The same applies to split-pins: always throw the old pin away and use a new one.

Jammed wheel nuts
Jammed wheel nuts are among the commonest examples of stiff fixings which the d-i-y mechanic must overcome. They are usually caused by the air guns in garages fitting the nuts with a force too great for the average wheel-brace.

A spider-wrench (fig. 17) is the easiest way to remove wheel nuts. If you have only the wheel-brace supplied with the car, you can get extra leverage by fitting a stout piece of pipe over the top of the brace to lengthen its handle. Fitting a spark-plug spanner on to the wheel-brace is another method.

The cranked type of wheel-brace is most effective when used by two people. Obstinate wheel nuts can generally be undone if one person kneels holding the brace, while the other operates it with his foot (fig. 18).

15 Split-pins are always folded back on to the nuts which they lock. They must be straightened before you can pull them out

16 Nuts with this plastic insert perform the same function as a split-pin. They can be removed with a little extra pressure

17 A spider wheel-brace is the most efficient device for freeing wheel nuts single-handed. Try to get as much lift as possible

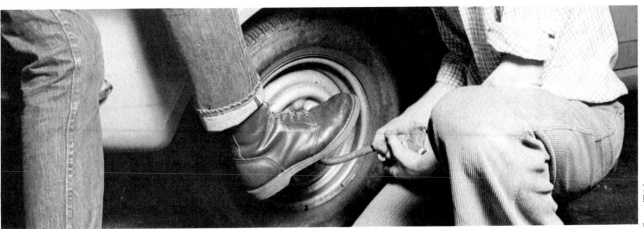
18 A cranked wheel-brace can be very effective if used as shown. Try stamping on the crank if a steady push with the foot fails

How to make it start

Symptom	Possible causes	Remedies
No response from starter motor and headlamps remain bright	Poor electrical connections Faulty solenoid Worn commutator brushes	Clean and retighten connection Replace solenoid Dismantle starter motor and renew brushes
No response from starter motor and headlamps dim Starter motor turns but fails to engage with engine fly-wheel	Flat battery Jammed starter motor pinion Starter motor pinion stuck on shaft Over-run clutch on motor shaft failed (pre-engaged type only)	Re-charge battery Push car in gear Clean pinion gear Replace over-run clutch

Two quite different symptoms may be noticed in a car which refuses to start. If the engine will not fire when the starter motor turns it over, the fault must be in the ignition or the fuel supply (see the panel at the top of page 44). But if the starter motor itself does not function, the fault must be in the motor or its associated electrics.

It is likely that the fault is not with the starter motor itself but with its power supply system. To check this possibility, in cases where there is no response when the starter is operated, begin again and turn the key just one position to put it into the ignition energizing section. The ignition and oil pressure warning light should come on and the fuel gauge register. If they do not, no power is leaving the battery. This will be because either the battery is flat or the connections at the terminals are at fault.

Flat battery
If the headlights or any other major power consumer have been left on for any length of time, the battery will have become completely flat and must be recharged before the engine can be started in the normal way.

Faulty battery post connections
If the battery itself is in order, the loss of power may be caused by faulty connections between it and the starter.

The 'post' connections on top of the battery are always suspect. In extreme conditions—icy weather, for example—a starter motor can take 400amps to turn the engine over. Any faulty connection will prevent such currents from flowing, but may nevertheless pass the much smaller currents demanded by the ignition lights.

A quick clue to the condition of the connections can be had by touching the positive terminal of the battery, marked +, immediately after you try to start the car. If it feels hot, the connection is poor.

Corrosion may have begun on the inside of the clamp, or on the post, or both. A quick whisk with sandpaper will restore the surface condition of both.

Clamps often become slightly oval inside through corrosion. So, when you replace the clamp, fix it in a slightly different position so that it presents a fresh face to the post.

With the hooded type of connection (fig. 3), a screw through the top locks the connection in place. If it has worked loose, tighten it. If this produces no result, remove the screw, lift off the hood and clean it and the post with sandpaper or emery paper.

If a battery connection will not come away from the post after it has been loosened, trickle hot water over it. Never try to pull or twist it free, as this risks cracking the top of the battery case and causing expensive damage.

Faulty battery cables
If you can find nothing wrong with the battery connections, next check the battery cables.

The braided metal lead to the earth connection is especially suspect, because corrosion can creep along it, attacking individual strands of the wire until those remaining cannot carry the starting load. It is easy to be misled by an apparently sound lead, as the corrosion often affects only the underside.

Lift the lead so that you can check it all round. If it is faulty, replace it.

The earth connection on the body of the car (at the other end of the braided lead) should also be examined, since rust can set up at the nut and bolt connection (fig. 2). Undo the connection, clean its faces with abrasive paper and bolt it back in place. The area of metal around the bolt may also need cleaning.

The insulated live lead from the battery tends not to suffer from corrosion as much as the earth connection does, but an over-filled cell or a fine crack in the battery case can allow acid to escape, settle on the lead and work its way under the insulation.

To test for this, bend the lead to and fro several times. If it is corroded you will feel the grating of the fractured wires—a sign that it must be replaced.

Turn the ignition key to the first stage again, and if the ignition light fails to come on, try the horn and the headlamps. If none works, the battery is completely flat.

If the battery is providing power, try to start the engine again. If the engine still fails to turn, switch on the headlights. This will produce one of the symptoms included in the panel above.

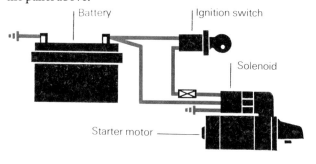

1 The pre-engaged starter motor circuit. With an inertia starter the solenoid is mounted in the engine compartment

If there is still no sign of life in the starter motor and the lights do not dim when you try to start the car, it is clear that no power is reaching the starter. When the starter motor turns it drains off power from the lights and causes them to dim. So if the motor fails to turn and the headlamps remain bright there are two possible faults. Either power is not reaching the motor, or the motor itself is defective.

Faulty wiring or ignition switch
To find a fault in the connections between the ignition switch and the starter motor, the wiring will have to be checked further down the line from the battery.

The starter motor itself is not likely to shake its connections loose, but check them anyway. The starter is usually fairly accessible from the engine compartment and is always fitted at the rear of the engine close to where the clutch housing bulges out into a bell shape. One, or in some cases two, thick cables go to it and can be checked for tightness by leaning down and twisting them. If they are loose, simply tighten up the nuts. The nuts may have fallen off the screw, in which case an emergency (only) repair can be made by fixing the cable in place with a length of wire twisted tightly round the thread of the screw.

The middle link in the starter circuit is the solenoid. This is an electro-magnetic switch which is connected between the battery and the starter motor and is controlled by the ignition switch. As the ignition key is turned (or the starter button pressed) power reaches the solenoid. This activates the solenoid and allows current to reach the starter motor. Its connections must be examined.

The solenoid will be mounted in one of two places—either on top of the starter motor or elsewhere in the engine compartment. The best way to find it is to look at the starter motor. If the solenoid is mounted on top of it you will see a small round metal case with wires leading from it (fig. 5). If not, follow the heavy black lead back from the starter motor. This will run directly to the solenoid (fig. 7).

Regardless of where the solenoid is, clean and tighten the connections on the thick black cables. It may be necessary to remove thin rubber covers from the terminals. These will pull off.

Once the terminals of these components have been cleaned and checked, try to start the engine again. If there is no improvement, the solenoid must be examined more closely.

The first task is to establish if the solenoid is working. Ask a friend to turn on the ignition in the normal way while you get as close as possible to the solenoid. You should hear a slight click as the solenoid is activated when the ignition is turned on. If you hear nothing, tap the solenoid with a spanner. As with a reluctant fuel pump, a slight jarring can sometimes free a sticking solenoid. If there is still no sound when the ignition is turned on, you will have one of two faults: either no power is reaching the solenoid from the ignition switch, or the solenoid itself is at fault.

To test the former either make or buy a test lamp (fig. 6). Attached to the solenoid are several thin leads. One of these is connected to the ignition switch and carries the power which turns on the solenoid. It is likely that it will be coloured either white with red stripes or black with yellow. It is also likely that this lead will be the only one attached to its particular terminal—all other light leads will connect to one of the heavy black cable terminals.

Disconnect this wire and attach it to one of the test lamp leads (fig. 8). Clip the other lamp lead to a good earthing point on the engine or the body of the car—the

2 The connections at either end of the earthing strap should be cleaned and the strap itself replaced if it has corroded badly

3 Hooded battery connections are usually reliable, but must be checked and thoroughly cleaned if starting becomes difficult

4 Be careful with these connectors. The posts are fragile and will snap off and ruin the battery if the nuts are over-tightened

5 A solenoid mounted on top of the starter motor. All electrical connections are made at the terminal on the right-hand side

surface of the metal must be free from grease, rust and paint. Turn the ignition to the starting position. If the bulb lights, electricity is reaching the solenoid.

If the bulb does not light, there is probably a loose connection at the other end of the wire in the ignition lock. Remove the ignition lock from the dash-board or steering column and check to see if the wire to the solenoid is loose (fig. 9). If this is not so, check the other leads, as the power supply into the switch may be at fault. If none of these is loose, check both the connections and the fuse at the fuse-box as these may be the cause of the fault. If all are sound it is likely that the ignition switch itself is at fault and will have to be replaced. When renewing an ignition switch, be sure to swap the leads one at a time to avoid mistakes.

Faulty solenoid

If you find that the ignition switch to solenoid lead now lights the test lamp, try to start the car again. If the symptoms persist, take a closer look at the solenoid itself. The solenoid switch itself must be tested and the best way of doing this is to by-pass it. If the starter motor shows signs of life when this is done the solenoid must be re-placed.

If the solenoid has a rubber-covered button at its centre turn on the ignition and press this firmly. This button over-rides the solenoid, so if pressing it makes any difference the solenoid is definitely faulty. If there is no such button, remove the rubber which covers the main terminals on the solenoid. Turn the ignition on and place a screw-driver across the terminals (fig. 10). This has the same effect as pressing the button and, though it will produce large, bright sparks, it is perfectly safe provided the screwdriver touches no other part of the car. If by-passing the solenoid produces no response in the starter motor, it is likely that there is a serious electrical fault in the motor itself.

Replacing a solenoid

The most important point in replacing a faulty solenoid is to ensure that the wires leading to it are reconnected correctly. The best way to do this is to make a quick sketch of the existing connections before you remove them.

If the solenoid is fixed in the engine compartment, dis-connect the wires, remove the bolts and clamp on the new solenoid. Carefully reconnect the leads and try to start the car again.

Solenoids which are mounted on the starter motor are slightly more difficult to replace. First, remove the starter motor itself (see below). The solenoid will be held by no more than four screws or bolts which will run vertically down from the solenoid into the body of the motor, or back from the front (fig. 11). Remove these and lift out the solenoid. When fitting the new one, ensure that the solenoid plunger is in position with the operating lever (fig. 13).

Faulty starter motor

If the solenoid and all the wiring are in good working order, the fault will almost certainly lie in the starter motor itself.

All starter motors work on the same basic principle: a small rotating cog (or pinion) engages with the engine fly-wheel, turning the crankshaft and therefore starting the engine. The only major difference between starter motors is the way in which the pinion engages with the fly-wheel.

In the first type, the inertia starter (fig. 18), when power reaches the motor its main shaft spins rapidly. The speed is sufficient to throw the pinion along the threaded sleeve

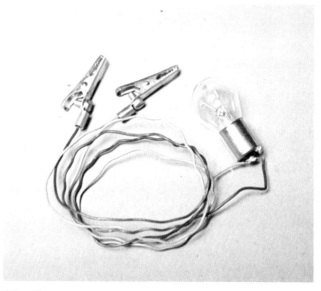

6 An efficient test lamp can be made by soldering two leads with crocodile clips to the terminals of a car indicator bulb

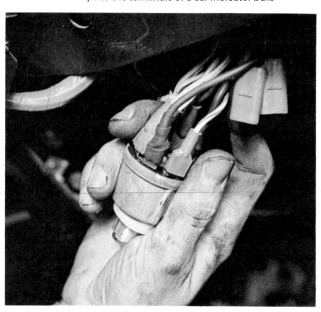

9 When checking the ignition switch see that the wire from the solenoid is firmly in place. It is next to the mechanic's thumb

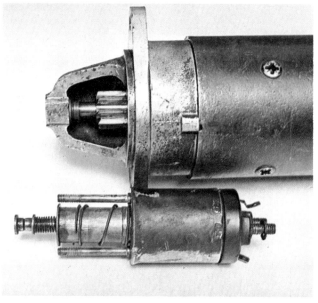

12 The solenoid removed. This type is very exposed to dirt and damp, so see that all the parts are cleaned and oiled well

7 A solenoid fixed to one wall of the engine compartment. The pointer shows the wire carrying power from the ignition switch

8 Testing this wire will be a problem if you cannot get a lead of the test lamp in to the connector. Use a safety pin as shown

10 By-pass the solenoid by putting a screwdriver across the main terminals. Be sure to use one with a well insulated handle

11 To remove the solenoid from a pre-engaged motor, first slacken the nut on the right and undo those above. Then pull it clear

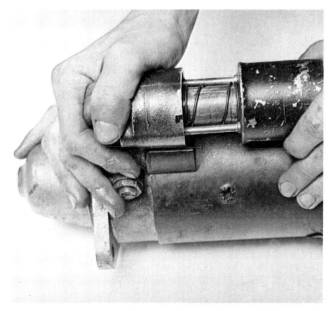

13 When replacing the solenoid it is essential that it connects with the lever, so push the solenoid back in very firmly

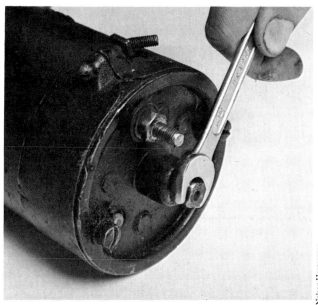

14 Inertia starter motors often have a square on the end of the main shaft. Turning this with a spanner may free a jammed pinion

Nelson Hargreaves

41

15 Cleaning the shaft of an inertia motor can be done with a paintbrush and petrol. Keep petrol from running into the motor

16 The coarse thread which the pinion moves up must also be free from dirt and grit if the motor is to work satisfactorily

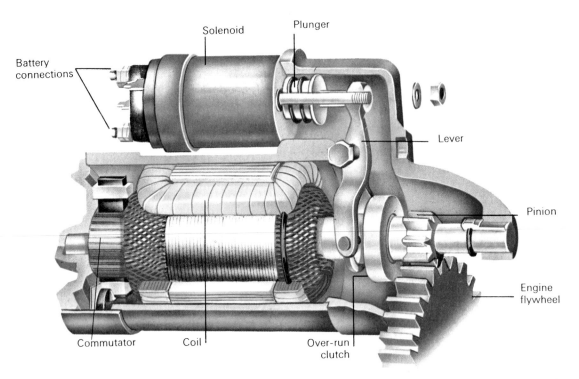

Solenoid

Plunger

Battery connections

Lever

Pinion

Engine flywheel

Commutator

Coil

Over-run clutch

17 (above) A pre-engaged starter motor
18 (below) An inertia starter motor

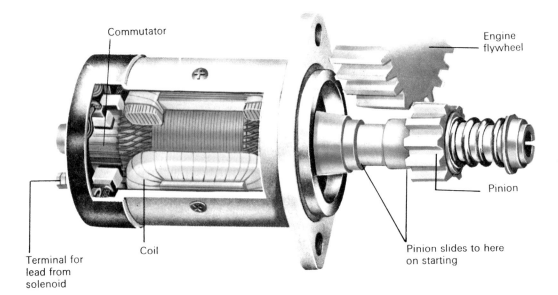

Commutator

Engine flywheel

Pinion

Terminal for lead from solenoid

Coil

Pinion slides to here on starting

on the shaft. This brings it into mesh with the engine fly-wheel and consequently starts the engine. When the engine fires its superior power and speed throws the pinion back up along the shaft and out of engagement with the fly-wheel.

The second mechanism is slightly different. The pinion of the 'pre-engaged' starter motor (fig. 17) is slid into position by the solenoid a fraction of a second before the shaft of the motor starts to turn. As current reaches the solenoid the plunger contracts sharply. This operates the lever shown in fig. 17, which pushes the pinion up the shaft and into position with the fly-wheel.

When the engine starts, the driver turns back the ignition key (or relaxes his pressure on the starter button) and so breaks the connection with the solenoid. So the plunger springs back from within the solenoid and brings the pinion back along the shaft.

Identification of the type of starter fitted to your car is simple. If the solenoid is bolted directly on to the starter you have one of the pre-engaged type, if the solenoid is mounted anywhere else you have the inertia type.

With the battery in good condition but the lights fading, it is clear that the starter motor is drawing power in the normal way. The fact that it is not turning indicates that the pinion has jammed in mesh with the fly-wheel. The procedure for freeing it will depend on the type of starter motor.

Most inertia starter motors have a square-ended shaft protruding through the back of the unit. This may be concealed by a metal cap. A spanner fitted on to this shaft and turned back and forth a few times should release the pinion (fig. 14).

19 Check the teeth of the pinion for wear. The teeth of this one are beginning to chew up badly. The pinion should be replaced

20 The teeth of this pinion are chipped on the right-hand side, but the wear is not so serious as to make replacement essential

If this fails to work and the car has a starting handle, turn off the ignition, check that the handbrake is on and that the car is in neutral. Crank the engine. There is a good chance that the pinion will slide clear of the flywheel. You will probably hear it if it does.

Starting handles are uncommon nowadays so alternatively, turn off the ignition, put the car in top gear and release the handbrake. Push the car forward a few feet and let it roll back – it will not roll far because the engine will act as a brake. Repeat this four or five times and the pinion should jump free. If not, the starter motor will have to be removed or at least have the bolts loosened (see page 55).

In pre-engaged starters, the fault is likely to be caused by the operating lever sticking. In order to clean this it will also be necessary to remove the starter. The procedure for removal is identical for all starters. It is not a difficult job, but it is a dirty one because the starter motor is fitted low down in the engine department and is usually covered with dirt, oil and grease.

Essential preliminaries are to disconnect the battery and make sure the handbrake is firmly applied. Disconnect all the wires attached to the motor and make a rough sketch of them in position if you think you will have any difficulty in replacing them correctly. The bolts securing the motor to the engine housing will be found at the join between the two—remove these and lift out the motor.

If it is an inertia motor, the action of removing it may free the pinion, in which case you will hear a metallic 'clonk' as it slides along the shaft. If you hear this, replace the motor immediately and try to start the car again.

If no such sound is heard you will have to clean the sliding gear. Do this with a wire brush (or wire wool) and petrol. Take care to stop petrol running down the shaft and into the body of the motor and do not use grease on the shaft of the motor. Work the starting gear up and down the shaft by hand to ease it. Refit the motor only when the pinion winds right up to the end of the shaft and springs back freely. If the pinion is found to be in bad condition (with worn or missing teeth) (figs. 19 and 20) or cleaning has little improvement the sliding gear must be dismantled.

On the pre-engaged type, the part to clean is the operating lever. To reach this you will have to remove the solenoid from the motor. This may allow you to reach in to clean and grease the pivot of the lever. If this fails to ease the lever, the motor will have to be dismantled further.

Motor failing to engage

If the motor turns but fails to engage with the fly-wheel, the cause again depends on the type of starter motor fitted (see above).

If it is of the inertia type, the starter pinion is likely to have jammed on its shaft. The motor must be removed and the sliding gear cleaned.

On the pre-engaged type of starter, this symptom is likely to have been caused by the operating lever seizing and preventing the pinion from engaging with the fly-wheel of the engine. The starter motor and solenoid must be removed before the lever can be freed.

It is also possible that the over-run clutch has failed. This is a device which prevents the engine from turning the motor after it has started in the fraction of a second before the solenoid withdraws the pinion.

When the starter motor jams

Procedures for dealing with a jammed starter motor are fully described on pages 50-54.

The points and plugs

Symptom	Possible causes	Remedies
Engine turns over but will not start	Tracking in the ignition	Wipe or spray dry, replace HT leads and distributor cap
	Worn contact brush	Replace brush
	Defective coil	Replace coil
	Cracked rotor arm	Renew rotor arm
	Dirty, incorrectly gapped or worn points	Clean, adjust or replace points
	Dirty, incorrectly gapped or worn spark-plugs	Clean, adjust or replace plugs
	Poor low tension connections	Clean or tighten connections
	No petrol in tank	Fill tank
	Faulty fuel pump	Repair or replace pump
	Blocked fuel line	Clear or replace pipe
	Blocked carburettor	Service carburettor
	Ignition timing wrong	Check timing

If your car refuses to start, even though the starter is turning the engine over normally, there are eight probable causes: tracking in the ignition circuit, a worn contact brush in the distributor cap, a cracked rotor arm, a defective coil, dirty or incorrectly gapped points, poor low tension circuit connections, dirty or defective spark-plugs, and incorrect ignition timing.

Another group of likely causes concern problems of fuel supply and include a failed petrol pump, blockages in the supply lines, a blocked carburettor, blocked filters and, of course, no petrol in the tank itself.

Testing the ignition
If the car will not start the first task is to see if the ignition circuit is functioning properly; to check, in short, that it is producing a spark.

The quickest way to do this is to use one of the HT leads which run from the distributor to the spark-plugs. Detach a lead from its spark-plug and remove any plastic cap which may conceal the metal socket into which the plug fits. If it proves difficult to remove find a nail which has a head that will fit firmly into the socket. Grip the lead by its plastic insulation and hold it no more than 6 mm ($\frac{1}{4}$in.) away from the engine block (fig. 2). With an assistant operating the starter, you should see a series of sparks jumping from the lead to the engine.

If not, there is clearly some fault with the ignition system.

The engine's failure to produce a spark can result from any of a number of causes, and the way to track down the actual cause is given in the accompanying chart (fig. 3).

Tracking in the ignition
Tracking is the term used when the electricity is not following its planned route to the spark-plugs, but is short-circuiting to another part of the car. This can be caused by damp settling on certain parts of the ignition system and by the appearance of cracks in the HT leads or the distributor cap, or both. The moisture and cracks both offer the current an alternative path and therefore allow it to leak away from the proper ignition circuit. In damp, misty weather this is a likely cause of non-starting.

If this is suspected, take a clean, dry cloth and thoroughly

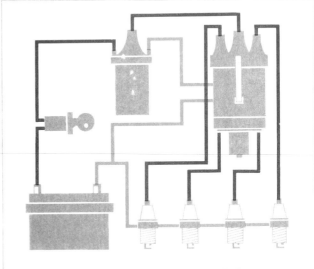

1 A typical ignition circuit for a four-cylinder car

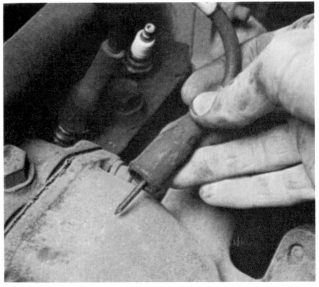

2 Checking the HT lead can be done without removing the plastic cap. Fit a nail firmly to the cap and hold it close to the engine

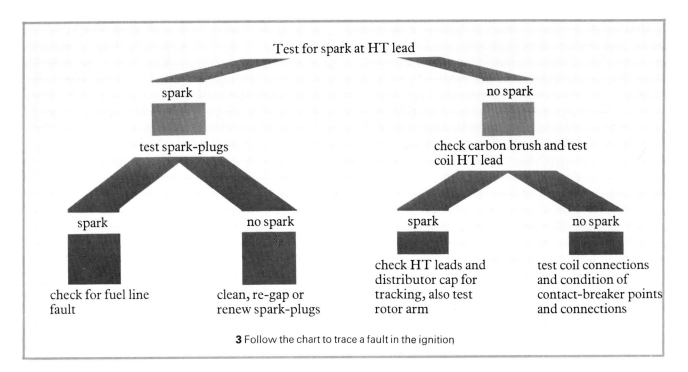

Test for spark at HT lead

spark → test spark-plugs

no spark → check carbon brush and test coil HT lead

test spark-plugs:
- spark → check for fuel line fault
- no spark → clean, re-gap or renew spark-plugs

check carbon brush and test coil HT lead:
- spark → check HT leads and distributor cap for tracking, also test rotor arm
- no spark → test coil connections and condition of contact-breaker points and connections

3 Follow the chart to trace a fault in the ignition

wipe dry each HT lead. With the ignition off, push a corner of the cloth into the sockets at the ends of the leads and wipe them dry too. Also wipe the tops of the spark-plugs dry. Replace the leads and trace them back to the distributor. Unclip the top of this and dry off the inside of the cap. Be very thorough here, as damp can settle in the most obscure places. Make a point of drying inside the sockets holding the HT leads. A good alternative to wiping dry is to spray the affected components with a damp-repellent aerosol such as WD40.

The HT leads should also be examined closely. If any have small cracks in the insulation you may have found the cause of the trouble. Look inside the distributor cap for cracks and forked marks showing the path of the current.

If any of the HT leads are found to be in poor condition they should all be replaced. If one has deteriorated, the chances are that the rest will be well on the way, so renewing them all now will save further trouble later. If the distributor cap is found to be faulty this too must be replaced, together with the HT leads. Spraying poorly insulated leads with a de-watering fluid is only a temporary cure.

Worn distributor contact brush
The contact brush is found on the inside of the distributor cap, right in the centre. It is a small, grey piece of carbon often held in a spring (fig. 5).

When the distributor cap is in place this brush makes contact with the rotor arm and carries HT current to it. If it is making less than perfect contact the efficiency of the ignition will suffer.

If the tip of the brush is burnt or chipped it must be replaced. Those mounted on a spring should be checked to see that they move up and down freely. If not, replacement is necessary. Distributors whose brush is fixed rigidly into the distributor cap must have the entire cap replaced if the brush has worn flush with the plastic.

Faulty ignition coil
The coil is a small, metal cylindrical component and is always fixed on or near the engine block. The best way to find it is to follow back the lead which runs to the centre of the distributor. This goes straight to the coil (fig. 6).

The coil's function is to boost low tension current (12

4 Wipe out the distributor cap very thoroughly if you suspect that damp may have settled inside. Use a clean, dry cloth

5 Check the carbon brush or fixed contact. Replace faulty carbons, or the complete cap if fixed contacts are fitted

Nelson Hargreaves

45

volts) from the battery into high tension current (up to 30,000 volts) for the spark-plugs. It is clearly essential that it be in good condition, and a fault in the coil is the cause of many failures to start.

The coil has three leads connected to its top surface. One brings LT current from the battery (via the ignition switch). This current passes through the coil and on through the second terminal, to the points. These are held by push-on connectors. The third and largest lead (fig. 7) carries HT current to the distributor cap.

The best means of checking the condition of the coil is through this last lead. Unclip the distributor cap and, having checked the contact brush (see above), hold an insulated screwdriver close to, but not touching, the contact brush. Make sure that the shaft of the screwdriver is also touching a good earthing point (fig. 8). Ask a friend to turn the engine over and a series of sparks should jump from the brush to the screwdriver. If so, the coil is in good order.

If sparks do not appear check the top of the coil. Wipe off any oil or grease that may have accumulated there. Next disconnect the HT lead from the top of the coil. This is usually held in place by a knurled plastic nut, the whole connection being protected by a thin rubber cover. Ease the rubber away and undo the plastic washer. Be careful here, as it is fragile and will crack if too much pressure is applied to it. If there is no nut the lead will simply be a push-fit into the top of the coil, in which case it can simply be eased out (fig. 9).

With the end of the lead exposed, examine the condition of the wires in the core. If they appear at all dirty or thin the wire must be cut back to expose the full core of wires, then reconnected.

Next, disconnect the thin leads and check the condition of their terminals (fig. 10). Clean them with abrasive paper if they are badly tarnished. Reconnect all the wires and test at the distributor cap again.

If there is still no response, turn the engine so that the contact-breaker points in the distributor are open. Connect one end of a test lamp (fig. 11) to the terminal which carries the wire to the distributor. Connect the other wire to earth (fig. 12). Turn on the ignition. If the lamp lights, current is clearly leaving the coil and it is therefore working properly. If it does not, one last check must be made before concluding that the coil is at fault. This will test if power is reaching the coil.

6 The ignition coil. It is usually fixed on the engine block by a steel clamp around the middle. Slacken this to remove the coil

7 The thin wires attached to the top of the coil carry power from the ignition switch and to the contact-breaker points

8 When testing the coil be careful to see that the shaft of the screwdriver is in firm contact with a good earthing point

9 To check the condition of the HT lead in the top of the coil, prise it out carefully. See that the contacts are clean

Nelson Hargreaves

To do this attach one of the test lamp leads to the other small terminal on the coil and connect the second lead to an earthing point (fig. 13). Turn on the ignition. If the bulb lights, power is flowing into the coil and, as the other tests have proved negative, the coil must be defective.

The coil is another part of the ignition that is not capable of being repaired, but must be replaced. This is not a complicated exercise as the coil is usually held in place by, at most, two bolts. The one point to watch is that the two thin leads are connected to the correct terminals on the new coil—so change them over one at a time.

Cracked rotor arm

The rotor arm is carried on top of the shaft in the body of the distributor. It is a thick plastic boss and has a shaped metal plate fixed on its top edge (fig. 14). It performs the highly important function of distributing the HT power to each of the spark-plugs in turn.

If the plastic cracks it can provide an alternative path for the current. To check for this, remove the rotor arm and look at it closely. If it appears to be slightly cracked, renew it. A more positive test is to remove the central lead from the distributor cap. With the rotor arm back in position,

get a friend to turn the engine while you hold the bare end of the lead close to the centre of the rotor arm (fig. 15). For once the absence of a spark is a good sign, and its presence is a bad one. If a spark is there it is obvious that the plastic body of the rotor arm is not preventing the current from running to earth, so it should be renewed.

Dirty electrodes

The electrodes which receive the current from the rotor arm are also a potential source of trouble. These are the brass studs in the distributor cap (fig. 16).

If any show a slight deposit of carbon, clean it off with a rag soaked in methylated spirits. If these contacts are pitted or badly burned the distributor cap must be replaced. Never attempt to clean the electrodes with an abrasive as this will widen the gap between the rotor arm and electrode.

Faulty points

The contact-breaker points control the timing of the surges of HT current which the coil sends to the distributor. They also influence the strength of the current. It is therefore essential that they be in good condition.

There are two main factors which affect them: incorrect

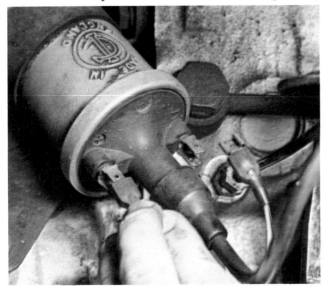

10 The low tension terminals should also be examined. Pull off the connectors and clean the copper blades if they are tarnished

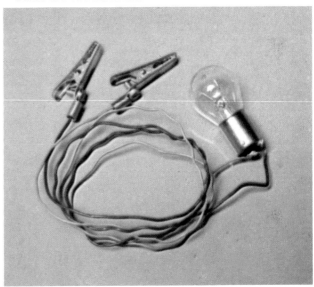

11 To make a test lamp, solder two wires to the terminals of a 12-volt bulb and attach crocodile clips to the other ends

12 To test the low tension windings of the coil, fix one clip to a terminal and the other to an earth. Then turn on the ignition

13 Do the same with the other terminal. If the bulb does not light, move the clips slightly to make a better connection

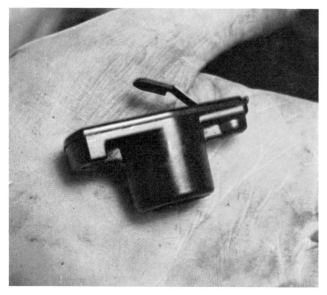

14 The rotor arm. Examine the metal plate for signs of wear and the plastic for cracks. Replace the arm if you find either

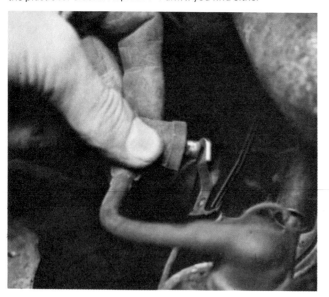

15 A good test for the rotor arm is to disconnect the HT lead from the coil and hold it above the rotor while the engine turns

16 The electrodes in the distributor cap must be in good order. Check that they are clean, but never clean them with an abrasive

gapping, and an accumulation of dirt.

The points gap is checked by sliding a feeler gauge between the contacts. First turn the engine over by hand until the points are fully open. The gap can then be measured when it is at its widest.

With the points open, check if they are clean. The slightest trace of dirt on them can be the 'last straw' in an engine that is already reluctant to start, so it is a good idea to clean them even if they do not appear to be particularly dirty. This can be done without removing the points. Rub each side of the contacts with fine glasspaper and blow out any dust which this might produce.

If, on the other hand, an inspection of the points shows that they are quite obviously dirty, they can be removed for a more thorough cleaning. In many respects, however, this may be more trouble than it is worth. Points have only a short life and, as they are crucial to the performance of the car, it is a good policy to replace them when they have clearly deteriorated. They should certainly be renewed if they are blackened or pitted.

Poor low-tension connections

The low tension circuit runs from the small terminal of the coil (see above) to the contact-breaker points. A fault at any of the connections in between could interrupt the circuit and cause the engine's failure to start.

Check for any signs of dirt or corrosion or loose connections. Clean or tighten as appropriate. If you dismantle any of these connections for cleaning, be careful to replace in the correct order the assortment of nylon and metal washers you will find. To be sure of doing this, lay out the washers on the wing of the car in the order in which you remove them.

Faulty spark-plugs

For the engine to start reliably the spark-plugs must be clean and correctly gapped.

If the HT lead held close to the block eventually produces a spark, yet the engine still refuses to fire, there is a good chance that the plugs are neither clean nor correctly gapped.

Remove the plugs, connect one to its HT lead and hold it against the engine—do not, of course, hold the plug itself, but the HT lead (fig. 17). Once the engine is turned over sparks should appear across the gap. If not, the plugs must be cleaned and gapped. If this produces no improvement the plugs will have to be replaced. Be careful not to over-tighten them.

Other possible faults

If all the tests described above prove that petrol is reaching the engine and that the plugs are sparking, then all that is left is a major fault such as slipped timing or a disconnected drive to the distributor or even faulty valve gear.

A quick check of the timing – a rough one, but it will do – is to remove No. 1 plug and bring the engine round until No. 1 piston is at the top if its compression stroke. Check this by holding your thumb over the plug-hole to feel for compression. When the piston is at TDC (top dead centre) on its compression stroke, the rotor arm should be pointing towards the lead to that cylinder with the points just about opening.

If it is widely out, then the timing has slipped for some reason and it will need much closer investigation to find out why (see pages 66–67).

Similarly, the valve timing may also have slipped and if no compression can be felt then a serious fault has arisen in the valve train.

Emergency starting procedures

Mechanical faults are not the only reasons for cars failing to start. Driver error is as frequently responsible.

On most cars the choke should be pulled out fully and the starter operated without touching the accelerator. The common habit of wildly pumping the accelerator—as much out of frustration as in a belief that it will help to start the car—will only swamp the engine with petrol and saturate the points of the plugs.

If your car is proving reluctant to start, do not keep the starter turning as this will rapidly flatten the battery. Operate it in short, sharp bursts of about five seconds.

On cold mornings the viscosity, or thickness, of the engine oil increases significantly, thus increasing the work of the starter motor. In such circumstances, let the clutch in when you turn the starter. This will take the weight of the gear-box off the load the starter motor is turning.

Using jump leads
If the battery will not turn the engine over at all, jump leads can be used to connect a sound battery to the flat one. Bring the car with the good battery as close as possible to the non-starter.

First connect the jump leads to the terminals of the flat battery. Then start up the car with the good battery. Connect the other ends of the leads to the terminals of this battery, making sure that positive terminal is connected to positive terminal, and switch on the ignition of the breakdown.

Never let uninsulated jump leads touch each other while they are connected to a good battery, or you will weld them together.

Wielding a starting handle
Some cars are equipped with starting handles, which engage with a notch on the pulley on the end of the crankshaft. Actually getting the handle on is often awkward, but lifting the bonnet and peering down between the engine and the radiator allows you to see a little

better. Have an assistant in the car with the ignition turned on and ready to press the throttle when the engine fires.

Once it is in position, grip the handle in one hand and ease the engine round until you feel its resistance becoming stiffer. This will mean that one of the pistons is coming up on to compression. Pause, then swing the handle over with as much momentum as possible.

Bump starting
Bump starting also allows a flat battery or broken starter motor to be by-passed.

It can be used, however, only if the car is standing on a hill or you have a group of volunteers willing to push the car. If so, turn on the ignition, pull out the choke and see that the car is in neutral. Then let off the handbrake and either allow the car to roll off down the hill or signal to the pushers that they should get going. Get the car up to about 5mph, engage third gear and let out the clutch. See that your assistants keep pushing after you have let the clutch out, as the momentum of the car alone is unlikely to be sufficient.

Once the engine fires, let in the clutch, stop the car, and rev the engine to keep it from stalling.

Tow starting
A car can be towed into life in much the same way, only with another car towing the non-starting car.

There is a correct way to attach the towing rope: it must be tied to a point on the car which is capable of taking the strain that towing will put on it. So do not attach the rope to any part of the steering or suspension, nor, on a front-wheel-drive car, to the drive shafts. Bumpers are also a bad fixing point.

Look under the car before you decide where to fix the rope, as some manufacturers provide towing points. Many transverse engined cars, for example, have hook-ended bolts where the sub-frame joins the body. If there is no obvious towing point available put the rope around an engine mounting bracket.

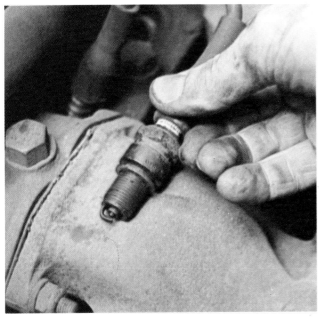

17 Test the spark plugs by holding the body of the plug against an earthing point on the engine. For safety use insulated pliers

18 Check all the electrical connections. The one on the right is badly frayed and could well prevent the engine from starting

The starter motor

Symptom	Possible causes	Remedies
Starter motor jammed	Pinion locked into ring gear	Try rapid disengagement methods
		Remove and refit starter motor
		Replace faulty components
	Faulty solenoid	Replace solenoid
Starter motor appears jammed	Faulty solenoid	Replace solenoid

The car starter motor has the mammoth task of turning over the cold engine, fighting thick oil and the engine compression. Surprisingly, starter motors seldom fail and usually have a long life. One fault from which they do occasionally suffer, and which renders the car useless, is jamming. The immediate remedy for this is usually simple but a continual failure of this sort will necessitate removing and cleaning the starter motor.

A starter motor is basically a powerful electric motor. It has only an occasional rather than a continuous use but, when it is used, a great deal is demanded from it. Modern multigrade oils have made the starter motor's work easier but, on a cold day, it may still use up to 400 amps of current or over 4.5 Kw (6 hp).

Considering the work it has to do, it is not surprising that the starter motor occasionally jams. Starter motor jamming may occur in either of two ways; the whole unit may jam with the pinion locked into the ring gear or the starter motor armature may refuse to revolve.

You need to understand the operation of the starter motor and its relationship to other components before you try to locate and cure any faults. There are, however, one or two easy disengagement methods you can apply that do not require this knowledge and it is suggested that these simple methods are tried first.

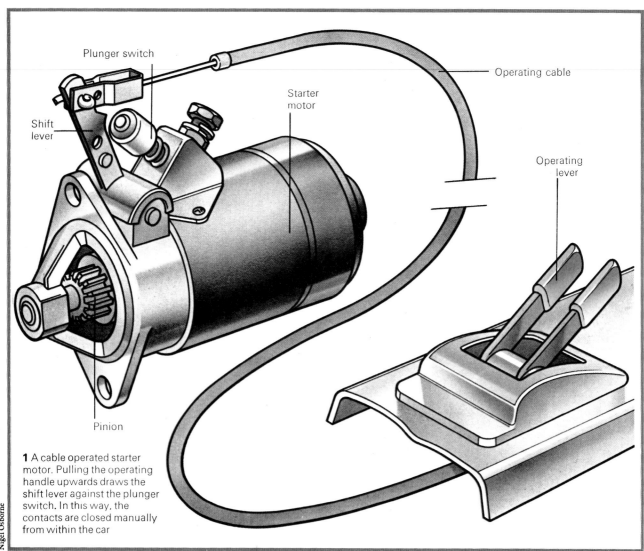

Plunger switch

Shift lever

Starter motor

Operating cable

Operating lever

Pinion

1 A cable operated starter motor. Pulling the operating handle upwards draws the shift lever against the plunger switch. In this way, the contacts are closed manually from within the car

Nigel Osborne

Rapid disengagement methods

These disengagement methods are sometimes sufficient in themselves to cure starting faults.

First switch off the engine and the ignition. Then tap the starter motor or its operating solenoid (see below) with a spanner. Now try to start the car again.

If tapping the starter and/or solenoid does not do the trick, try to jerk the gearing free. There are two methods of doing this and the method suitable for your car depends on the type of transmission fitted.

On cars with manual transmission, switch off the ignition, partially apply the handbrake and select second gear. Then rock the car backwards and forwards. This will turn the engine slightly and is often enough to throw the starting gear out of engagement. After rocking the car a few times you can try to start the car again.

On cars with automatic transmission, there is a method that can be used if you have an inertia starter motor (see below). Inertia starter motors often have a square ended shaft protruding through the back of the unit, sometimes concealed by a metal cap. Turning this shaft backwards and forwards a few times should release the pinion. If you do not have an inertia starter motor of this sort, you may have a starting handle that you can use to rock the engine.

If none of these methods works, you will have to inspect more thoroughly the starter motor and/or its solenoid.

How starter motors work

A typical starter motor is shown in figs. 2 and 3. This powerful electric motor is connected mechanically to the engine flywheel when starting the car. Once the car has started, the starter motor is rapidly disengaged.

There are two methods used on modern cars to engage and disengage the starter. Both begin by forcing the starter pinion (a gear on the motor) into mesh with a much larger gear on the flywheel. This flywheel gear, the ring gear, forms a ring around the flywheel (fig. 5). As soon as the engine has started and turns faster than the starter motor, the pinion is disengaged from the ring gear.

In old cars, and some more modern cars such as the Fiat 126, the starter motor is operated by a cable. This cable connects the starter either to a lever on the floor next to the driver's seat or to a pull knob on the fascia. Applying the lever or knob closes heavy duty contacts, needed because of the large current drawn from the battery, and the starter motor armature rotates. The pinion is thrown up the armature shaft along helical splines and meshes with the ring gear, turning the engine.

In some contemporary cars, such as Mk I Minis, the contacts are in the form of a pushbutton which is situated on the floor by the driver's seat.

In most modern cars, such partly mechanical systems have been replaced by an all-electric system using a solenoid.

Starter motor solenoids

The starter motor solenoid (a plunger which is forced along the centre of a cylinder by a magnetic field) is triggered by a low current from the 'start' position of the ignition switch. Operating the solenoid closes the heavy duty contacts to actuate the starter motor.

Two main types of solenoid are used with starter motors. The older type, still used on many cars, is mounted complete with its switch contacts in the engine compartment. It is usually positioned close to the starter motor to avoid the need for long runs of heavy cable. It may have an extension of the solenoid shaft, covered by a rubber bulb, sticking out on one side. Pressing this extension, the by-pass switch,

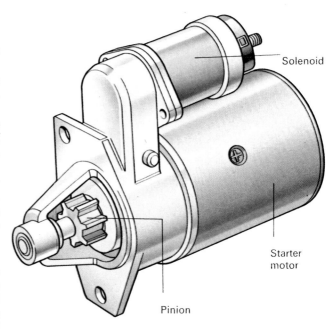

2 A typical pre-engaged starter motor. It is easily recognised by the solenoid fitted to the top of the unit

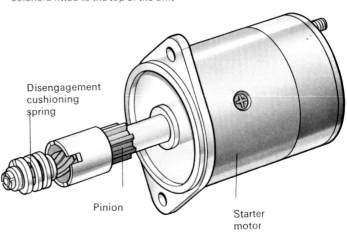

3 A typical inertia starter motor. The solenoid is not integral, it is mounted elsewhere inside the engine compartment

operates the solenoid manually. A starter using a solenoid of this type is called an 'inertia' starter motor.

More recent types of solenoid are mounted on top of the starter motor and have two functions. They not only operate as the main switch, they also bring the pinion into engagement with the ring gear. This replaces the older, cruder disengagement system where the throwing action of the turning starter armature is used. The combined solenoid/starter motor system is called a 'pre-engaged starter' and is much quieter in operation than the older inertia type and more popular with manufacturers.

Finding out which type of starter motor you have in your car is simply a matter of locating the starter and looking at it: pre-engaged starter motors have their cylindrical solenoid mounted on top of them (fig. 2).

Jammed starter motor

If the engine will not start or turn over when the starter switch is operated, and there is no electrical supply fault (pages 38-39), it is likely that the starter motor has jammed. The first check that you should make is that the battery is charged and the terminals are sound. Switch on the headlamps; this will give an immediate indication of the state of the battery—if they light up, the battery is charged.

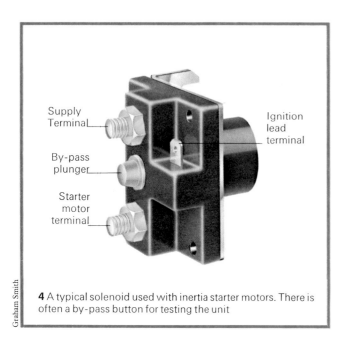

4 A typical solenoid used with inertia starter motors. There is often a by-pass button for testing the unit

Supply Terminal

By-pass plunger

Starter motor terminal

Ignition lead terminal

Graham Smith

Next, switch the ignition key to the start position. If the headlights remain bright there must be a fault in the starter electrics or operating switches (see 'faulty solenoid', below), for no power is reaching the starter motor.

But if the headlights dim considerably, the starter gear is jammed in its driving position with the engine. This may be due to one of two things: the starter solenoid is not working properly, or the starter motor itself is faulty.

Faulty solenoid

A fault in the solenoid may be responsible for either form of starter motor jamming. The solenoid may keep the contacts closed, maintaining the spinning action of the armature and preventing the pinion from lifting out of the ring gear. Alternatively, the solenoid may keep the contacts open, preventing power reaching the motor and not allowing the armature to spin or the pinion to make contact with the ring gear. In either case the car cannot be started.

The first stage of locating solenoid faults lies in determining whether or not the starter is engaged. To do this, inspect the pinion end of the starter motor.

If it is free from the ring gear, the solenoid may be either

keeping the contacts open, or (in pre-engaged starters) refusing to engage the pinion in the ring gear. If your car has a by-pass switch, press it. If the starter now works the solenoid itself is faulty and must be replaced. If there is no by-pass switch, as with pre-engaged motors, you will have to bridge the main terminals (often covered by a rubber case) on the solenoid with an insulated screwdriver. Again, if the starter now works the solenoid itself is faulty.

If the starter motor pinion is locked into the ring gear and the rapid disengagement methods (see above) did not work, you will have to dismantle the starter motor (see below), rectify the fault and then re-assemble the starter with the pinion free and test the solenoid.

Replacing a faulty solenoid

Removing and replacing a starter motor solenoid is a relatively easy job, the most important thing being the correct reconnection of the wiring.

If the solenoid is separate from the starter motor, first disconnect the wires, noting their correct positions. Then unbolt the faulty unit and replace it with the new one. Finally, refit the wires.

Solenoids which are part of a pre-engaged starter motor are slightly harder to replace. You will first have to remove the starter motor (see below). Then undo the solenoid mounting bolts that run vertically down from the solenoid into the body of the motor. Remove these bolts and lift out the solenoid. Take care when fitting the new solenoid that the solenoid plunger is in position with the operating lever.

Removing the starter motor

The removal method for starter motors varies slightly from car to car and is also dependent on the type of starter motor fitted. Which type your car has may be hard to establish, since sometimes cars from the same manufacturer, and in the same model range, have different types.

In any case, starter motors of either type are not difficult to remove. They are usually bolted to the clutch bell-housing low down at one side of the engine block. One notable exception is the original front wheel drive Triumph 1300, which has its ring gear mounted at the front of the engine with the starter brackets on one side. Its operation normally has a slight ringing sound (do not confuse this with the sound of a broken drive-spring).

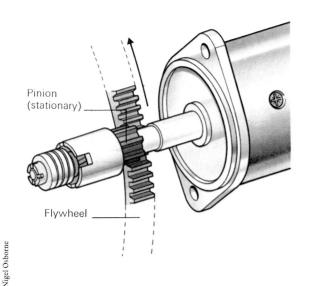

Pinion (stationary)

Flywheel

5 When the inertia starter motor is not being used the pinion rests in front of, and out of contact with, the engine flywheel

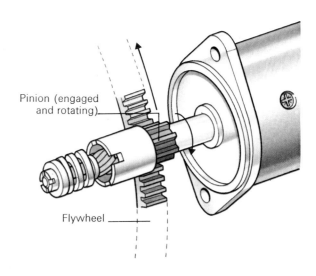

Pinion (engaged and rotating)

Flywheel

6 When the solenoid contacts are closed, the commutator starts to spin, throwing the pinion backwards to mesh with the flywheel

Nigel Osborne

7 When removing either the solenoid or the starter motor, always disconnect the positive terminal on the battery

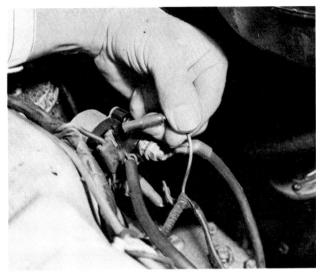

8 On the Cortina Mk 2, the solenoid is mounted securely on a wheel arch in the engine compartment. Remove the ignition lead

9 Next, disconnect the supply lead. This lead comes straight from the battery and is usually a bolt-on connection

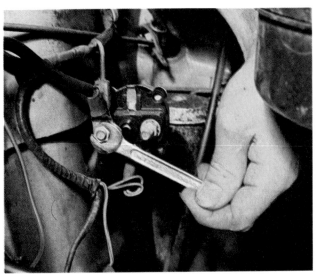

10 Then remove the starter motor supply lead and any supply leads to the accessories on the other solenoid terminal

The basic removal method, which can be adapted for most cars, is as follows.

First, disconnect the live battery terminal to prevent the risk of shorting. Then remove the main feed wire from the terminal on the starter motor. On pre-engaged starters, you will also have to remove the solenoid feed cable. Take care when removing the main terminal nut that you do not allow the terminal screw to move, as this may damage the inner wiring. On cars with a ballast resistor, remove the by-pass cable on the solenoid.

Next, remove the screws or nuts holding the starter to the engine. (You may have to remove any components that are in the way before doing this.)

Finally, slide the starter motor out of its housing.

Starter motor inspection

Most faults are caused by poor connections, but there may be mechanical causes. Parts that are likely to be involved in a jammed starter are mainly the armature and the pinion. In particular, examine the pinion for worn or broken teeth. On the inertia type of starter motor, make sure that the pinion moves freely on its splines right back to the buffer spring. Any faults in this area will require the replacement of the Bendix drive or even the whole starter motor. Replace any faulty components that you discover. While

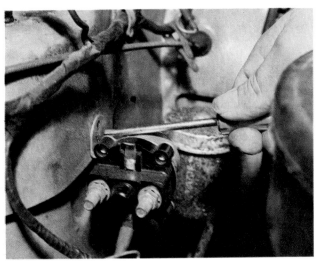

11 The solenoid is held on this wheel arch by means of a bracket. Unscrew the bracket and remove the solenoid

you have the starter motor out, take the opportunity to examine the ring gear on the flywheel. Turn the engine by hand to expose this a section at a time. Any damage on the ring gear will mean replacing the flywheel. This particular type of replacement is described in the chapter on clutch

Nelson Hargreaves

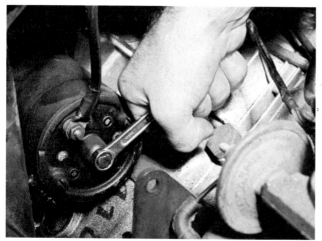

12 If the starter motor has a rear extension of the armature fitted with a bolt, this can be used to free a jammed pinion

13 An alternative, and much more crude, method is to jarr the pinion free by striking the starter motor with a hammer

14 Removing the starter motor on the Cortina Mk 2 is relatively easy, there are no access problems. Remove the supply lead

15 Then undo the starter motor mounting bolts. These hold the unit on to the bell-housing. There is one underneath the car

16 There is another accessible from the engine compartment. Remove it, supporting the motor by hand

17 Finally, loosen the brush cover and slide it back to inspect the condition of the motor

Nelson Hargreaves

maintenance (pages 74-79). Repair is not a practical consideration.

After re-assembly of either type of starter motor, it should be tested before you re-fit it to the engine. To do this, hold the starter against the engine (or on the earth terminal of the battery if yours is a positive-earth car). Then connect a jump lead between the live terminal on the battery and the main starter motor terminal. Hold the starter body very tightly while doing this; the torque is tremendous and the starter will try to jump out of your hand. Wear rubber gloves or rubber soled shoes while doing this, otherwise you may receive a small electric shock. When the armature and pinion spin freely, it is safe to re-fit the starter in the car. If it does not spin freely, check your re-assembly carefully for mistakes and rectify them. When all is well, re-fit the starter and try to start the car in the normal way.

Take care, while refitting the starter motor, that you inspect all the retaining bolts. The unit takes a great deal of physical strain and any weakness in these bolts may cause them to snap off, creating more starting problems.

Renewing brushes

Starter motor brushes which are less than ⅜in. long must be replaced. To make a simple inspection remove the dust cover clamp ring, revealing the brushes and the commutator.

If the brushes are worn the end plate must be removed in order to replace them. First, undo the nut on the main supply terminal and take off the washers and spacer, noting their order for re-assembly. Next, unscrew the two long bolts (through bolts) and slide them out carefully to avoid any chance of damage to the field windings. The end plate can now be levered away from the body.

There are four brushes, two with insulated leads which go to the field windings, and two uninsulated leads which are on the end plate. Note that one of the insulated leads is longer then the other.

Before dealing with the brushes, examine the commutator. If it is damaged or badly worn there is no point in going further because a new motor will have to be fitted. If it is merely a bit dirty, clean it with a strip of fine glasspaper by wrapping the strip round the commutator and using a sawing action, moving round to give even treatment. Unlike a dynamo, the divisions between the commutator segments must under no circumstances be undercut. Taking care that grit does not get into the starter body, clean off with methylated spirit.

If new brushes are to be fitted they have to be soldered into place. The insulated leads are copper cored and are joined to the aluminium field windings by a special process, so you will have to solder the new brush leads to 'pig-tails' from the originals. Cut through the old leads leaving at least ½in. Clean the ends of old and new leads and make a loop at the end of the new one. Hook the new lead through the loop and solder the two together to make a secure joint. The uninsulated leads are attached to the end plate and are treated in the same way.

When replacing the brushes in their holders do not, at first, let the spiral tension springs (clock springs) bear on top of the brushes. Hook them up so they rest on the edges of the holders; this makes it easier to refit the end plate. Slide the end plate into position, making sure it locates on a notch in the motor body. Insert the long bolts carefully, once again to avoid possible damage to the field windings, and tighten them but do not overtighten. Replace the washers and nylon spacer in their correct positions and tighten the main supply terminal fixing nut. If the nut is loose the terminal bolt may turn when re-fitting the power cable which could damage the internal connection.

When the end plate is secure, a small screwdriver or hooked piece of strong wire can be used to lift the clock springs and move them so they bear on the tops of the brushes. Replace the dust cover.

If your car is fitted with a face-type commutator starter, do not use any sort of abrasive to clean the segments as they are fairly thin. Use methylated spirit on a clean non-linting cloth. New brushes in the end plate are simply pressed into their holders and are kept in contact with the commutator face by coil springs. The field winding brush leads (insulated), however, have to be soldered in the same way as for the drum commutator starter described above.

With a pre-engaged starter, the procedure for replacing the brushes is much the same as for the inertia starter, except that you may have to remove the solenoid to gain access.

18 Remove rear end bush cover and shims and remove U clip. Keep everything in the correct order for re-assembly

19 Ease away commutator end plate to expose brush assembly. Renew brushes if less than 10mm (³/₈in) long

20 Field winding brushes are pressure soldered to their posts, cut leads ¹/₄in from posts and solder new brushes to these tags

21 Check brushes move freely. If not, use a fine file to ease them. Check brush springs for equal pressure

Engine temperature problems

Symptom	Possible causes	Remedies
Engine runs too cool or too hot	Faulty thermostat	Replace thermostat
Engine appears to run too cool or too hot	Faulty needle gauge	Replace needle gauge
	Faulty sender unit	Replace sender unit

Your car engine runs most efficiently within a specific temperature range. An engine that remains too cool will stall at idling speeds unless you use the choke. An engine that becomes too hot may seize.

The combustion of petrol in the cylinders creates a great deal of heat and the cooling system is designed to keep this within strict limits. Water-cooled engines are cooled by water flowing through the engine block and absorbing much of the heat. The hot water then flows into the radiator matrix where it is cooled by air flow.

If this water flows too fast, the engine remains cold. If it flows too slowly, or not at all, the engine overheats. The thermostat's job is to control the flow of water, thus keeping the engine within the required range of temperatures.

An engine that fails to reach working temperature, therefore, indicates that the thermostat is faulty.

The temperature gauge
The temperature gauge works independently of the thermostat. Its job is merely to sense the temperature of the cooling water and warn the driver of over- or under-heating.

Temperature gauges can, however, malfunction and consequently give a false reading.

So your first check if your engine does not appear to be reaching working temperature ought logically to be on the temperature gauge. But, in practice, it is better to check the thermostat first, for two reasons: firstly, because it is the more likely to go wrong, and secondly because it is generally easier to get at.

Faulty thermostat
Fig. 1 shows a typical thermostat. It is usually fitted at the base of the top water hose where it enters the cylinder block, although it may be found at other places along this hose. As long as the water passing through this thermostat to or from the radiator is cold, the thermostat stays closed. This restricts the flow of water through the engine block, reducing the cooling effect. The water temperature rises as the engine heat increases and the thermostat gradually opens. The water flow then increases until the engine starts to cool down again. This opening and closing of the thermostat continues until a balance is reached and the engine is maintained at its working temperature.

If the thermostat jams open, the water flow remains fast and the engine will take longer to reach a working temperature. The engine will tend to stall at idling speed unless you use the choke and your petrol consumption will, therefore, greatly increase. Most car heaters use hot water from the cooling system and, if the engine is running cool, these heaters will blow only cold air.

If the thermostat jams closed, the water flow is greatly reduced, it remains in the engine block a great deal longer and the engine will rapidly overheat. The car heater will also become over-efficient. If the engine is allowed to run at too high a temperature for any length of time, it will eventually seize.

If you suspect that a faulty thermostat is causing the problem, remove and inspect it as soon as possible.

Testing the thermostat
To test a thermostat, you will have to remove it from the cooling system. To prevent scalding your hands, it is best to work on the car while the engine is cold.

First, find the thermostat. To do this, trace the top main radiator hose from the top of the radiator back to the engine head. The thermostat is held in a large metal or plastic bulge, the thermostat housing (fig. 6), usually being held on to the engine block by two or three bolts.

Next, you will have to partially drain the cooling system. The method of doing this depends on whether you have an open or a sealed cooling system. Your owner's handbook will tell you the type and capacity of the system.

You can now remove the thermostat. To do this, undo the retaining bolts holding the housing on the cylinder block. Then ease the housing over the studs and remove it. Finally, lift out the thermostat and remove and discard the thermostat gasket.

The first test is a visual inspection of the thermostat. The spring (fig. 9) should be expanded and there should be little—if any—gap between the disc and the body. If this is not the case, it is likely that the thermostat is jammed open.

Next, immerse the thermostat in a bucket of water and gradually heat the water. Use a thermometer to note the temperature of the water. When it reaches between 80°C and 90°C, the thermostat should open fully. Allow the water to cool. The thermostat should gradually close. If the thermostat remains fully open or fully closed, it is faulty and should be renewed.

Fitting a new thermostat is the reversal of the removal method and a new gasket should be used. After refitting the thermostat, you will have to refill the cooling system.

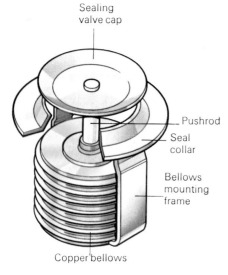

Sealing valve cap

Pushrod

Seal collar

Bellows mounting frame

Copper bellows

1 A typical thermostat used in water-cooled engines. The copper bellows expand with heat, opening the valve

Nigel Osborne

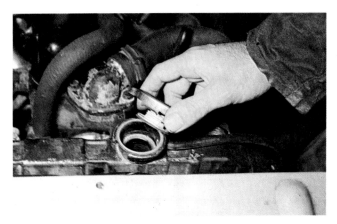

2 Before examining the thermostat, drain the water out of the cooling system. With the engine cold, remove the radiator cap

3 Next, locate and undo the drain plug. This is usually at the base of the radiator under the car

4 The main radiator hose leads from the top of the radiator to the thermostat housing. Undo the jubilee clip at the housing end

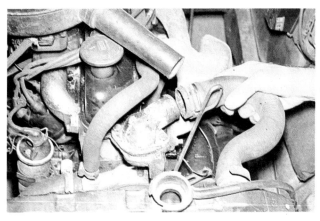

5 Pull the hose away from the housing pipe. Any sediment in the pipe or hose indicates that the system needs flushing

6 The thermostat housing is held onto the engine block by bolts. Clean away any built up sediment and undo these bolts

7 Lift off the thermostat housing. There is a gasket fitted between the housing and the block. Replace this with a new one

8 Next, lift out the thermostat. This may be partially seized into the engine block. If so, carefully lever it out

9 The thermostat out of its housing. Clean away any sediment and inspect the condition of the thermostat spring

Jake Wynter

10 To test the action of the thermostat, put it in a bucket of cold water. Gradually add hot water and watch the valve

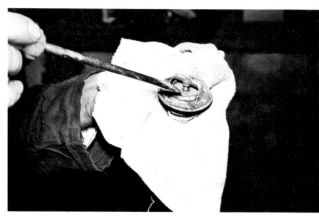

11 Initially, the valve should be sealed shut—as above. As the hot water is added the valve should slowly open

12 If the thermostat is faulty it will stay in the closed valve condition. There is no way to repair it, fit a new one

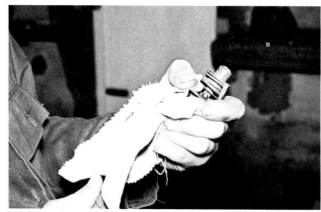

13 A properly working thermostat should open up completely before the water reaches boiling point

14 The temperature gauge sender unit can be seen inside the opening on the engine block. It should be clear of sediment

15 The electrical connection to this sender unit has sheared away from its terminal. A new unit will have to be fitted

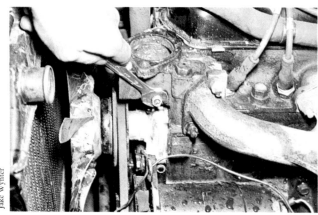

16 To remove and replace the sender unit, unscrew it from the engine block. It may be seized, If so use penetrating oil

17 To test a sender unit without removing it from the engine block, pour boiling water over it through the block opening

Jake Wynter

58

After filling the cooling system, test drive the car. Keep driving until the engine would normally have reached full working temperature. Park the car and push in the choke to make sure that the engine does not stall. Next, try the car heater. This should be fully controllable throughout the engine's temperature range. Finally, look at the temperature gauge (if fitted). It should register normal, but if not the thermostat is not neccessarily still at fault. It may be due to the temperature gauge itself.

Faulty temperature gauge

A large number of cars are fitted with a temperature gauge as standard equipment. Gauges vary in terms of the information they give. The most common type have three calibrations: 'Cold', 'Normal' and 'Hot'. Other gauges may have just 'Cold' and 'Hot', where the mid-position between 'Cold' and 'Hot' is normal, or may have a needle gauge covering the temperature range of the engine.

All these gauges serve the same function—to inform the driver of the temperature of the engine. In normal practice the gauge should read 'Cold' or its equivalent when you start the engine. It should then gradually rise to 'Normal' after about 5 km (3 miles). It should never register 'Hot'. If the gauge does not alter, it may be faulty.

In icy weather, the engine may actually fail to reach working temperature and you should use a radiator baffle (a piece of card or silver foil fixed in front of the radiator grille that reduces the amount of air flowing through the radiator). The engine should then reach working temperature. In normal or warm weather, this should not be necessary.

How temperature gauges work

Before you test the temperature gauge it helps to know how it works.

Basically, the temperature gauge consists of two main components: the sender and the needle gauge.

The sender is fitted into a hot part of the cooling system and reacts to the heat of the water to operate the needle gauge. There are three types of sender unit:

1. The older, vapour pressure sender. This consists of a bulb full of a volatile liquid. As the water temperature increases, the liquid expands and travels along a connecting pipe to the needle gauge on the fascia. The liquid moves the needle to the corresponding mark (fig. 19).

2. The thermal gauge sender. This consists of two contacts screwed into the cylinder block. As the water temperature in the block increases, the contacts vibrate and create a current. This current moves the needle in the gauge to the corresponding graduation mark on the needle gauge (fig. 20) on the car's fascia.

3. The semi-conductor sender. This consists of a pellet made of a material that increases electrical resistance as the temperature falls. Similarly, the resistance falls as the temperature rises. This has the effect of controlling the needle gauge movement (fig. 18).

At the other end of the system, there are three types of needle gauge units:

1. The capillary controlled gauge. This type is used with the vapour pressure sender. The capillary tube connects the volatile liquid in the sender to a needle in the gauge. As the liquid expands, it moves the needle in the gauge.

2. The moving iron gauge. This type is used with the semi-conductor sender unit. As the current from the semi-conductor alters, the magnetic field created by the coils in the gauge alters. This magnetic field controls the movement of the needle.

3. The bi-metallic arm gauge. This unit works with either the thermal gauge sender unit or the semi-conductor sender unit. It consists of a bi-metallic strip surrounded by a coil. As the current from the sender passes through the coil, the arm (bi-metallic strip) bends. This arm is connected to the needle in the gauge and when the arm bends its needle is moved.

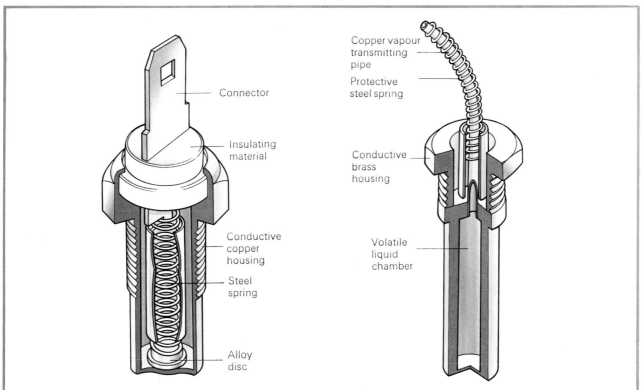

18 A typical semi-conductor sender unit. The electrical resistance of the alloy disc reduces as the temperature rises

19 A typical vapour pressure sender unit. The vapour expands in the chamber and passes along the copper pipe to the gauge

Connector

Insulating material

Conductive copper housing

Steel spring

Alloy disc

Copper vapour transmitting pipe

Protective steel spring

Conductive brass housing

Volatile liquid chamber

Nigel Osborne

Testing the needle gauge

Testing the needle gauge by itself involves the use of test meters that are not usually owned by home mechanics owing to their expense and low rate of use. If you do not own a Universal meter, the best course is to test the sender unit by trying it out with a needle gauge which you know does work (see below). Then, if the sender unit is in order, you know by a process of elimination that it is the original needle gauge which is faulty and which needs to be replaced.

As the cooling system relies on perishable components like rubber hoses and paper gaskets, testing the gauge and sender is a worthwhile part of routine maintenance.

Testing the sender unit

The most difficult part of testing the sender unit lies in locating it. The safest way of doing this is to trace the electrical wire from the loom to the component, using the car handbook circuit diagram. It will probably be located somewhere on the cylinder head, usually near the thermostat housing. On a few cars the sender is tapped into the water jacket further down on the block.

You cannot do this with vapour pressure sender units, however, as they are not electrical. To locate these sender units, trace the capillary tube from the needle gauge straight to the sender unit. It is not difficult, but you must be careful not to confuse it with any other sender unit, for example the one for the oil pressure gauge. If you are not sure which type of sender unit is fitted to your car, consult your local specialist dealer.

When you have located the sender unit, remove any surrounding dirt and carefully unscrew the unit from the cylinder block. It should be free from rust, dirt and water scale. If it is not, carefully clean away any deposits from both the sender and its hole in the cylinder block.

To test semi-conductor or thermal gauge units, first select a meter that you know is working—for instance, the petrol gauge. Disconnect the supply wire from both the sender unit and the petrol gauge. Join the positive terminals from the sender unit with the wire to the supply terminal on the petrol gauge. Connect another wire from the body of the sender unit to a good earth point. Finally, place the sender unit in a bowl of hot water. The petrol gauge needle should start to move. If it does not, the sender unit is faulty.

Reassemble the petrol gauge and its wiring. If the sender unit is faulty, fit a new one. Otherwise, try your cleaned-up sender unit, this time connecting it to the temperature gauge. When you immerse it in the hot water again the gauge should indicate 'Hot'. If it does not, the temperature gauge is faulty and should be replaced with a completely new unit.

When you refit the sender unit in the cylinder block it is a good idea to wipe a gasket sealer or some high temperature grease on the threaded part of the unit. If a gasket or copper washer is used between the unit and the block make sure that you fit a new one.

With vapour pressure sender units and gauges it is not advisable to test the sender unit further than cleaning it. This is because the capillary tube and vapour bulb are delicate. The money you might save by doing the job yourself is not worth the risk of damaging either the old unit or any new unit you fit. For this reason, it is better to take the gauge and sender to a specialist dealer for inspection and, if necessary, replacement.

Replacing a temperature gauge

Many temperature gauges are now part of a sealed unit instrument cluster. If one of these is faulty, it is best left to a dealer for your make of car for removal and replacement. Tampering with these combined instruments involves a risk of damaging the other instruments.

If the gauge is individually mounted, you need only unclip or unscrew the unit, disconnect the wiring and fit a new unit. Try to transfer the wires one at a time to avoid mistakes; otherwise, label them or note their respective colours. Finally, take the car for a short drive and check the action of the new temperature gauge. If it does not work, then you must check all your wiring for any wrong connections and rectify where necessary.

22 Reassemble the components and refill the cooling system with water. Run the engine for a while and then top up again

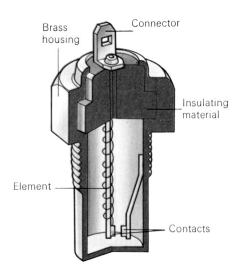

Brass housing — Connector — Insulating material — Element — Contacts

Nigel Osborne

20 A typical thermal gauge sender unit. The two contacts within the unit vibrate as the temperature increases

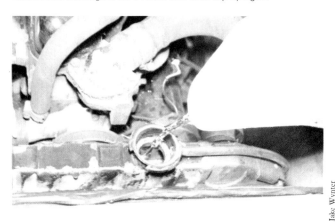

Jake Wynter

21 When you have poured the boiling water over the sender unit in the engine block, look at the gauge. It should read "Hot"

The carburettor

Modern carburettors are what is usually called 'tamperproof'. The mixture has been set at the factory and the adjuster sealed. In fact, the majority of carburettors on European cars are not really tamperproof as very 'often all you need to do to get at the mixture adjustment is to remove a plug or shroud, and sometimes not even that. Once the adjuster has been exposed, tuning can be carried out.

Although it is not yet illegal in Britain, unlike some continental countries, the only way to tune a carburettor efficiently is to use a CO (carbon monoxide) meter to analyse the exhaust gas, and as few ordinary motorists possess one, tuning is probably best left to a specialist. There are, however, a number of maintenance tasks which the owner can and should do.

SU and Stromberg

With SU and Stromberg carburettors, at approximately 3000 mile intervals, unscrew the cap on the suction chamber (dashpot), remove the damper unit, and check the oil level in the suction piston guide rod. For the SU carburettor the level should be 13 mm ($\frac{1}{2}$in) above the top of the rod, for the Stromberg 6.5 mm ($\frac{1}{4}$in.) below. Use SAE 20 or 20W/50 for the SU, and Zenith special oil for Stromberg.

All carburettors are equipped with needle valves which regulate the flow of petrol from the fuel pump to the float chamber. If the needle sticks open because of dirt the carburettor will flood. Try cleaning the valve by swilling it with clean petrol and blowing through it. If this does not work it is probably too worn and needs replacing.

Another thing which can cause flooding is an incorrect float level. The way in which the float chamber is secured varies from make to make but should not be difficult to find. The way in which the level is set also varies and if the information is not in the owner's handbook, check with the manufacturer.

The choke cable adjustment is important, not only to ensure that the choke mechanism is fully off when the knob on the dashboard is pushed right home, but also that it comes into full operation when the control is pulled out.

With most fixed jet carburettors, the choke cable operates a flap in the carburettor air intake. This can be seen if the air cleaner is removed. The flap should blank off the intake when in the closed (cold start) position, and return to the vertical when the choke control is pushed fully home.

The SU carburettor has no flap. Instead, when the choke control is pulled out, it pulls the jet downwards allowing a greater flow of fuel. When it is pushed in, the jet should be raised until it touches the underside of the jet adjusting nut.

Strombergs have a special metering valve in the carburettor body to which a cam lever is attached. When the choke control is pulled out the lever turns. Check that when the control is pushed home the lever returns to its stop on the body of the carburettor.

Do not forget that although an incorrectly adjusted choke cable or richly set mixture will cause excessive fuel consumption, a clogged air cleaner will have much the same effect.

An occasional drop of light oil on all pivot points on the carburettor, not forgetting the pedal inside the car, will also help to keep the linkages moving smoothly. This gives more precise throttle control and aids fuel economy.

1 All Stromberg carburettors are designed with variable jets. This is the 150CD model

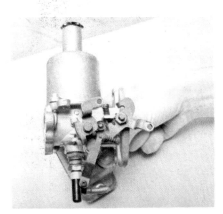

2 SU carburettors are also of the variable jet design. The HS2 model is illustrated

3 The Weber 32 DGV 15B is of the fixed-jet design and is fitted with twin venturi

4 The Zenith 361V EP carburettor is fitted to some Vauxhalls. It is a fixed-jet model

5 This Zenith 361V model differs slightly, as it is a conversion for fitment to Fords

6 The Nikki carburettor is a popular tuning modification, especially on Leyland Minis

Distributor problems

Symptom	Possible causes	Remedies
Engine "pinks"	Mechanical advance not working	Repair or replace mechanical advance
	Vacuum advance not working	Repair or replace vacuum advance
	Timing over advanced	Re-set timing
	Wrong grade of petrol	Use higher octane petrol

The timing of the spark which ignites the petrol/air mix in the combustion chamber is critical to the performance and economy of your car. As the engine speed changes, the time at which the spark must occur changes correspondingly. The distributor has two completely separate mechanisms designed to alter the time of the spark—the mechanical advance system (usually known as the centrifugal advance) and the vacuum advance system.

The most common indication that one or both timing devices are malfunctioning is 'pinking'—a metallic knocking noise, generally accompanied by a failure to run smoothly and a general lack of performance.

After the spark from the ignition system has ignited the compressed petrol/air mix in the compression chamber, there is a brief delay before the burning mixture expands to produce maximum pressure. If the spark is timed correctly, this delay occurs while the piston passes over TDC (top dead centre), and the burning mixture exerts its maximum force when the piston is in the ideal position to transfer this

pressure in the combustion stroke on to the crankpin and, eventually, into forward motion.

As the engine speed increases two things happen to alter the ideal time for the spark. First, the piston completes the combustion stroke faster and there is less time available for full combustion of the petrol/air mix. Second, the petrol/air mix becomes less dense and therefore less compressed at TDC, with the result that the time needed for full combustion is longer. For both these reasons ignition must take place earlier in the cycle.

To match the timing of the spark accurately with the need for the spark, the distributor is fitted with the automatic advance mechanisms. Although the mechanical advance and the vacuum advance systems are designed to operate separately, they work best in combination and it is rare for only one to be fitted.

Several other automatic advance or retard devices may be fitted to cars for emission control. These other systems are specific to a particular make and model of car and are usually sealed units, making them difficult to repair or inspect. They are described at the end of this chapter.

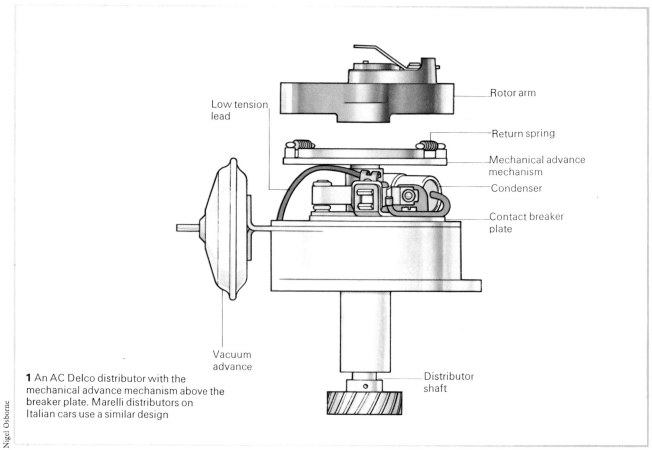

Low tension lead

Rotor arm

Return spring

Mechanical advance mechanism

Condenser

Contact breaker plate

Vacuum advance

Distributor shaft

1 An AC Delco distributor with the mechanical advance mechanism above the breaker plate. Marelli distributors on Italian cars use a similar design

Nigel Osborne

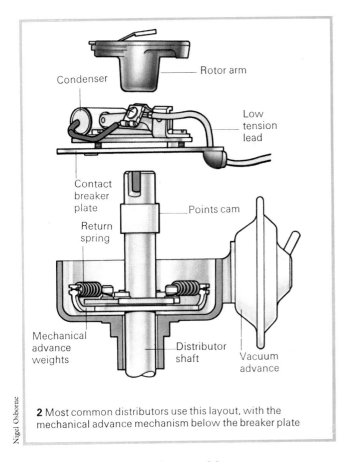

2 Most common distributors use this layout, with the mechanical advance mechanism below the breaker plate

Nigel Osborne

Mechanical advance, where and how

The mechanical advance system is fitted inside the distributor and it is possible to remove and replace the various parts. The system consists of two weights and two springs. They are below the distributor baseplate on most distributors (fig. 2), but above it on AC Delco distributors fitted to Vauxhall and Holden cars and Marelli distributors on Italian cars. In all forms of distributors equipped with a mechanical advance system, the part of the distributor shaft which carries the contact breaker cam is separate from the main shaft and has a small amount of free play. (See page 118 for further information on the ignition system.) One end of each weight is pivotted on a circular drive plate which moves with the distributor main shaft (fig. 3). The other end of each weight is attached to the breaker cam by a small spring. As the distributor main shaft rotates, these weights tend to continue in a straight line due to inertia. The pivotted ends of the weights rotate with the distributor drive plate and the weights are thrown away from the centre (fig. 3). This effect is called movement by centrifugal force. The force increases as the distributor shaft and drive

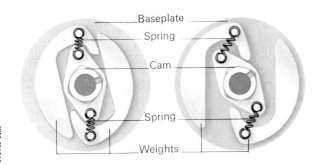

Trevor Hill

3 When the engine is not running, the mechanical advance weights are in the position shown on the left. The distributor shaft turns when the engine is running, and at high speeds this moves the weights by centrifugal force to the position shown on the right

plate move faster. The ends of the weights apply tension to the contact breaker cam through the springs, turning the cam in relation to the mainshaft, and causing the points to open earlier in the compression stroke at higher speeds. The timing is thereby advanced.

In electronic systems, the same effect is achieved by similar means. In magnetic electronic ignition systems the breaker cam is replaced by an induction cam. Advancing this induction cam advances the magnetically induced spark. In optical electronic ignition systems the breaker cam is replaced by light interrupting blades – with a blade for every cylinder. Advancing the blades cuts the light trigger earlier and advances the ignition spark.

With both conventional and electronic ignition systems, the weights and springs are designed to match the special requirements of the particular make and model of car. Although the mechanical advance system combines with the vacuum advance system to maintain perfect ignition timing at all engine speeds, for the purpose of inspection and repair the mechanical advance system should be regarded as operating independently.

Checking for faulty mechanical advance

The mechanical advance system, like other automatic systems, depends on the distributor contact points, rotor arm, cap and shaft being in good working condition. Check and if necessary replace these before looking at the advance system.

Take off the distributor cap and rotor arm. In the AC Delco distributors on Vauxhalls and Holdens and in Marrellis the weights will be immediately visible. On most other distributors, you will also have to remove the contact breaker points and the capacitor, lift off the plastic sleeve at the base of the rotor shaft, and remove the distributor baseplate. The weights will then be exposed. Carry out the following checks:

1. The weights should be free to move out against the tensioning springs. All wiring should be routed clear of these weights and no other obstruction should be near them.
2. Replace the rotor arm and then turn the engine by hand, taking notice of the direction of rotation. Now gently press the cam in this direction using the rotor arm, and release it. The cam should spring back under the tension of the springs. If this does not happen, remove and clean the weights and pivotpoints, having carefully noted their position for reassembly. Replace the weights and fit new tension springs. Make sure you use the correct springs for your make, model and year of car.
3. The mechanical advance weights should not become damaged and cleaning them should be sufficient. If this is not the case the operation of the distributor must be faulty and it should be replaced completely.

Finally, replace the distributor components in reverse order and retime the ignition (see pages 66-67).

Vacuum advance system, where and how

The vacuum advance system is designed to provide additional advance to increase the timing accuracy given by the mechanical advance system at varying driving speeds.

During normal running conditions, the down movement of the piston on the combustion stroke produces a partial vacuum in the inlet manifold. The throttle butterfly in the venturi stays open and this partial vacuum draws an increased amount of petrol/air mix through. During certain running conditions, notably cruising, the butterfly is only partially open. The vacuum increases and less petrol/air mix is therefore drawn into the cylinders. The reduced

4 Working on the mechanical and vacuum advance mechanisms is much easier if you first remove the carburettor air filter

5 With the ignition switched off, disconnect the positive terminal from the battery. Then remove the coil lead from the distributor

6 Next, label the plug leads to help replace them in the correct order, then remove them from the distributor cap

7 Unclip the cap and remove it. On some cars, like this Cortina Mk II, the cap can be removed with all the leads still in place

Nelson Hargreaves

8 You can now start work on the mechanical advance mechanism. It is under the breaker plate on this distributor. Remove the rotor arm

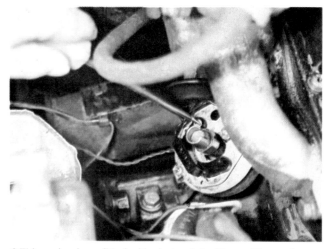

9 This car has been fitted with electronic ignition, with a reed receiver instead of contact breakers. Unscrew and remove this

amount of petrol/air mix takes longer to ignite and the spark must therefore be advanced to maintain maximum power. The vacuum advance uses this extra vacuum to do this automatically. And, because the vacuum both causes the need for the advance and supplies advance, the solution is at all times perfectly matched to the problem. In its simplest form, the vacuum advance system consists of a chamber with an airtight diaphragm sealing the carburettor from the distributor and connected to both by a pipe (fig. 16). The chamber is found attached to the side of the distributor and

can easily be recognised by its shape (fig. 19). A spring is fitted inside the chamber so that when no vacuum is present, the diaphragm is held against the pipe leading from the chamber to the distributor. This effectively seals the distributor from the chamber. When the vacuum is produced in the carburettor inlet manifold, the diaphragm is drawn away from the distributor. The diaphragm is connected to the distributor base plate by a linkage system, and as the diaphragm is drawn against the spring, the linkage moves the base plate. This moves the contact breakers so that they are

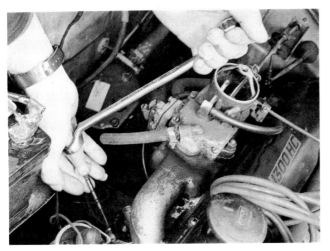

10 The contact breaker plate is held on by two screws. Undo these, using a ring spanner as a lever if the screws are tight

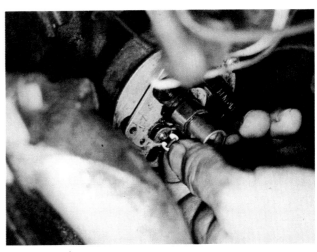

11 On this distributor, the breaker plate is also held on by two circlips. Press the pivot post down and remove the larger clip

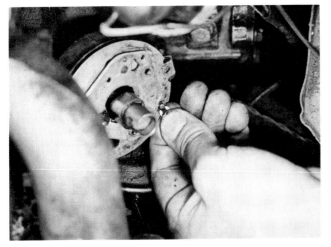

12 Then remove the second, smaller circlip. Take care to keep these circlips and remember their positions

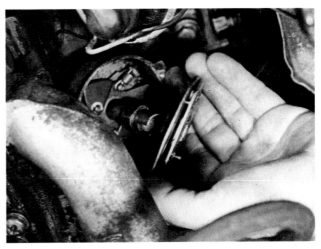

13 The breaker plate is then removed by lifting it over the shaft. Clean the breaker plate and store it for re-use

14 The mechanical advance weights and springs are then exposed. Make sure that they are clean and unobstructed

15 Turning the rotor arm clockwise on this distributor moves the mechanical advance weights. A faulty mechanism will not move

opened earlier by the cam on the distributor shaft and the spark timing is advanced. The vacuum and diaphragm action have the same effect on electronic ignition systems.

Checking the vacuum advance system

The vacuum advance system will only work if the piping from the carburettor to the diaphragm, the diaphragm itself, and the diaphragm chamber on the carburettor side are all airtight. Carry out the following checks:

First, remove the distributor cap. Next disconnect the vacuum unit from the carburettor and suck the open end of the pipe. Move the base plate gently forward with a screwdriver. Remove the screwdriver and the base plate should remain in the new position as long as your tongue maintains the suction. Removing your tongue should allow the breaker plate to spring back to its original position.

If the breaker plate does not move, first make sure that there is no obstruction—all wiring should be routed free of the breaker plate. Next, check that the piping is unblocked. To do this, remove the piping from the diaphragm chamber

16 To check the operation of the vacuum advance unit, first remove the tube from the base of the carburettor

17 Take the cap off the distributor and then suck the open end of the pipe. The suction should move the breaker plate slightly

18 If the breaker plate does not move, the pipe may be blocked. Remove the other end of the pipe and blow through it to clear it

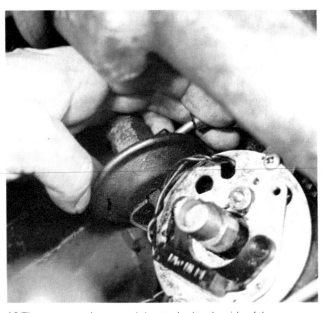

19 The vacuum advance unit is attached to the side of the distributor and it is easily recognizable by its shape

20 To remove a faulty vacuum advance unit, undo the retaining bolts on the side of the distributor and lift out the linkage arm

and blow through it. If the piping is clear, unbroken and in good condition, the fault is most likely to be in the diaphragm. It may be a ruptured diaphragm, a jammed spring, or a faulty air seal. Alternatively, but rarely, the linkage from the diaphragm to the breaker plate may be broken or damaged. If any of these is the cause you will have to fit a new unit. The vacuum unit is held onto the distributor by a bracket and by connecting linkage. Undo the bracket and fine tuning nut holding the linkage to the breaker plate. Take care to retain the spring on the linkage. Fitting the new unit is the reverse of removal.

Finally, retime the ignition.

Timing the ignition

There are two ways of setting the ignition timing: statically or stroboscopically. A few cars such as Audi, Datsun, and Volvo must be set with a strobe light, but the static method can be used to establish a starting point. Most cars with electronic ignition should be set with a strobe light.

You must first locate the timing marks and identify the one which indicates top dead centre (TDC). In most cases

Nelson Hargreaves

there will be either a notch in the crankshaft pulley and a series of pointers on the cylinder block, or vice versa. Some cars, notably transverse engine models, have the marks on the flywheel which can be viewed through an inspection hole in the housing (covered by a plate when not in use).

The spark which fires the mixture must be timed to occur a few degrees of crankshaft rotation before the timing cylinder reaches TDC. The timing cylinder is usually No. 1, but in rare cases it may be No. 4, No. 6, or No. 8. (Check your handbook). If there is no advance mark, or more than one, use a disc of cardboard the same size as the crankshaft pulley and mark out the angle of advance with a protractor. Hold this against the pulley and identify the correct advance mark, or make one with a dab of white paint or a filed line.

Static timing
Remove all the spark-plugs and press your thumb firmly over the plug hole in the timing cylinder. Turn the engine over by pulling on the fan belt, or by using a spanner on the crankshaft pulley nut, until your thumb is forced off the plug hole by pressure. This means the timing cylinder is on the compression stroke.

Line up the timing marks at the correct number of degrees before TDC. Remove the distributor cap and check that the rotor arm is pointing at the stud for the timing cylinder. Then connect a test light between the terminal at the side of the distributor and earth. Turn on the ignition.

Slacken the distributor clamp bolt and slowly rotate the distributor until the test bulb lights. This shows the contact breaker points have opened. Make sure the rotor arm remains stationary. You will have to turn the distributor to and fro a few times to find the exact moment the bulb lights. Retighten the clamp bolt making sure the distributor does not move.

Stroboscopic timing
Since timing with a strobe light is done with the engine running at a required speed, a tachometer is needed to see that the revs are correct. With some cars strobe timing must be done with the vacuum advance disconnected and the carburettor vacuum connection plugged (check handbook). It is a good idea to dab the timing marks with white paint to make them clearly visible. The strobe light is connected in series with the timing cylinder plug lead so that it flashes each time the plug fires.

Start the engine and set the throttle stop to obtain the correct rpm. Point the strobe light at the timing marks and if the timing is correct the moving timing mark should appear to be stationary opposite the fixed mark.

Adjustment can be made on the Vernier or by loosening the clamp bolt and turning the distributor until the marks line up. If you turn the distributor, make quite sure it does not move before the clamp bolt has been fully tightened.

You can also check the operation of the mechanical advance mechanism with a strobe. Disconnect the vacuum pipe, blip the throttle, and you should see the timing mark apparently moving backwards. As the revs are allowed to drop to the original revs, the marks should line up again.

Safety precautions
Some strobe lights have leads which connect to the battery as well as to No. 1 spark-plug. When using these, always connect first to the battery, then to No. 1 plug. When disconnecting, always remove first the No. 1 plug leads, then the battery leads. This way you will avoid getting a high voltage shock if you touch the battery connections.

21 With the timing marks aligned and the vernier scale (if one is fitted) centred, slacken the distributor clamp bolt, located at the base of the distributor near the engine

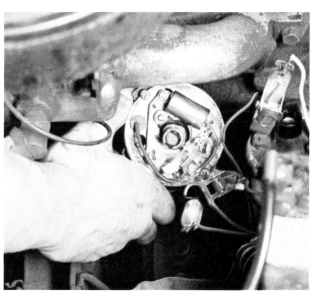

22 The light should come on as the marks align. If it does not, rotate the distributor until it does. Now retighten the clamp on the base. Make any final fine adjustment with the vernier scale

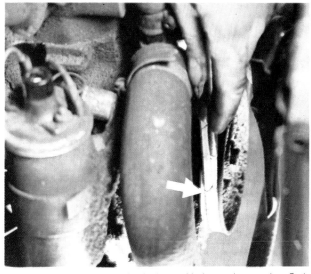

23 Stroboscopic ignition timing is done with the engine running. So it is necessary to make sure the pulley timing mark stands out. Pick it out with a thin line of white paint

Maintaining the oil pressure

One of the simplest and yet most vital ways to keep your car's engine in good condition is to keep it well lubricated. This usually just means maintaining the oil level and changing the oil and filter at the specified intervals. Over a long period of time, however, the oil pressure essential for efficient lubrication may begin to drop due either to a worn oil pump or to some form of blockage in the sump.

If the oil pressure does start to drop then the bearings will receive less oil than they need and as a consequence will wear. So to protect your engine it is a good idea to service certain key components in the lubrication system, such as the oil pressure relief valve and the oil pump. Servicing the internal oil strainer and the oil pickup system requires the sump to be dropped. This may not be possible without first removing the engine – a task not recommended to the inexperienced mechanic (see pages 70 to 73).

So unless you have reason to suspect that a particular component is faulty, the best approach is to check first those parts which are most accessible.

Servicing the pressure relief valve
The oil pressure relief valve (figs. 12 and 13), as its name suggests, relieves excess pressure in the oil circuit by lifting off its seat against its spring at a predetermined load. Many engines have these valves fitted externally to the block, filter casting or oil pump housing, but as their location is so variable you will have to refer to your manual or local main dealer for this information.

Oil pressure relief valves are of two types but both operate on the same principle. A large hexagonal nut locates either a spring and ball, or spring and piston assembly, which closes off a return oilway to the sump or pump inlet. When the oil pressure exceeds a certain amount, the ball or piston of the valve is forced off its seat and oil escapes down the return circuit, thus lowering the pressure in the system.

Checks which apply to all relief valves include checking the ball or piston for excessive wear which will take the form of pitting or scoring. The spring is difficult to check for faults unless it is obviously badly worn or broken. In fact, as the spring and valve assembly can be obtained relatively cheaply, it is probably more sensible to replace them anyway.

Also, check down the valve hole with a torch (a small mirror may be needed) to see that the seating is free from marks. If not, it is often possible to lap (remove the ridges from) a marked seat using a small quantity of fine valve grinding paste on the end of the valve if it is of the piston type. Extreme care should be taken to ensure that all the paste is removed before re-assembly. This can normally be done with a rag on the end of a stick. Ball seatings can often be restored by giving the ball a sharp tap on to the seat with a brass drift and hammer. This also needs to be done carefully, especially if your engine is made from alloy.

Some types of pressure relief valve are adjustable, so when you come to refit one, check with your manual for the correct setting. Adjustment is carried out either by a screwbolt and locknut or by means of shims under the head of the securing bolt.

Servicing the oil pump
Whether you service the oil pump next will depend on whether it is fitted externally or is within the sump. In the latter case the sump will have to be removed first, the method for which is given below.

As with the pressure relief valve you will have to consult your manual for the location of the pump as their positions are variable. Once found the pump's securing bolts should be removed (fig. 1) allowing the pump to be moved free (fig. 2). In some cases this will be the trickiest part and you may have to remove some other engine components to gain working space. Still worse, on cars such as the Triumph

1 Once you have found the oil pump remove the securing bolts. This Ford Escort pump has three

2 With the pump's securing bolts, and any other obvious obstructions removed, move the pump out of its location

3 This pump was removed with the oil filter still in position. The old gasket must be cleaned off prior to re-fitting the pump

George Wright

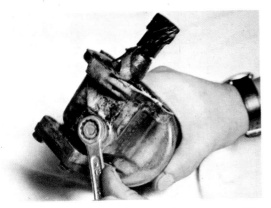

4 To remove the oil filter casing the bolt on top of the pump must be undone. Always replace the oil filter with a new one

5 In order to examine the condition of the gears inside the pump, undo the four retaining bolts of the cover

George Wright

6 With the retaining bolts removed, lift the cover off. There is no gasket used here, merely a rubber O-ring

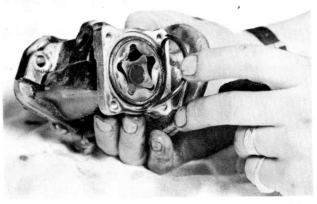

7 The O-ring should be prised out of its location in the body of the pump. Always use a new O-ring on re-assembly

Dolomite the front engine mounting has to be undone and the engine has to be jacked up to allow enough clearance for the pump to be removed.

Removal of pumps which are inside the sump is quite easy once the sump has been dropped. One of the most important points to watch for when releasing the mountings, however, is that you do not strain the pipes, especially if the union nut is a large one.

There are three common types of oil pump (see below and page 70) and they can all be checked for wear visually and by using feeler gauges. All three are simple in design and the way they function is obvious. The three types are: gear pump, which relies on the meshing of a drive gear and an idler gear to push the oil round, eccentric vane pump and eccentric rotor pump, both of which employ the offset drive of the vane or rotor within the pump housing to 'squeeze' the oil and thus push it out under pressure. Once removed from the car, dismantle the pump for inspection (figs. 3 to 7).

Wear checks common to all three involve checking the rubbing and rotating surfaces for ridging or scoring. If any such signs of wear are present the pump should be renewed. Remember that the oil pump is an important component and relative to its value to the engine is not that expensive to replace.

If no serious wear marks are evident, the next check on gear type pumps is to measure the clearance between the outer face of the gear teeth and the housing with a feeler gauge (fig. 8). The pump must be clean for this check. The wear limit here will vary according to the manufacturer's specification and the diameter of the gears. A typical maximum width measurement measured in several places around the edge of the housing would be 0.1270 mm

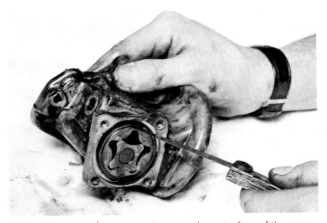

8 You can check the clearance between the outer face of the gear teeth and the housing with a clean feeler gauge

9 Also check for wear on the gear teeth. This is done by using the gauge to measure the slack between the mesh of the gears

10 To ascertain if there is any play in the drive shaft, first remove the idler gear then rock the shaft in its housing

11 To check the end float on the gears, place a straight edge across them and the housing. Then measure the clearance

12 On this Escort the oil pressure relief valve was in the pump. To remove it, the retainer was prised out of its seating

13 The oil pressure relief valve. It consists of a piston (on the left), a spring and a retaining cap

(0.005in.). Wear on the gear teeth can be found by checking the slack between the mesh of the gears (fig. 9); this normally should not exceed 0.2032 mm (0.008in.). The idler gear must be removed next (fig. 10) so that the amount of play in the drive shaft can be ascertained. This is done by trying to rock the gear in its housing hole. Play here should be no more than just perceptible. Finally, check the end float on the gears by placing a straight edge across both the gears and the housing and measuring the gap under it with feelers (fig. 11). The maximum clearance here is typically 0.1270 mm (0.005in.).

The same end-float measurements should be done on the end of the rotor type pumps. The clearances are usually a bit less, but refer to your manual for the exact figures. The lobe construction rotor types should be measured for the clearance between the tips of the inner rotor and the thickest part of the lobe on the outer rotor. This is usually 0.1524 mm (0.006in.), and the clearance between the outer rotor and the housing should be no greater than 0.2032 mm (0.008in.).

When measuring the side clearance on the end of the vanes on the eccentric vane type, each one should be measured in turn at its fully retracted position in relation to the housing, the maximum clearance is usually 0.1270 mm (0.005in.). The rotor drive spindle should be rocked in the housing to check for excessive play. Special care should be taken to note the order of the parts as you remove them as outer rotors are often designed to fit in one direction only with a chamfered edge facing into the body and spacer rings need to be fitted in the correct position.

When you are checking the pump be critical in your assessment of any wear; it is always better to renew a pump which is only slightly worn than to refit it and run the risk of low oil pressure and the extensive and expensive engine damage which may ensue.

Oil filter service

Some engines with 'internal' oil filters do not need the sump to be removed to be inspected. The sump on the Volkswagen air-cooled engine is part of the main casting and cannot be removed anyway. In many cases, the flat-four engine does not have an external filter and the internal filter screen should be cleaned during oil changes. This filter is covered by a circular pressed-steel plate with a central drain plug. After the oil has been drained, the cover can be removed from its position in the centre of the sump by removing the circle of bolts around its edge.

Similarly, some Fiats have their filters external to the sump. Usually these are of the centrifugal type and are located on the end of the crankshaft pulley.

With these few exceptions, however, the majority of internal filters are located within the sump and thus require the sump to be removed first.

Sump removal

In order to remove the sump it is necessary to have good access to the underside of the car. Obviously a pit will make the job a lot easier but ramps will be adequate if they lift the car by at least 25 cm (10in.). Alternatively, if you have no ramps, you may be able to make do with wooden blocks under a chassis-member, but be absolutely sure that the car is firmly supported before you crawl underneath it. Chock the rear wheels and pull on the handbrake.

The engine should be hot to allow the oil to drain out easily. The oil cannot be drained before the car is driven on to ramps, but where jacks are being used you might find that the oil will drain out more quickly if the car is on the flat. For, depending on where the drain plug is, draining the sump with the car at an angle may be a problem.

The sump and the general area around the sump should be thoroughly cleaned before sump removal is attempted. If everything is particularly oily, the whole engine and under-bonnet area should be washed down in a suitable place before the car is raised. This will not only reduce the risk of getting dirt in your eyes when you are working underneath, but it will also make sure that the exposed parts of the engine have the best chance of not being contaminated with harmful particles of dirt and grit.

Before the sump can be removed, you may have to unbolt various items (figs. 14 and 15) like stabilizer bars which prevent the sump fastenings from being reached or prevent the sump from being dropped once the bolts have been removed. You will most likely have to remove lower shield panels; these may be steel panels secured by screws or simple cardboard splash shields fastened with clips.

Where the engine has to be detached from one or more of its mountings and raised up slightly to provide the necessary clearance, you will need an engine crane or hoist. It is unlikely that you will be able to raise the engine with a jack without its getting in the way and it may be very unwise to use the jack anywhere near the gearbox housing. This would put an undue strain on the gearbox cross-member mountings and could damage other components as the engine would be raised at an abnormal angle. There is also a greater risk of the jack slipping when it is used well off the centre of the engine where most weight is concentrated.

With a crane or hoist in place over the engine, strong ropes or cables should be attached to it to take the weight—the best positions are slightly towards the front. As the ropes cannot be slung under the sump you will have to find other suitable attachment points. Bear in mind that the engine must be supported evenly to avoid the possibility of it tilting as it is raised.

There are several items which must be disconnected or removed (figs. 16 to 19) before the engine can be raised even a little. The most obvious are the radiator hoses, exhaust-pipe-to-manifold connection, earth straps and fuel lines. When the most obvious restrictions have been removed the weight of the engine can be taken up by the lifting equipment and the appropriate nuts and bolts removed from the engine mountings (fig. 20). Making frequent checks that nothing is being distorted or crushed, the engine can then be slowly raised. If the engine has to be raised fairly high before the sump will clear, you should watch out for any signs of strain at the gearbox end of the propshaft or the back of the engine distorting the bulkhead—lower the engine, if necessary, to remove any parts which are coming close to being strained.

It is a good point to remember that where a manufacturer states that a sump can be removed without lifting the engine slightly, it may be less of a struggle to remove if the engine is raised a little—half an hour spent lifting the engine may save you hours of struggling on your back under the car trying to manoeuvre the sump and its bolts clear of and away from numerous obstructions.

The sump can be fastened by bolts which screw into the engine block, or by nuts above, or by nuts and studs. Often there is a combination of all three. Do not waste time idly turning a bolt with a free nut above it but check your manual or feel around the edge of the block first. Some sumps are held by less common fixings such as Allen bolts; these have an internal hexagon drive and you will need special keys. Check with your local dealer.

You may find that the common 13 mm ($\frac{1}{2}$in.) drive socket heads are too large to get close enough to the wall of the sump to undo the bolts. If this is the case then there is no alternative but to use an open-ended spanner and to undo the bolts a flat at a time.

If you have already checked on the relative accessibility (figs. 21 to 23) of the sump bolts you may find that there is a special tool you can hire which will make the job a lot easier. Often the most useful addition to your tool kit will be a 7 mm ($\frac{1}{4}$in.) drive socket set. Where Allen socket head bolts are used it is usually a simple matter to cut a piece off the key wrench and press it securely into one of the smaller sockets. Using extensions and a universal joint or flexible drive you should be able to remove and replace awkwardly

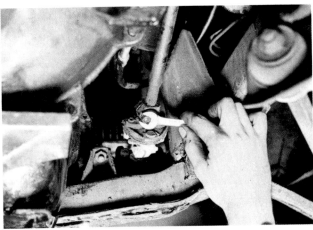

14 You may need to pull down the engine support-member to give the sump clearance. First unbolt the steering-column at the rack

15 Now remove the support-member bolts. To gain enough clearance you will probably need to do this at both sides

16 With the water drained from the radiator, remove the hoses. You need to do this if you are going to raise the engine

George Wright

placed fastenings with reasonable care.

Once the bolts are removed (fig. 24) you may have to tap the sump gently to break the seal. For this use your hand or a wooden mallet and, as you do it, try to keep as much of your body out of the way as possible, for when the sump comes free (fig. 25) the residual oil will come with it.

Where the sump has to be carefully manoeuvred out of place take care not to bend the oil pickup pipe (fig. 26) as the sump drops. You will often find that the dipstick has to be removed if the sump comes out sideways.

With the sump removed, the oil strainer (fig. 26) and the bottom of the sump can be examined. The relative positions of the pickup pipe, the strainer and the pump (if fitted to

the crankcase) are very variable, as are their design and manner of fixing.

The pickup pipe may be held by a large union and bolted fixing brackets which have to be removed before this, or the pump, can be removed. Alternatively, on some designs the pickup pipe and strainer may be incorporated in the pump and the pump bolts need only be undone to remove the whole assembly.

As parts are dismantled make a note of the location of shims, gaskets and O-rings—gaskets and O-rings should be renewed on re-assembly. Also make a note of the position of the oil pump drive shaft if this is detachable.

The sump and oil strainer and the pump should all be

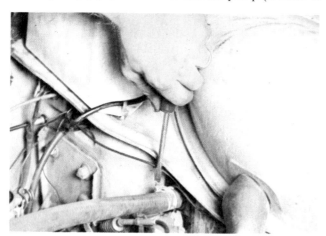
17 Also disconnect the heater hoses at the engine bulkhead. It is a good idea to examine the hoses and clips for wear

18 Disconnect the exhaust down-pipe from the manifold. Tie the pipe out of the way so that the mountings are not strained

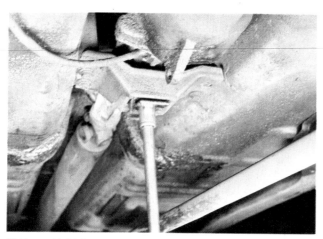
19 If you think it is necessary, remove the gearbox cross-member bolt. This will allow you to raise the engine slightly higher

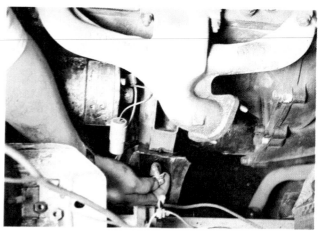
20 With the weight of the engine taken up by a jack or hoist remove the engine mounting bolts

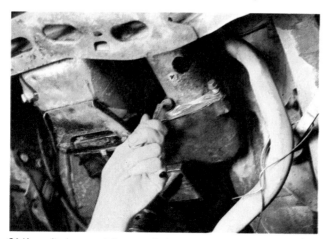
21 If you find some of the sump bolts obscured by the starter motor, undo its retaining bolts and move it out of the way

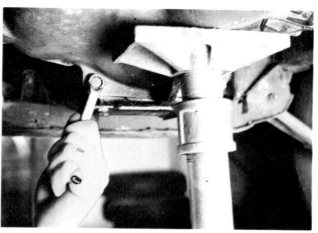
22 Now undo the bolts connecting the sump reinforcing plate to the bell-housing. There are two of these

23 With the sump reinforcing plate bolts undone, you can now withdraw the dust cover for the clutch assembly

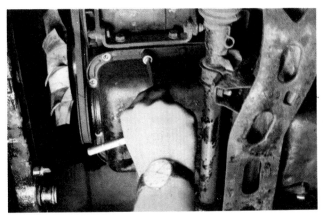

24 Making sure that you have access to all of the sump retaining bolts, work your way around the sump and remove them

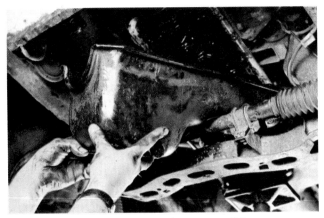

25 With the retaining bolts removed, you can pull the sump away from the rest of the engine. Beware of any oil left in the sump

26 The oil strainer attached to the oil pickup pipe. Inspect the strainer for holes or damage caused during removal of the sump

George Wright

27 Sludge containing small particles of metal worn away from the engine, hence the grey colour. Always clean the sump thoroughly

28 Before replacing the sump make sure that you have removed all of the old gasket. Use a locking compound on the new gasket

washed thoroughly in paraffin (kerosene), petrol or white spirit (fig. 27). All parts should be dismantled as far as possible to aid cleaning and all traces of the old gasket should be removed (fig. 28) from mating surfaces. The pump should then be serviced as described above.

Re-assembly

Re-assembly is virtually a reversal of dismantling but check all points where the possibility of poor sealing could have caused trouble on the oil pickup side, especially any small fatigue cracks which could have developed in the pickup pipe drawing oil up from the sump. New gaskets and O-rings are best lightly smeared with an efficient sealer such as silicone rubber gasket compound—just the lightest coating is all you need. Use slightly thicker applications when sticking sealing strips where the sump may mate to

the bearing caps. A blob of sealer where the edge of the cap meets the flat mating face of the block will often help. Silicone rubber is particularly useful as it also acts as a lubricant to settle the sump and gasket on rounded surfaces. When assembling part-gaskets (as opposed to one-piece types), make sure that any mating chamfers are fitted the correct way round and that tiny pieces are not left out.

Before final assembly, carefully check the manufacturer's instructions about the priming of the pump and oil galleries. In some cases the system is self-priming but may need to be aided initially by packing the inside of the pump with Vaseline before re-assembly.

Carefully check for evidence of oil pressure once the engine is fired up. There may be a delay of a few seconds before the oil circulates properly. For this reason the idle speed should be kept as slow as possible during this period.

Clutch maintenance

Clutch problems can be caused by a variety of faults, and the cure varies from the easier clutch adjustment to the harder clutch overhaul. D-i-y will save you a great deal in service costs and ensures a thorough job.

The clutch is the first stage in the transmission of power from the engine to the final drive mechanism. It forms a link between the engine and the gearbox. Since it must transmit the full torque of the engine against the complete weight of the car, it is liable to wear and need repair and replacement.

The structure of the clutch is illustrated in fig. 1. This is a generalized diagram, and the actual mechanism will vary from car to car.

Symptoms of faulty clutch

Clutch problems basically fall into four categories:
1. Snatch
2. Excessive slippage and drag
3. Judder or take-up faults
4. Squeak

A common cause of snatch, (where the clutch takes effect suddenly instead of smoothly sliding into operation), can be a distortion of the clutch plate due to overheating. To establish this as the fault, you should first check that the engine and gearbox mounts, the sub-frame attachments, the prop-shaft and the rear axle are all securely attached to their various points. If these elements are at all loose, the excess freedom of movement will cause resistance to smooth clutch engagement.

If this check finds nothing wrong you can be sure that clutch plate distortion is the problem, and should consider an overhaul to exchange the buckled parts for new ones.

Excessive slippage or drag (where the gearbox becomes stiff or the car tries to creep when held in gear with the clutch pedal on the floor) very often indicates maladjustment of the operating mechanism or faulty hydraulics.

To check for drag, have the car at rest with the engine running and engage first gear. Then, without letting the pedal off the floor, select neutral followed by first again. If there is any resistance at all to the second engagement of first gear, clutch drag is present and the operating mechanism should be adjusted as described below.

If resetting the adjustment makes no improvement, overhaul is the only course of action.

Judder or take-up trouble can be caused by the faults that cause snatch, or maladjustment. Squeal can be caused by faulty linings, or a worn or dry release bearing.

Clutch adjustment

Many clutch problems are caused by maladjustment. As the clutch wears, the free play (essential in both cable and hydraulic operating mechanisms to allow the full spring pressure to be exerted) will decrease. If this free play decreases too much, the condition will be reached where the engagement does not fully release, causing drag and a stiffness of gear change. If the adjustment is set correctly, the centre plate of the clutch should disconnect completely before the pedal is floored and there should be a small amount of noticeable free play at the top of the pedal

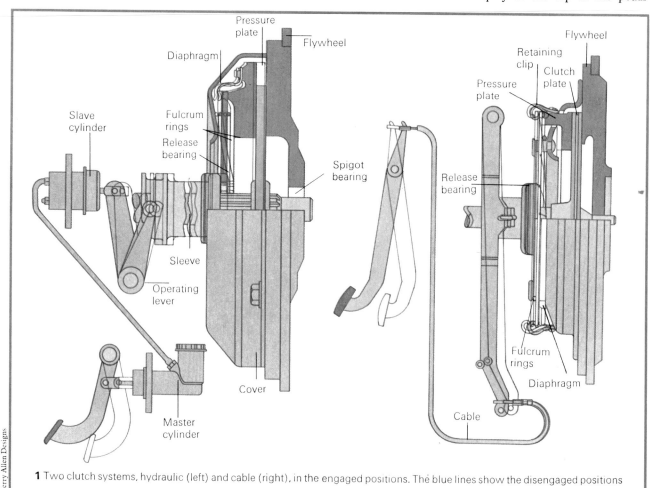

1 Two clutch systems, hydraulic (left) and cable (right), in the engaged positions. The blue lines show the disengaged positions

2 In cable operated systems, the brake and clutch pedals should be at the same height. The above example needs adjustment

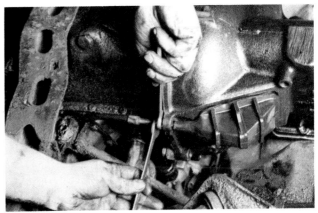

3 Use two spanners to slacken the lock nut, found on the bell housing, and turn the adjusting nut until the two pedals are level

movement. This free play is normally specified as about 6 mm (0.25in.) at the release lever end of the system, or about 20 mm (0.75in.) at the pedal.

Adjusting the mechanism should be carried out at the release lever end of the cable system, or at the slave cylinder piston rod (fig. 1) in hydraulic systems. Some hydraulic systems are self-compensating and have no provision for adjusting the free play.

Hydraulic system adjustments

With the hydraulic system, the adjustment is usually provided at the slave cylinder with a screw and lock nut on the pushrod (fig. 4).

You should slacken the lock nut using two spanners, and screw the operating ball nut (fig. 4) a few turns.

Now check the free play and, when correct, retighten the lock nut.

When air enters the hydraulic system, the fluid becomes partially compressible and the clutch will not free completely. Pumping the pedal is a temporary cure, but the permanent solution lies in bleeding the system and checking for leaks.

To do this, first top-up the reservoir (see fig. 1) and make sure that it never empties during the bleeding process.

Next, you should remove any floor covering which might restrict the full pedal travel, carefully wipe away any road dirt from the bleed nipple located on the slave cylinder (fig. 4) and attach a rubber tube to this bleed nipple.

You should then immerse the other end of the tube into a clean glass containing a little hydraulic fluid. Hydraulic fluid is very corrosive to paintwork and a great deal of care should be taken in handling it.

Next, slacken the bleed nipple by half to one third of a turn, then have a friend push the pedal slowly to the floor and give it several short, sharp jabs, followed by another long full stroke while you check the fluid being expelled into the glass for bubbles of air.

Finally, have the friend slide his foot off the pedal sideways, to allow the pedal to spring back sharply.

This procedure should be repeated until clear, air-free fluid is being pumped into the glass jar, then retighten the nipple in the middle of a full stroke. Remove the rubber tube and jar, top up the reservoir to the correct level, clean round the neck and replace the cap.

If the system fails to improve with bleeding, a defective cylinder seal is indicated.

Cable system adjustments

The main problems arising with a cable system are liable to be due to maladjustment from either clutch wear or cable stretch, or from partial or complete parting of the strands forming the cable.

If the clutch action is very stiff, first check that the cable has not been displaced. It should take up a smoothly curved arc between the pedal and the release lever without any sharp kinks and, if possible, it should not bend back upon itself in an 'S' shape.

If the clutch cable strands have partially or completely separated, the only answer is to remove the cable and fit a new one. The new cable will usually have shaped ends which prevent the inner cable from being withdrawn, but during manufacture the unit will have been thoroughly lubricated to protect the strands from wear.

To remove the cable, first you should detach the clutch cable support bracket on the clutch bell housing and swing it aside (fig. 18).

Next slacken the clutch cable adjuster nut and lock nut, peel back the rubber gaiter and pull the clutch inner cable from its fixing (fig. 18). Utmost care should be taken during this operation, for the release arm should not be moved more than 12.75 mm (0.25in.) or the arm may become

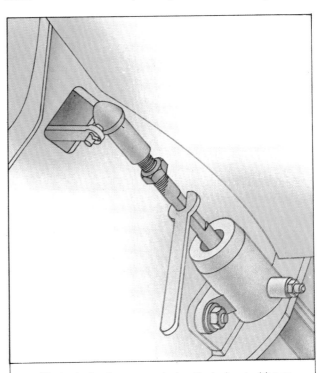

4 In the hydraulic system, slacken the lock nut with two spanners, then turn the adjusting screw as shown above

5 To remove the clutch, you must first undo and remove the gear lever. To do this you first unscrew the baseplate retaining screws

6 Next, use a screwdriver to prise apart and lift off the gear lever circlip which holds the rubber gaiter in place

7 You can now lift off the rubber gaiter to expose the gear lever locking tabs. Bend these up with a screwdriver

8 The gear lever domed cap can now be unscrewed and the gear lever lifted out from the transmission housing

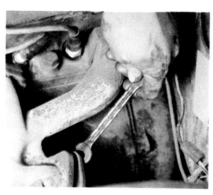

9 The next step is to unbolt the exhaust downpipe from the exhaust manifold. You can then wire the pipe out of the way

10 While still under the bonnet, you can locate some of the bellhousing bolts — usually four

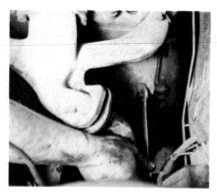

11 Depending on the make of car, it may be easier to undo as many bolts in the engine bay as you can, before getting underneath

12 Next, undo the bolt holding the starter motor lead and remove this lead. Then undo the three starter motor retaining bolts

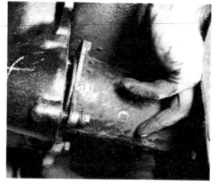

13 The starter motor can then be lifted free from the flywheel and either held to one side or totally removed

detached from the release bearing retainer. This would mean removing the gearbox to replace the arm.

You should now remove the rubber bung from the engine rear bulkhead which will provide access to the cable connection on the foot pedal. This will enable you to lever the cable eye and pin from the clips on the pedal lever.

Finally, remove the pin from the cable eye and withdraw the clutch cable assembly from the fascia panel and put this to one side.

The cable replacement is the reversal of the above procedure and should be followed by readjusting the cable.

The adjustment procedure is very similar to that described for the hydraulic clutch system. The main difference is that the screw and lock nut are on the cable end, adjacent to the release lever (fig. 1).

When all adjustments and checks do not relieve slip, judder, squeak, drag or snatch, the clutch unit itself must be removed for attention. If this is the case you should be prepared to devote a weekend to the job.

Clutch removal

If you have reached the stage where an overhaul cannot be avoided, never buy replacement parts until you have stripped out the old parts. This is because there are three elements which are always available separately, and they may not all need replacement.

Procedures for clutch overhaul differ considerably according to the mechanical layout of the engine and transmission in the car.

This chapter will deal with the conventional front-engine layout as used in the Ford range (excluding Fiesta), Morris Marina, Vauxhalls and similar cars.

In the majority of front-engined rear-wheel drive cars, the gearbox can be removed and the clutch serviced without removing the engine.

A careful study of the access to the transmission bell housing retaining bolts (see fig. 10) will be a good indication as to whether the gearbox can be separated without removing the engine.

14 With the starter motor removed, it will be easier to reach hidden bellhousing nuts and bolts in the engine bay

15 The lower two bell house retaining bolts can now be reached and undone. At this stage, do not move the gearbox

16 If a dustcover is fitted to the flywheel the retaining bolts can now be undone. Two or three bolts are usually used

17 The flywheel dustcover can now be slid free from between the flywheel and the gearbox. Clean the cover before refitting

18 The clutch cable can now be removed. To do this, slacken the locknut and turn the adjusting screw until the cable pulls free

19 The gearbox cross member is held in place by four bolts, two on each side. Undo in turn, leaving the centre bolt

20 Now the four side bolts have been removed, the centre bolt can be undone and removed, freeing the gearbox

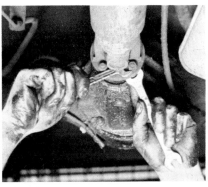

21 Scratch a mating mark on the propeller shaft and the rear axle flanges. Then undo the four bolts holding the propeller shaft

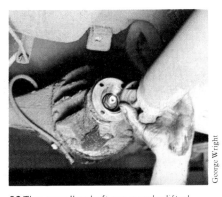

22 The propeller shaft can now be lifted free from the rear axle flange. It is best to support the propeller shaft by hand

If you have enough room to operate your spanners satisfactorily and there appears to be enough clearance to ease the gearbox back at least 50 mm (2in.) when everything is disconnected, the job should be started by jacking up the rear of the car and mounting the axle on securely positioned stands. This is assuming no hoist or pit are available. An alternative is to drive the car up on ramps at the rear.

Having carried out one of these procedures, chock the front wheels securely to prevent the car from moving forward.

Place the gear lever in neutral and remove the carpets or any console from the transmission tunnel inside the car, then remove any rubber gaiter that may be fitted.

Most gear levers are attached to the top of the transmission housing by a domed screw cap or a flange held down by set bolts (fig. 5).

If you cannot turn the domed cap by hand after you have pressed any locking tabs up flat (fig. 7), and no spanner is available, or there is insufficient access for a proper

grip, it can be sometimes loosened by a sharp tap with a blunt chisel. You should take care not to damage the cap.

Before proceeding any further, where possible drain the oil from the gearbox. To do this you should undo the gearbox drain plug and then drain the oil into a clean container. When all the oil has drained out, replace the drain plug. The oil collected in the container can be reused when topping up.

Exhaust system removal

With some engine layouts, it may be necessary to remove the exhaust system before being able to reach the clutch plate mechanism (for example, this will be necessary with the Morris Marina). If this is the case you should disconnect the exhaust downpipe from the manifold and either remove the pipe or reposition it out of the way by wiring it to some part of the structure.

It will also be necessary to remove the speedometer

23 The other end of the propeller shaft is then lifted out from the gearbox. This shaft should be stored in a safe place

24 To prevent any residue gearbox oil from seeping out as the unit is tilted, use a bung or a polythene bag held by a band

25 Before removing the gearbox, disconnect the speedometer circlip with a screwdriver

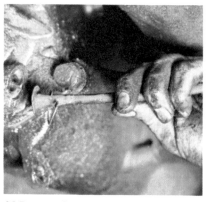

26 Remove the speedometer cable from the gearbox by lifting it out. Put it aside

27 Depending on space, you may need help to lower the gearbox which is usually heavy

28 By slackening the retaining bolts a little in turn, remove the clutch assembly

cable. To do this you should detach the speedometer cable circlip, knurled nut, or single bolt and withdraw the assembly. If an automatic reversing light is fitted, you should disconnect it by pulling the plug off the switch in the side of the gearbox.

Starter motor removal
You should now disconnect the main battery cable and remove the starter motor.

To remove the starter motor, first disconnect the starter motor cable from the terminal on the starter motor end cover (fig. 12). Next, undo and remove the nuts, bolts and spring washers which secure the starter motor to the clutch and flywheel housing. Then lift the starter motor away by manipulating the drive gear out of the ring gear area (fig. 13) and then from the engine compartment.

Drive shaft removal
The next step is to remove the drive shaft (propeller shaft).

You should first mark the rear axle flange (fig. 21) with a file to allow you to reassemble it in the same position to maintain balance.

Every car has universal joints at the end of the shaft. Undo three of the four bolts at either joint, then, with an assistant supporting the weight of the shaft, undo the remaining two bolts and withdraw the unit.

If the drive shaft is fitted with a centre bearing, you should detach this bearing's housing from the reinforcement in the floor before loosening each end.

Some cars have one universal joint between the drive shaft and the differential, and a sliding splined joint at the gearbox end. This has no flange, but simply pushes into the gearbox tail housing. Pull the drive shaft rearwards to disengage the splines (fig. 23).

Finally, seal the gearbox extension housing with a plastic cap or polythene bag held by a rubber band. This will prevent any residue oil from draining out as the gearbox is tilted backwards.

Clutch disconnection
With a cable operated clutch, you should next slacken off the adjustment, as described before, sufficiently to allow you to remove the cable end from the release lever.

With hydraulic operation, you should seal the vent hole in the reservoir (fig. 1) with non-porous sticky tape to prevent the loss of hydraulic fluid. Then, either detach the slave cylinder completely from the release lever and the transmission housing, or detach the hydraulic pipe from the slave cylinder (fig. 1).

With self-adjusting hydraulic systems, you should use wire or string to prevent the piston rod from being pushed out by the spring inside the cylinder.

The next stage is to undo the bolts connecting the bellhousing to the engine block. Most cars use three or four nuts at the top of the bellhousing, and there are usually dowels as well.

The final step is to remove the gearbox mounting. Before you undo the bolts, pass a rope around the tail housing and up into the car through the gearlever hole in the floor. As you release the bolts, you should have an assistant take the weight of the unit by keeping the rope taut. Ease the unit backwards to disengage the input shaft splines from the clutch centre plate, then lower it.

Clutch assembly removal
The engine flywheel will now be revealed with the clutch assembly attached to it by a ring of six or eight bolts. All that remains to be done is to remove the actual clutch

29 The pressure or cover plate should not be scored. If it is, replace it

30 Examine the friction or driven plate for wear down to the rivets, or scoring

31 Examine the flywheel. If badly scored, replace it; if not, degrease the surface

32 Reassemble the components and lightly secure the retaining bolts in position

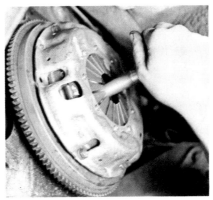

33 Insert the clutch aligning tool fully and tighten the bolts. Remove the tool

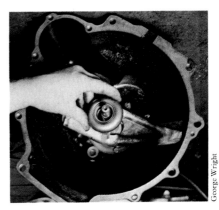

34 Before refitting the gearbox, clean the bellhousing and fit a new release bearing

assembly. To do this, slacken each of the retaining bolts a little in turn. The clutch springs will tend to force the cover off as these bolts are released, and the clutch assembly will come away in two parts.

You will now be able to see the state of the linings, the presence of any distortion or contamination of the centre plate, and the condition of the thrust race. The thrust race will have been removed with the release lever as part of the gearbox assembly (fig. 34).

Replacement clutch parts are available as three separate elements: a pressure plate; a driven plate; and the release bearings. It is worth considering the work inolved in getting access to the clutch before skimping on the extent of the overhaul. Clutch parts wear together, so it is false economy to replace only one part, such as the driven plate, as the other parts will soon wear out.

Clutch re-assembly
If the flywheel has been badly scored, it may be necessary to fit a new one and in this case you should always use new locking tabs for the retaining bolts.

Examine the spigot bearing in the flywheel centre. If it is worn, replace it, otherwise smear with HMP grease.

If the flywheel is in good condition, clean it thoroughly with methylated spirits, and in either case you should clean the face of the new pressure plate in this way.

Next, lightly grease the splines in the centre plate and position the centre plate with the protruding side away from the flywheel. To do this you will need to borrow or make a special aligning tool because if the centre plate is not perfectly central the gearbox will not mate with the engine without distorting the centre plate. The aligning tool, which can be made quite quickly in wood, consists of a two-diameter mandrel (fig. 33). The tool's smallest dia-

meter must be a snug fit in the crankshaft spigot bearing (fig. 33), and the larger diameter must be a similarly snug fit inside the centre plate splines.

The centre plate assembly should be offered up to the flywheel and, having done this, you should start all the retaining bolts in their threaded holes. Then, position the aligning tool and continue to tighten the cover plate bolts in turn by small amounts to compress the clutch springs gradually. When you have tightened them all completely, you can remove the aligning tool.

The next step is to replace the gearbox. This can be a tricky job due to its weight. First lightly grease the input shaft splines, then check to see if there is a blank spline which should correctly align with the clutch centre plate splines. Make sure you never let the shaft take the weight of the gearbox, then gently ease the unit home. Never attempt to force it into position.

Now refit the crossmember and the bellhousing bolts, then reconnect the speedometer, the reversing light lead if fitted, and the clutch operating mechanism. Once you have done this, remove the tape previously placed over the reservoir vent (if you have a hydraulic system), and bleed the system as described on page 75.

Before replacing the drive shaft, check the free play of the system and adjust it to the correct amount, refit the starter motor and reconnect the battery lead.

You can now replace the drive shaft. To do this, align the file marks made on the rear flange and fit new self-locking nuts.

Finally, reconnect the exhaust system and refit the gear lever and interior trim. Lower the car to the ground and test the clutch.

The new clutch linings may require a short time to bed in and once they have, the adjustment may need resetting.

The gear lever and linkage

Symptom	Possible causes	Remedies
Gears difficult to engage or operate	Gear linkage worn, broken or out of adjustment	Replace or readjust linkage
	Engine mountings loose or broken	Replace or tighten
	Clutch wrongly adjusted	Readjust
	Internal gearbox fault	Dismantle gearbox and fit replacement part

A difficult gearchange accompanied by the gnashing and grinding of teeth is a condition that sends many motorists scurrying to their nearest gearbox replacement stockist. But the problem may not be as serious as it appears. A simple check for faults in the gear change linkage system may reveal the cause to be a defect in a minor or relatively inexpensive component.

On all cars the gears are selected by a gear lever near to the driver's hand. This may be mounted on the floor pan, on the steering column or even on the dashboard of the car. It is connected either directly or by linkage to the gear selector mechanism inside the gearbox casing.

The position of the gearbox in the car and the general design layout determines whether or not a linkage system is used. For example, if the engine and gearbox are at the rear of the car some form of linkage will be needed so that the gear lever is in a convenient position for the driver. But a front-engined car which has a gearbox extending backwards towards the driver, may need only a short linkage, or even none at all with the gear lever protruding directly from the gearbox. Figs. 1-3 and 8-9 show the appearance of the various types of linkage, to help you decide which sort your car has.

The linkage transmits the gear lever movements to the gearbox to mesh or unmesh the gears. Where linkage is used the gearchange mechanism is called remote. There are three basic types of remote linkage. The most common uses a system of rods from the gear lever to the gearbox. Cables or a combination of rods and cables are the other types but these are less commonly found.

If the component members of the linkage are slack, worn or broken, it may be difficult or impossible to change gear. The gear lever will not transmit the correct movement through the linkage to locate the precise position of the gears in the gearbox. Therefore, start the faultfinding procedure at the gearbox end of the linkage. This section of linkage is found between the lower end of the column rod and the gearbox. The lower linkage is likely to be very similar on both internal and external rod systems and can be dealt with in the same way. Faults can then be traced backwards through the system to the gear lever. This approach could save much unnecessary dismantling of the column-rods should a fault be found in the exposed lower linkage.

This chapter also deals with cable gear change linkage.

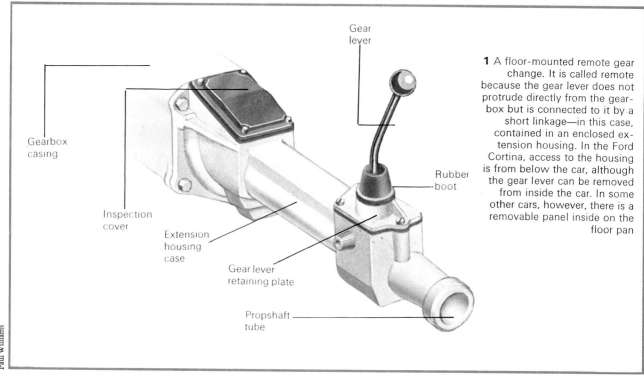

Gear lever

Gearbox casing

Inspection cover

Extension housing case

Gear lever retaining plate

Propshaft tube

Rubber boot

1 A floor-mounted remote gear change. It is called remote because the gear lever does not protrude directly from the gearbox but is connected to it by a short linkage—in this case, contained in an enclosed extension housing. In the Ford Cortina, access to the housing is from below the car, although the gear lever can be removed from inside the car. In some other cars, however, there is a removable panel inside on the floor pan

Remote rod linkage

Rod gear change linkage, in conjunction with a floor mounted gear lever, may be used no matter where the gearbox is situated. There are two types, the extension housing and external rod. They both operate on a similar principle but differ in the way they are mounted on the car.

The housed linkage is located in a casing which extends from the gearbox to the gear lever and is completely enclosed (fig. 1). The linkage is usually of fixed length and rarely has provision for adjustment. The linkage components therefore have to be dismantled to find the cause of the fault and cure it.

Dismantling extension housings

You can gain access to the linkage inside an extension housing by removing its inspection cover either from inside the car or from below it, according to the make and model. If access is from inside the car you may have to remove any rubber matting, carpet, covering trim or even the seats to get at the housing cover. If access is from below, the car will have to be jacked up and supported. The propeller shaft ('propshaft') and exhaust pipe may also need to be taken off.

Before starting work make sure that the gear lever is in neutral so that the car can still be moved if required once you have begun. The gearbox oil may also need to be drained off.

Start by unscrewing the knob from the gear lever stalk. Most gear levers have a flexible rubber gaiter or boot attached to the floor of the car and a tight push fit around the lever (fig. 5). This keeps noise and road dirt out of the car where the lever passes through the hole in the floor to its housing. Use a screwdriver to remove the small screws that secure the gaiter to the floor pan and pull it off the gear lever stalk (figs. 6 and 7).

The housing cover is held to the housing body by four or more bolts, so remove these with a spanner. The cover can now be pulled from the housing body. According to the design, the linkage and gear lever mounting may be contained in the cover and will come away with it. Alternatively the cover may come off leaving the gear lever and linkage in the main housing. But these differences do not radically affect the general principles of the dismantling and examination procedure.

Examine the connection between the rod linkage and the gear lever (fig. 12). It is at this point, along with the ball joint on which the gear lever moves, that faults most commonly occur. The connection assembly may be one of several basically similar types. One type uses a ring which encloses the ball joint and can sometimes be removed only when the ball joint is dismantled. But the simplest is a slotted rod which fits over a corresponding flat on the lower end of the gear lever and pivots on a bolt secured with a nut. This is sometimes called a clevis fork. A common variation is the bracket hinge joint held in the same way.

Before undoing the nut and bolt, hold the lever and rod and feel for excessive play or movement. The joint usually contains bushes and if these are worn will cause a very sloppy movement of the linkage. The bushes may be metal or tough nylon (fig. 13). These can be drifted or prised out and renewed if they are faulty.

Follow the linkage along its route towards the gearbox end. Examine any other joint in a similar manner. On the type where the linkage comes away with the cover the rod may pass through a bush or small bearing in the cover webbing. This supports the rod where the internal gear lever arm enters the gearbox. Slide and rotate the linkage through the bearing or bush to ensure that it is operating smoothly and correctly (fig. 14). If any signs of wear or slackness are found drift out the part and replace it. The internal gear lever arm usually has a ball-end which locates in a corresponding cup inside the gearbox. Look for severe scratches or heavy wear marks on the ball itself (fig. 15).

The arm may be attached to the rod with a small screw or retaining pin. Replace the arm if the ball is faulty. If the arm is integral with the rod shaft the unit will have to be replaced as a whole.

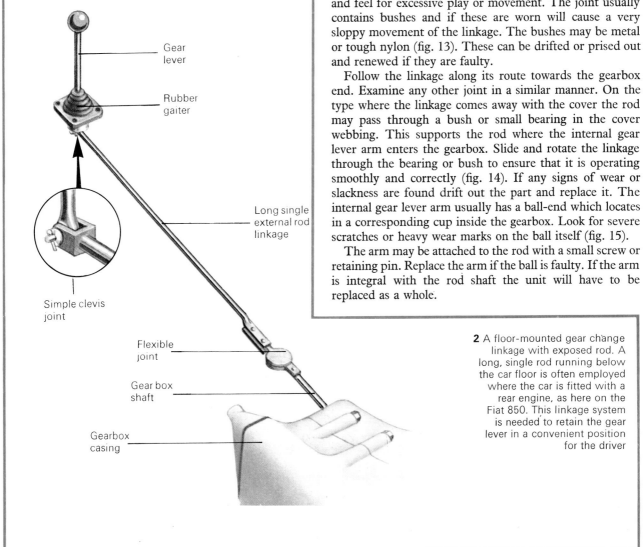

Gear lever

Rubber gaiter

Long single external rod linkage

Simple clevis joint

Flexible joint

Gear box shaft

Gearbox casing

2 A floor-mounted gear change linkage with exposed rod. A long, single rod running below the car floor is often employed where the car is fitted with a rear engine, as here on the Fiat 850. This linkage system is needed to retain the gear lever in a convenient position for the driver

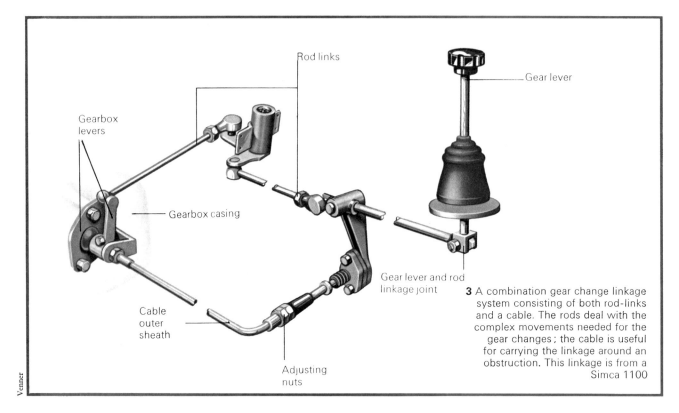

Rod links

Gear lever

Gearbox levers

Gearbox casing

Gear lever and rod linkage joint

Cable outer sheath

Adjusting nuts

3 A combination gear change linkage system consisting of both rod-links and a cable. The rods deal with the complex movements needed for the gear changes; the cable is useful for carrying the linkage around an obstruction. This linkage is from a Simca 1100

Venner

The type in which the linkage is contained in the main housing body may not have an internal gear lever visible. The rod enters the gearbox directly. However, the last section of the rod may be connected with a split-pin and washer to a shaft which enters the gearbox. Check that the pin has not broken and that the washers are not worn. Replace the parts if necessary.

It now remains to check the operation of the gear lever mounting. This can be done only when it has been disconnected from the linkage. The mounting for most floor-mounted levers is basically the same but there are countless design differences.

The lever pivots on one or two ball joints which are set in hemispherical cups. The lever is usually held in position by a spring-loaded retainer plate or cup over the entire ball joint assembly (fig. 17).

The cup or plate will be seen surrounding the gear lever on the top side of the lever stalk. This needs to be removed to release the lever. Use a spanner to remove the bolts from the plate type. Unscrew, or push down and twist, to remove the retainer cup type. Pull the retainer off over the gear lever. A further dished or shaped washer, made from either nylon or metal, will then be revealed. This is particularly vulnerable to wear and should be replaced as a matter of course when reassembling. It holds down the springs and often the nylon type breaks up, allowing the springs to lose their tension and causing a gear engagement problem (figs. 18 to 21).

Pull off the washer and springs from the lever. Check the length of an old spring against a new one at your local dealer and replace them if there is an appreciable difference.

The ball joint should now be found resting on its shoulder on the bottom end of the lever. It may be retained by a circlip or be a tight push fit. Check that the circlip is not broken or bent or that the push fit type has not become loose. Examine the two mating surfaces of the ball joint for wear, particularly where a combination of metal and nylon components is used. If the ball is deeply ridged or lipped then pull it off the lever and replace it. Similarly unbolt or prise the lower cup from its mounting for inspection.

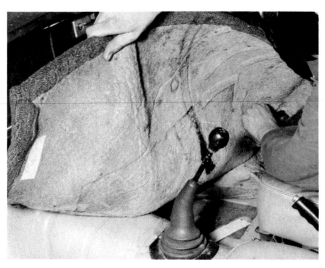

4 To gain access to any gear lever retaining plate or remote housing panel, the carpet or covering trim must first be removed

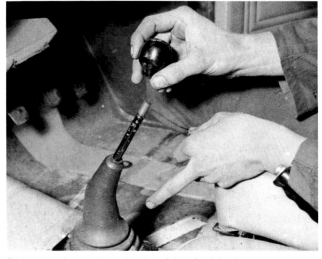

5 Unscrew the gear lever knob and then look for the screws which retain the protective rubber gaiter or boot round the gear lever

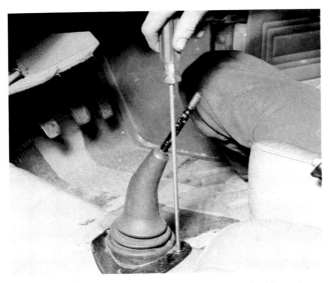

6 Use a screwdriver to remove the small, cross-head self-tapping screws which hold the gaiter retaining plate in position

7 Pull off the gaiter retaining plate and then the gaiter itself. The latter may be a tight fit on the gear lever shaft

Finally reassemble the linkage and gear lever making sure that everything is working smoothly. Grease all moving metal parts and test the gear change.

External rod linkages

The external rod type is simply an exposed rod linkage system usually running under the floor pan from a gear lever mounting bracket to the gearbox (fig. 2). This system is often used where the gear lever is situated a long way from the gearbox. Even slight wear is amplified by the long length of the linkage, so a means of adjustment is often provided and this should be checked before attempting to dismantle anything.

Adjusting rod linkages

Rod linkage adjustment usually alters both the axial and backwards and forwards (longitudinal) movement of the selector mechanism relative to the gear change lever. On some cars both adjustments can be made by slackening a single clamp. This may be found almost anywhere along the

length of the rod, and is usually accessible from either below the car or, occasionally, through an inspection cover inside the car. Finding the correct position so that all gears can be engaged may be a matter of trial and error.

If the problem is in the movement up and down the 'H' of the gate, for example, when engaging first gear, or going from first gear to second, then the rod linkage may not be moving far enough backwards or forwards. So slacken the clamp, pull the rod links slightly apart longitudinally, tighten the clamp and try the gear lever again.

If the problem is across the 'H' gate the axial movement of the rods may be at fault. Try slackening the clamp, then twisting the rods relative to each other, but do not alter their length. Retighten the clamp and try the gear lever. It should now move further across in one direction. Do this until exactly the right position is found.

Other linkages may require very careful adjustment to extremely fine tolerances, sometimes to fractions of a millimetre. The gear lever may even need to be set at a certain number of degrees from the vertical in a specific

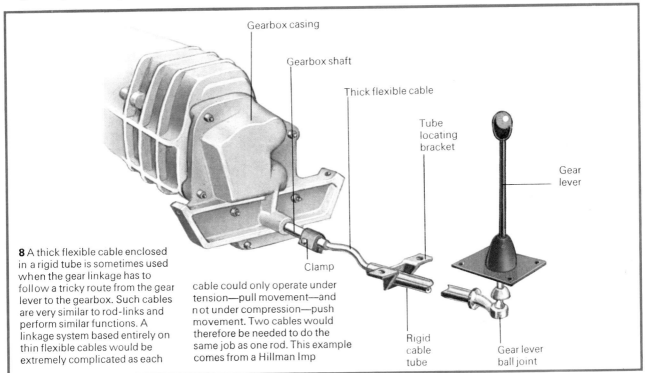

Gearbox casing

Gearbox shaft

Thick flexible cable

Tube locating bracket

Gear lever

Clamp

Rigid cable tube

Gear lever ball joint

8 A thick flexible cable enclosed in a rigid tube is sometimes used when the gear linkage has to follow a tricky route from the gear lever to the gearbox. Such cables are very similar to rod-links and perform similar functions. A linkage system based entirely on thin flexible cables would be extremely complicated as each cable could only operate under tension—pull movement—and not under compression—push movement. Two cables would therefore be needed to do the same job as one rod. This example comes from a Hillman Imp

Nelson Hargreaves

Paul Williams

position before you can adjust it. Such wide variation in the procedure means that you will have to consult a manual for your particular car.

Dismantling external rods

Some external linkages have two rods instead of one connected to the gear lever (fig. 9). One of the rods is connected to the gearbox through a lever or plunger mechanism on the gearbox casing, and is usually the rod connected nearer the top of the gear lever. This is called the shift rod. The other rod may be connected to a lever on the gearbox and is called the selector relay rod.

The joints between the linkages tend to be straight-forward clevis forks so check these in the manner described above. The gear lever mounting is also similar to the housed type so follow the dismantling and faultfinding guide for that type.

External rods sometimes pass through insulated brackets, especially where this linkage is used on rear engined cars. The brackets prevent a long length of rod from flexing or moving out of alignment. If the insulating material (it may be rubber or nylon) in the bracket has rotted or worn, the bracket will not stop the rods from bending. Even though the amount of movement may be slight, it could be enough to cause an engagement fault. Examine the bracket and insulation. If signs of wear or damage are apparent replace

10 To remove the extension housing which encloses a remote gear change, remove the bolts that secure it to the gearbox

the parts. The brackets are usually bolted to the car floor pan and can be removed with a spanner. The nylon type may need lubricating occasionally so that the rod passes through the bracket smoothly. Put some grease on this type and then try the gear change to see if it makes any difference before replacing the parts.

Cable gear change linkage

Gearchange linkage based solely on cables is rarely used because of the specialized and relatively complicated set-up

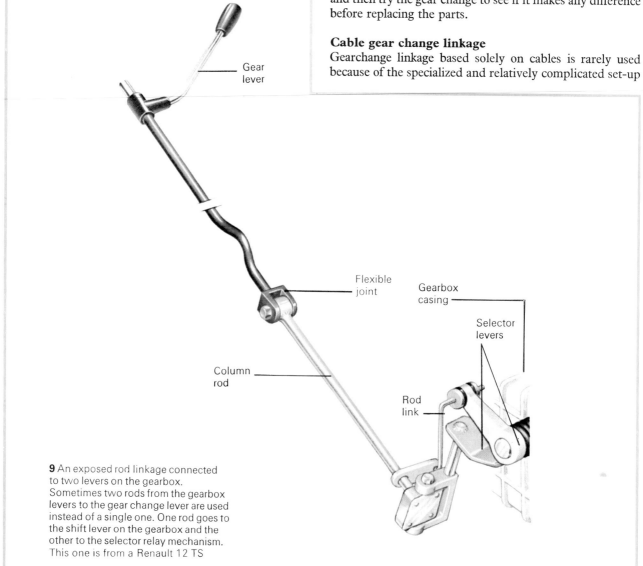

9 An exposed rod linkage connected to two levers on the gearbox. Sometimes two rods from the gearbox levers to the gear change lever are used instead of a single one. One rod goes to the shift lever on the gearbox and the other to the selector relay mechanism. This one is from a Renault 12 TS

Gear lever

Flexible joint

Gearbox casing

Selector levers

Column rod

Rod link

11 Separate the housing from the gearbox. If the car floor-pan has an access panel, this can be done from inside

12 Hold the rod linkage and the gear lever and try to twist them against each other ; this will show up any play in the joint

13 The gear lever and rod link joint may contain a small metal or nylon bush. Prise it out and replace it if the joint is slack

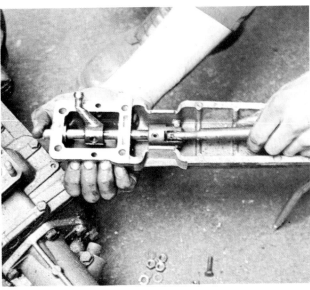

14 The housing may contain a bush to support the rod linkage where the internal gear lever joins it. Test for play here

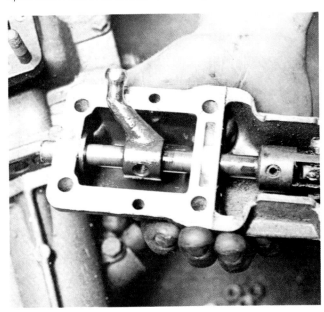

15 Examine the ball end of the internal gear lever for scratches and wear. If it is badly damaged it must be replaced

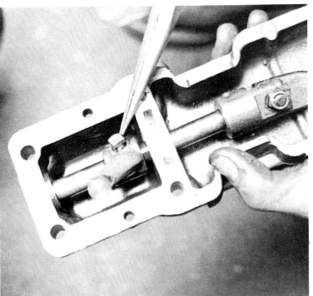

16 The internal gear lever may be held to the rod shaft by a bolt or retaining pin. Undo this to remove the lever

17 To remove the gear lever from its mounting first take off the retaining plate. This may be a push-turn fit or screwed in place

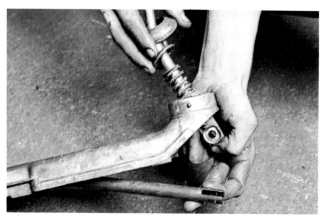

18 A nylon bush, a spring and the gear lever ball-joint are found under the retaining plate. Pull these off the gear lever shaft

19 Examine all the components for wear. Test the tension of the spring by measuring its length and comparing it with a new one

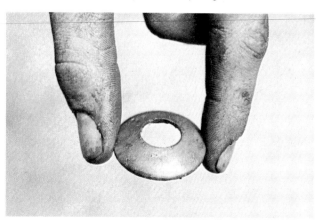

20 The nylon bush keeps the gear lever spring under tension and is subject to heavy wear, so replace it as a matter of course

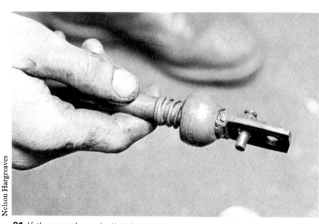

21 If the gear lever ball-joint is worn, replace it. But if the ball and lever are integral, the whole unit must be changed

required to make the system work. Long conventional cables can only be used where a 'pull' movement is required, that is when the cable is under tension. Their flexible nature makes them unsuitable for 'push' or compression movement. So two or more cables may be required to perform the same job as a single rigid rod. The cables that are used for the entire linkage therefore, are of a special type. They resemble thick flexible rods and are usually sheathed in thick metal tubes to prevent them from buckling under the strain of compression (fig. 8). Faults often occur when the cables stretch from continual tension and this throws the linkage out of adjustment.

Adjusting cable linkage
Both conventional cable linkage and the multi-tubed type can be adjusted to accommodate slackness arising from stretch. Adjustment of a conventional cable is normally made by a locknut on the threaded ends of the outer cable sheath. Tightening the nut effectively lengthens the sheath or tube. This may be a trial and error system until all the gears can be engaged.

You may need specific instructions from a manual to adjust the multi-tubed type as this can prove a little more difficult. Fixed clearances and a certain order of procedure may be essential. Or the cables may need to be adjusted rather than the sheaths or tubes, which remain a fixed length.

If the adjusting mechanism on any type of cable has already been moved to the limit of its travel the cable has overstretched and must be replaced.

Removing conventional cables
Remove the cable by slackening the adjuster nuts on the sheath completely. Remove also the nuts which secure the sheath to its mounting bracket. The inner cable can then be pulled off the gear lever actuating arm. The arm is usually a forked rod into which slots a nipple or ball on the end of the cable. The other end of the cable is often attached by a clevis fork joint to a lever protruding from the gearbox. Check that the split pin and washer or nut and bolt at the joint are intact or properly in place before removal. Fit a new cable, readjust the linkage and try the gear change. If a problem still exists the fault may be in the gear lever mounting. This is likely to be similar to those already described.

Combination cable and rod linkage
The faultfinding procedure for the type of linkage which combines both cables and rods can be adapted from the methods described above.

Nelson Hargreaves

Brake maintenance

Symptoms	Possible causes	Remedies
Brakes need pumping or heavy pressure to operate (spongy brakes)	Air in hydraulic fluid (single circuit system) Air in hydraulic fluid (double circuit system)	Bleed hydraulic system Bleed front, rear or both hydraulic systems
Pressure differential warning light stays on (dual circuit systems)	Pressure in one dual circuit system greater than pressure in other circuit Pressure differential warning activator faulty	Re-set pressure differential warning activator Remove and renew pressure differential warning activator

Effective brakes are essential for the safety of all road users. They must be fully responsive to the amount of pressure applied to the brake pedal. If your brakes are spongy and need pumping or heavy pressure to operate, lives—including your own—are at risk until the fault is rectified.

All braking systems on modern cars are hydraulic. They rely on those properties of a fluid which prevent it being compressed. Air, on the other hand, is compressible and if air enters the system the vital property of the fluid is destroyed. As air in the fluid is the main cause of spongy brakes, your first job is to locate the cause of the air entering the braking system.

How air enters the system
There are five major ways in which air can find its way into the hydraulic braking fluid in the car:

1. The master cylinder reservoir has been allowed to empty. This usually happens when a mechanic works on the brakes without topping up the reservoir, although it can also result from a severe leak in the system.

2. The brake hydraulic pipes or hoses rupture. This may be due to the age of the components or can result from an accident. Examine the pipes and hoses very carefully and replace any ruptured sections before replenishing the brake fluid.

3. Leaking seals. A leak in the seals will not only allow fluid to leave the system, it will also allow air to enter. Examine the seals and replace any damaged or leaking ones.

4. Dirt has been allowed to enter the system. This usually results from a mechanic working on the brakes without previously cleaning the components. Dirt may lodge in a seal, damaging the rubber and making it leak, or grit can damage the pistons in the brake or master cylinders. If this happens you will have to drain the system, flush it with methylated spirits and replace any damaged parts, then re-fill the system.

5. Old or incorrect fluid has been used. Brake fluid that has been bled from the system will appear to be air-free after about 24 hours. Although it is often done, it must not be re-used. It may contain dissolved air and, even more dangerous, in may have absorbed water vapour from the air. It is vital to re-fill the system with entirely new fluid. Using the wrong type of fluid may also damage the seals, so always use the brake fluid recommended for your car. If the wrong fluid has been used, drain the system, flush it with methylated spirits, renew all the seals and re-fill the system with the correct fluid. Always bleed the braking system when re-filling it.

Flushing the system
To drain the hydraulic system, use the bleeding method described below that suits your car but with the following additional steps.

Instead of filling the master cylinder reservoir with brake fluid, fill it with methylated spirits. Carry out the bleeding process, continuously topping up the reservoir with methylated spirits, until the brake fluid stops appearing and the spirits appears instead. Do this for each wheel. Now start to fill the reservoir with brake fluid and repeat the bleeding process at each wheel until brake fluid appears again. Make sure that you continue this stage of the process for long enough to clear all the methylated spirits out of the system.

Types of braking systems
The method for bleeding the brake hydraulics varies according to the type of system fitted to your car. There are two major types used by motor cars—the single circuit and the dual circuit system.

The single circuit system is the most common. Fig. 1 shows a typical single system. The front wheels and the rear wheels are all served by the same hydraulic circuit. There is a single master cylinder that controls the pressure applied to all four wheels when the brake pedal is depressed.

The dual circuit system separates the wheels into two groups, giving additional safety. Fig. 2 shows a typical dual circuit layout. In this one, the front wheels are served by one circuit and the rear wheels by the other; in others, each circuit works on diagonally-opposite wheels. The master cylinder is divided into two sections, completely isolated from each other. A single activating rod passes through both chambers via a fluid-proof seal. There is a single piston attached to the rod in each chamber. The front piston and chamber serve the front wheel circuit and the rear chamber and piston serve the rear wheel circuit.

Your car handbook should tell you which brake system is fitted to your car. If it does not, you should consult your authorized dealer.

Bleeding single circuit systems
To bleed the system, you will need the help of a friend and the following: a clean glass jar, not a food container, a length of tubing—the end of which should be a tight fit over the bleed nipple—and a can of the correct grade and

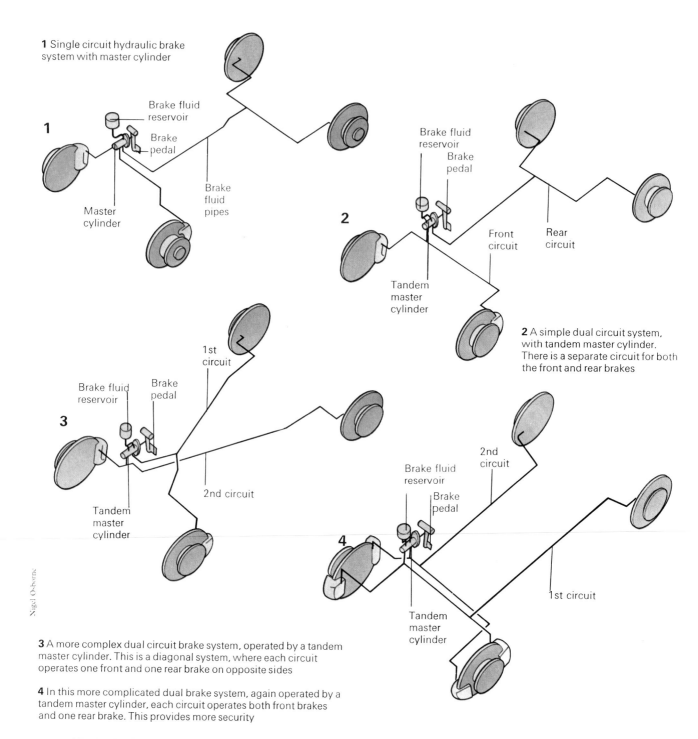

1 Single circuit hydraulic brake system with master cylinder

Brake fluid reservoir

Brake pedal

Brake fluid pipes

Master cylinder

Brake fluid reservoir

Brake pedal

Front circuit

Rear circuit

Tandem master cylinder

2 A simple dual circuit system, with tandem master cylinder. There is a separate circuit for both the front and rear brakes

1st circuit

Brake fluid reservoir

Brake pedal

2nd circuit

Tandem master cylinder

2nd circuit

Brake fluid reservoir

Brake pedal

Tandem master cylinder

1st circuit

3 A more complex dual circuit brake system, operated by a tandem master cylinder. This is a diagonal system, where each circuit operates one front and one rear brake on opposite sides

4 In this more complicated dual brake system, again operated by a tandem master cylinder, each circuit operates both front brakes and one rear brake. This provides more security

Nigel Osborne

type of brake fluid which is suitable for your car.

Before you carry out the work, first clean the area around the bleed nipple on each wheel with a stiff brush and petrol.

Next, clean the area around the top of the master cylinder reservoir cap. Remove the cap and fill the reservoir with the correct brake fluid. You will need to top this up frequently while carrying out the bleeding operation.

The two most common types of master cylinder are the Girling and the Lockheed. Although there are differences in operation, the basic principle is the same.

Starting with the wheel furthest from the master cylinder, attach the tube to the bleed nipple and put the other, open, end of the tube in the glass jar. Fill the jar with enough brake fluid to keep the end of the tube covered throughout the operation.

Unscrew the bleed nipple until the pumping action on the brake pedal forces brake fluid into the jar. Continue pumping until the fluid entering the jar is completely free of air bubbles. Hold the brake pedal in the last position and

tighten the bleed nipple. Repeat this process for each of the other three wheels. Before road testing, pump the pedal hard and hold it down with maximum pressure for two minutes. Then examine all the pipes and connections—including the bleed nipples. If any leaks appear you will have to repair them and bleed the system again. If no leaks appear, try the brakes carefully while driving the car along an empty road.

Bleeding dual circuit systems

Bleeding dual circuit brake hydraulic systems is similar to bleeding single circuit systems. The only difference is that you bleed both the wheels in one circuit first, check the system, then bleed both wheels of the other circuit if the fault persists.

Although bleeding the hydraulic system is the only cure for air in the fluid, it will not remove other contaminants. If there is any possibility of contamination or if the wrong type of brake fluid has been used, you must drain the

5 Many cars with dual circuit brake systems incorporate a warning lamp, operated by the pressure differential warning activator

6 To re-set this on the Volvo 244, you will have to bleed both brake circuits at the same time. First remove the road wheels

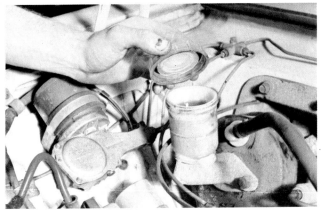

7 Either your handbook or dealer will tell you which wheels are on which circuit. Now remove the brake fluid reservoir cap

8 Thoroughly clean the grease and dirt away from the bleed nipples. You will need two helpers for the next stages

9 Have one helper connect a pipe to the bleed nipple for one circuit. This pipe should be immersed in a jar of brake fluid

10 Have another helper prepare the bleed nipple for the other circuit. Then pump the brake pedal to build up pressure

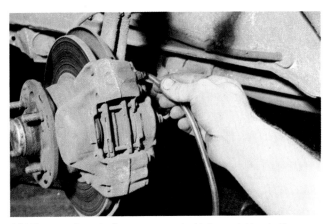

11 When you have built up pressure, hold the pedal in a half depressed position and bleed both nipples at once

12 The pedal will give way beneath your foot eventually. Call out when the pedal is fully depressed to close the bleed nipples

Nelson Hargreaves

13 You may have to repeat the bleeding several times before the light goes out. Remember to top up the fluid reservoir each time

14 The pressure differential warning activator is reset when the light goes out. Do not confuse this with the handbrake light

system, flush it with methylated spirits and fill it with the correct fluid. Having done this, it is advisable to bleed the system to make sure that air has not entered.

To bleed the system, you will again need a clean glass jar, a length of tubing that makes a tight fit over the bleed nipples and a can of the correct grade of brake fluid.

On systems without a pressure differential warning activator (see panel, page 87) or fitted with an automatic re-set type of activator, proceed as follows:

First, clean the areas around the bleed nipples and attach a bleed tube to the nipple on the left hand rear wheel. Place the other end of the bleed tube in the clean glass jar and pour in enough brake fluid to keep the tube covered throughout the operation.

Next, open the bleed valve with a spanner. Your helper should press down on the brake pedal as soon as you have

15 To flush a hydraulic brake system, first bleed off the brake fluid. Then fill the reservoir with methylated spirits

16 Next, connect a clean pipe to each bleed nipple and place the end of each pipe into an empty jar. Then pump the brake pedal

slackened the bleed nipple. Have him slowly release the pedal, wait a few minutes to allow the master cylinder to compensate, then depress the pedal again. Repeat this process until the fluid coming out of the tube is completely free of air bubbles. While doing this, make sure that the level of fluid in the master cylinder never drops below the minimum mark. When the fluid is completely air free, re-tighten the bleed nipple with the pedal fully depressed.

Repeat this process for the other rear wheel bleed nipple. Then test the braking system. If the brakes are no longer spongy, the front system may be free from air contamination and there is no need to bleed it. However, as you have everything ready, it is safest to do so anyway and be completely sure.

The bleeding method differs slightly for cars which have a dual circuit system with a pressure differential warning activator without an automatic re-set. Use a light pressure on the brake pedal and do not press it fully to the floor. Do not check the feel of the brakes until you have completely bled both systems.

After you have bled the system, the last remaining job on dual circuit brake hydraulic systems is to re-set the pressure differential warning activator, assuming that the re-setting is non-automatic.

Pressure differential warning activator
The dual circuit brake hydraulic system often has a built-in warning device that tells the driver, by means of a warning lamp inside the car, when either of the two systems has a lower pressure than the other. This device is called a pressure differential warning activator (fig. 19). It consists of a piston fitted in a connecting pipe between the two circuits. If the pressure in either circuit drops, the pressure in

17 Bleed each wheel in turn until the methylated spirits coming through the pipe is clean. Then empty the reservoir

the other circuit pushes the piston towards the weakened circuit. This displacement of the piston completes the electrical circuit of the warning light, illuminating the lamp on the fascia in front of the driver. If the lamp lights, it indicates either air in one circuit, a leak in the hydraulic pipes or hoses, a failed seal or a leaking master cylinder.

Check all the components of both circuits. If they are sound the problem is caused by air in the hydraulics. There is no direct method of finding which circuit has the air contamination and you will have to bleed each circuit in turn until the brakes operate normally.

Automatic re-set
On some systems the pressure differential warning activator has automatic re-set. This will, as the name implies, automatically re-set the activator as soon as the fault is rectified. Check your car handbook to find if there is an automatic re-set or contact your dealer for the information.

Re-setting pressure differential warning activator
If the warning light of the pressure differential warning activator remains on after correcting the fault and it is non-automatic, you will have to re-set it.

There are two alternative methods for doing this. First try the method described below. If this does not work, figs. 5 to 14 show the second method. Only if neither of these methods work should you suspect the pressure differential warning activator itself.

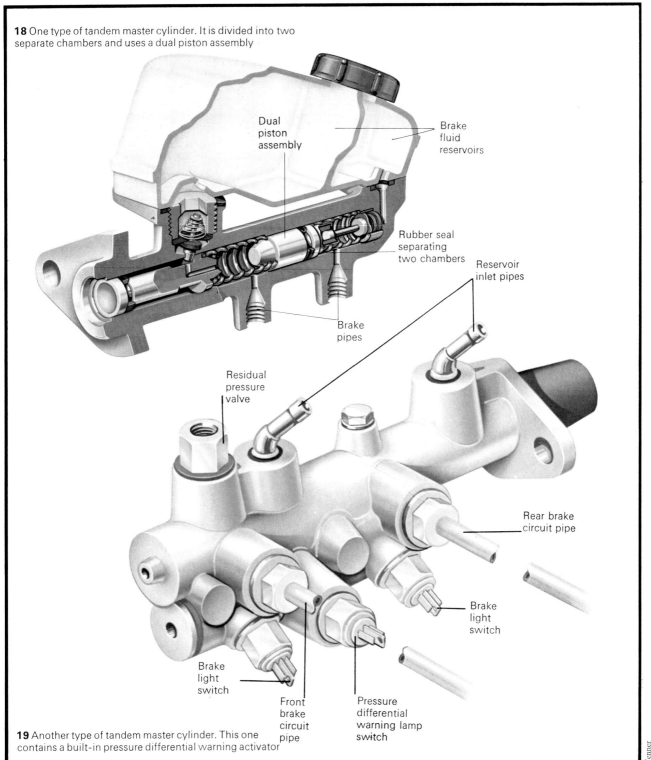

18 One type of tandem master cylinder. It is divided into two separate chambers and uses a dual piston assembly

Dual piston assembly

Brake fluid reservoirs

Rubber seal separating two chambers

Reservoir inlet pipes

Brake pipes

Residual pressure valve

Rear brake circuit pipe

Brake light switch

Brake light switch

Front brake circuit pipe

Pressure differential warning lamp switch

19 Another type of tandem master cylinder. This one contains a built-in pressure differential warning activator

Venner

20 Soak up the excess methylated spirits with a clean cloth. Use the spirit-soaked cloth to clean the chamber inside and out

21 Re-fill the brake fluid reservoir with new brake fluid. Do not use old fluid as this may have water dissolved in it

22 Again bleed each wheel in turn until the methylated spirits is flushed out by clean brake fluid. Keep topping up the reservoir

23 When all the methylated spirits has left the system, bleed the brakes. Re-set any dual circuit warning activators

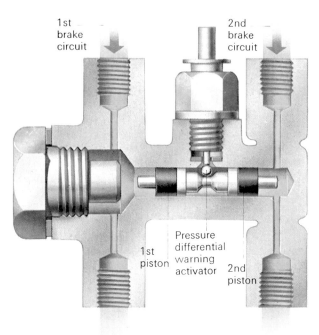

1st brake circuit   2nd brake circuit

1st piston   Pressure differential warning activator   2nd piston

Paul Williams

24 A cut-away of a tandem master cylinder incorporating a pressure differential warning activator

First, make sure that the master cylinder reservoir is full, then switch on the engine and run it at idling speed.

Attach a bleed tube to the front right-hand brake caliper bleed nipple and place the other, open, end of the tube in a clean glass jar. Fill the jar with enough brake fluid to completely cover the tube during the operation.

Next, have your assistant apply a gentle pressure to the brake pedal while you slowly open the bleed nipple. Bleed the system until the warning light goes out, having told your assistant to stop depressing the pedal as soon as this happens. Then re-tighten the bleed nipple with the brake pedal held in the same depressed position.

If the warning light fails to go out or if you were too slow in closing the bleed nipple which would cause the light to come back on, it is the opposite system that has the greater pressure. You should therefore repeat this process for the right-hand rear wheel brake caliper bleed nipple.

When the lamp goes out and the bleed nipple is re-tightened, remove the bleed tube, switch off the engine and top up the master cylinder reservoir.

If the pressure differential warning activator light still will not go out, the unit itself is faulty. The warning activator is a single unit connected between the two circuits of the dual braking system. It cannot be overhauled and must be replaced complete. To do this you will have to disconnect it from the hydraulic pipes.

There are two positions for the pressure differential warning activator. It may be an integral part of the tandem master cylinder (see fig. 19 and fig. 24). In this case you will have to remove and replace the whole tandem master cylinder/pressure differential warning activator assembly. Alternatively, it may be a separate unit. When removing either type, remember that brake fluid is highly corrosive, so wear gloves to keep it from dripping on to any paintwork. Before removing the faulty unit, buy the new part and have it near you in order to fit it as quickly as possible. This will prevent too much brake fluid draining away. Top up the master cylinder both before and after carrying out the job.

Nelson Hargreaves

Wheel bearings

Wheel bearings perform an important function in the smooth running of your car, but they are frequently overlooked when routine checks are made. Adjustment is critical. Loose bearings wear rapidly and may cause erratic tyre wear. Bearings that are too tight can heat up and seize and there is a chance that the car may lose a wheel—with possibly dire consequences. Conversely, correctly adjusted, free-running, bearings can aid fuel economy, as they offer minimal resistance to the rotation of the wheels.

There are two types of wheel bearing, the tapered roller and the ball. Most bearings consist of an inner and an outer track, with the ball or roller bearings held in a cage to keep them evenly spaced. The outer track of each bearing is an interference fit with the hub, the inner track holding the bearing itself. To complicate matters, the bearing fitted nearer to the stub axle housing is referred to as the inner bearing; that nearer to the hub securing nut is known as the outer bearing.

The track on a ball bearing—sometimes known as a ball race—will normally have a raised internal lip on one side (commonly known as the thrust side) while roller bearings normally have a tapered shape which serves the same function. This is to provide the necessary side location of the wheel, which must be as friction-free as possible. That is why the correct side clearance of a wheel bearing is so important. Insufficient clearance will cause friction and consequent heat build-up, which can rapidly destroy bearings. Too much clearance can accelerate wear through incorrect contact of the bearing faces.

Most tapered roller bearings are adjustable. Non-adjustable bearings of this type are rare. The majority of ball bearings are non-adjustable.

Wheel bearings are made of steel and require a lubricant. The most convenient is high-melting point grease, normally retained in the hub by a seal. This bears against a shoulder, within the hub, often referred to as the seal land. On cars fitted with disc wheels of the bolt-on type, the hub has a small grease cap covering the securing nut.

Before you begin even to check your wheel bearings, you must find out which type your car has by consulting either your handbook or your local dealer. It is vitally important that you tighten the hubs to the manufacturer's specified torque figures. Accidents have occurred where adjustable bearings have seized after being tightened to a torque figure far in excess of the load the unit was designed to take.

Checking wheel bearings
Wheel bearings must be checked for wear and faults at the regular service intervals, as stated in the vehicle handbook. Some service schedules recommend washing out the bearings after high mileages and repacking them with fresh grease. This has become increasingly unnecessary due to modern lubricants having a far longer life.

Three checks should be carried out. For all of them the car will have to be raised and supported firmly on axle stands, after disconnecting the battery.

The first check should be made on the bearing adjustment. The best method is to hold the wheel lightly at the top and bottom of the tyre and attempt to rock it in the vertical plane (fig. 3). The ideal state of adjustment for adjustable bearings is barely perceptible play. If non-adjustable bearings are fitted (these have no adjustment details in the manual, only a torque figure) they should normally have

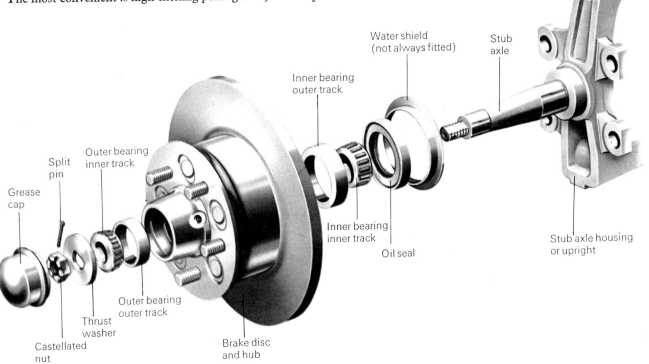

1 Exploded drawing showing adjustable, tapered roller bearings fitted to a disc brake hub

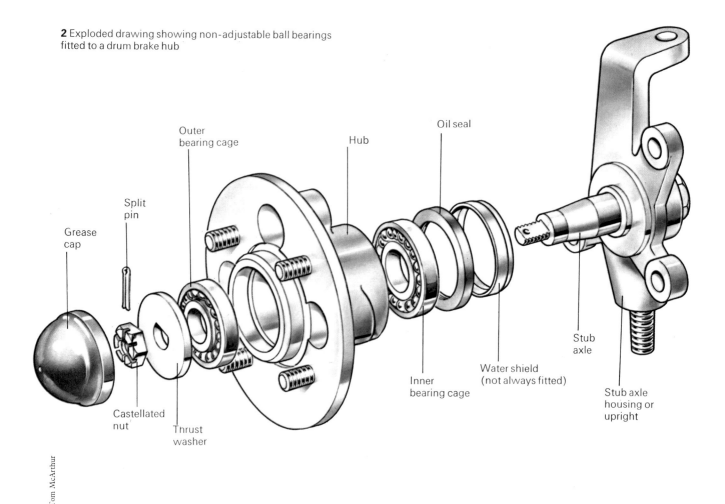

2 Exploded drawing showing non-adjustable ball bearings fitted to a drum brake hub

Grease cap

Split pin

Outer bearing cage

Hub

Oil seal

Castellated nut

Thrust washer

Inner bearing cage

Water shield (not always fitted)

Stub axle

Stub axle housing or upright

Tom McArthur

very little or no play (or end-float). The maximum permissible end-float on non-adjustable bearings is in the region of 0.15 millimetres. This can generally be measured by inserting a feeler gauge between the inner track of the outer bearing and the thrust washer (fig. 1). The thickness of feeler gauge blade required to take up the end-float gives a guide to the amount of wear present.

It is not always possible to use this method, however, as the lip of the hub may partly shield the securing nut, preventing the insertion of the feeler gauge blade.

Adjustable bearings can usually be checked in the same manner. A problem will arise if your car has wire wheels, for the splined hubs often mean that the outer bearing and the thrust washer are buried well within the hub. This can also occur on disc wheels for the same reasons as outlined for non-adjustable bearings. In these cases, the only answer is to use the wheel rocking test.

The second test involves giving the wheel a good spin by hand and listening for any roughness in the bearings as the wheel rotates freely. To carry out this test, you may have to slacken off any adjusters on drum brakes or retract the pads slightly on disc brakes. Rubbing brakes may cause too much wheel drag and any noise from this source may mask bearing noises. Disc pads can be gently levered back from the disc. They should be changed when the lining thickness is down to 3mm ($\frac{1}{8}$in.). Faulty bearings make a "shushing" sound and badly worn bearings may "rumble" or "click" as the wheel spins. A small amount of noise may simply be due to lack of grease.

The third check is to study the condition of the grease, even if there is no excessive end-float or noise in the bearings. Remove the wheel, then prise the small grease cap from the centre of the hub. This is usually made from thin

steel and is a push fit or it may sometimes be threaded. In rare cases the caps on the left hand side of the car may have left-handed threads which must be turned clockwise to remove. (This may also be the case with the central bearing nut where the caps have a left-hand thread.) The push fit types are either plain or have a raised lip round the edge. The latter type is simply levered out with a screwdriver, moving round the edge. The plain variety can often be levered out with care, but may have to be gripped lightly with a pair of pliers and slowly worked out. Take care not to distort the cap. A few light taps with a soft-faced hammer usually shifts stubborn caps.

If the car has wire wheels on centre-lock hubs, you may have to wait until you have removed the hub to gauge the condition of the grease.

If the grease around the outer bearing has a brownish tinge and a waxy quality, it has dried out. It may even have an unpleasant smell. This is also a sign that it has oxidized and although probably still serviceable it should be renewed. If the grease has taken on a whitish appearance or contains any white spots, it is probable that it has become contaminated with water. Again, the remedy is to carefully clean out the old grease and lubricate the hub with a fresh supply.

Removing the hub

To clean and repack the hub with fresh grease or to renew the bearings, you will have to remove the hub. This is a fairly simple job on most hubs. The procedure for this is described on the next page. Where the car is fitted with drum brakes, remove the drum. Some older vehicles, such as Ford's Anglia 105E model, have a one-piece drum and hub which makes the job easier (fig. 7). If the car is fitted

3 The first check that can be made is to grip the wheel at the top and the bottom and rock it in the vertical plane

4 If the grease round the outer bearing has a brownish tinge and a waxy quality, it has dried out and should be replaced

with disc brakes, the caliper will have to be removed by undoing the bolts anchoring it to the stub axle.

There will be a locking device on the central bearing retaining nut. This could be a locking tab, which must be renewed when disturbed, a locking nut or, more commonly, a castellated nut or pressed-steel castellated cover, retained by a split-pin. A new split-pin should be fitted each time the nut is disturbed as the pin becomes fatigued if the ends are bent over too many times.

To remove locking nuts, you will need to use two spanners of similar size in order to hold the inner nut as the outer is loosened.

Split-pin removal is just a matter of squeezing the tails of the pin into line and pulling it out. Remove the hub nut and thrust washer. If the hub is fitted with adjustable bearings, the outer bearing should be supported as the hub is pulled off the stub axle, otherwise it could drop out.

The inner track on the inner bearing of adjustable bearings will sometimes be a tight fit on the stub axle and some force may be needed to remove the hub as the bearing is held by the grease seal. Removing the hub may leave the inner race and the seal on the axle.

It is often extremely difficult to remove this part of the bearing without damaging both the bearing and the seal. Normal practice for removing the bearing is to tap a thin chisel carefully between the face of the upright and the axle, and the edge of the bearing track. Work round the edge, being careful to hold the chisel at an angle where it does not mark the axle. When you have a gap large enough to take a screwdriver blade, use two screwdrivers at opposite sides as levers to remove the bearing. In extreme cases a bearing extractor will have to be obtained. You can either borrow or hire one.

Hubs with non-adjustable bearings are often a tight fit on the axle and may need a suitable hub puller.

A method of removing hubs which prove difficult to pull off is to fit the road wheel loosely with the outer side facing the hub and two or three wheel nuts in position. The wheel can be carefully jerked outwards to act as an impact hammer.

It may be more convenient to remove the disc on disc-brake hubs before working on the bearings. Lightly scribe marks near one of the retaining bolts on the disc and near the respective bolt hole on the mounting flange on the hub, to ensure that the disc is returned to the same position. This helps to maintain the balance of the unit.

Splined hubs, as fitted to centre-lock wire wheels, require a slightly different removal technique. As the securing nut and split-pin are hidden by the splined section of the hub, access holes are pre-drilled by the manufacturers. Working end on to the hub, bend back the legs of the split-pin, then work it out from the stub axle through one of the access holes (fig. 9). The nut can then be loosened with a socket and extension and the hub removed.

Removing non-adjustable bearings
Be careful not to damage non-adjustable bearings if they are only being removed for cleaning and degreasing. Unfortunately, this is not always an easy task. Non-adjustable bearings will have a distance piece between the two inner tracks which carry the bearings, the two being held together by the two outer tracks. Some hubs have sufficient room inside to enable you to push the distance piece, which also acts as a thrust washer, to one side. This is possible because it is no longer held in place by the stub axle, the hub having been removed. This type of hub is, however, fairly rare. When you drift out the bearings, you

5 On this particular car, a Chrysler Imp, the speedometer drive cam is positioned in the nearside front hub. Remove it first

6 Where the vehicle is fitted with drum brakes, remove the drum. You may find you have to slacken the adjusters to do this

Nelson Hargreaves

95

7 Some cars, such as the Ford Anglia, have a one-piece brake drum and hub. Once the drum is removed, the bearings can be extracted

8 If the hub proves difficult to remove, reverse the road wheel and attach it by two wheel nuts, then jerk the wheel outwards

9 Where splined, centre-lock hubs are fitted, the manufacturers pre-drill access holes. Ease the split pin out through one

10 With the hub securing nuts removed, try to ease the hub from the axle. Be careful that the outer bearing does not drop out

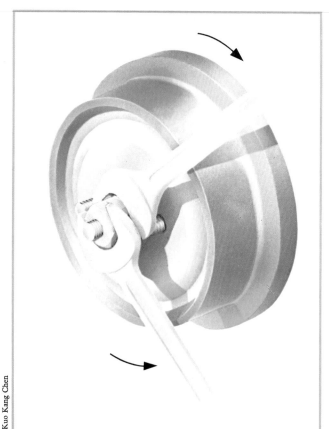

11 Where the hub is held in position by two nuts, hold the inner steady with one spanner, and slacken the locknut with another

should never allow the drift to act on the inner tracks, as this may deform them with consequent damage to the bearings when the hub is refitted. If you do not have enough room in the hub to push the distance piece to one side, it is almost certain that you will have to destroy the bearings to remove them, by drifting them out against the inner races.

Warming the hub by immersing it in hot water sometimes allows the bearing to be removed more easily. Never apply flame to heat the hub. If a non-adjustable bearing comes apart, renew both bearings.

Once the outer bearing has been removed, the inner bearing can be drifted out bringing the seal out with it. Many hubs have internal longitudinal slots opposing each other to allow the outer track of either the inner or outer bearings to be engaged with a thin drift. Tap each side evenly to remove the bearing.

Removing adjustable bearings
Adjustable bearings are usually much simpler to remove. If the seal is damaged or worn, it can simply be prised out and the inner bearing inner track pulled out to allow you to drift the outer bearing outer track from the hub. If the seal is worth using again and the bearings only need repacking, drift out the inner bearing outer track to clean the hub.

Cleaning and checking the bearings
Petrol is the best cleaning fluid for removing dirt and grease, but should be used with caution owing to its inflammable nature. Wash the bearings separately from the hub if they are to be used again, in order to avoid unnecessarily subjecting them to dirt from the hub body; one tiny piece of grit can wreck a bearing or seriously limit its life. Wash the bearings in a clean tray of petrol using a clean paint brush.

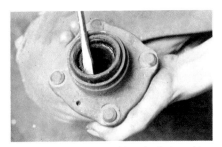

12 If you are only repacking the hubs with fresh grease, be careful not to damage the oil seal when you prise it out

13 Once the oil seal has been removed, the inner bearing inner track can be extracted and set to one side

14 Most hubs have longitudinal slots that allow you to drift out the outer tracks of the inner and outer bearings

15 Begin drifting out the outer tracks with a screwdriver. Apply even pressure to each half of the track to avoid damage

16 When you have loosened both outer tracks, lift them from the hub, which can then be thoroughly cleaned

Never spin a dry bearing excessively fast, especially if blowing it out with an air line.

Once all the parts are spotlessly clean, they should be inspected for wear and damage regardless of whether any noises were present during the check, as faults can sometimes be spotted which have not shown up in the form of noise.

Check the internal surfaces in the hub into which the bearing tracks fit. A polished appearance, sometimes accompanied by light scoring round the bore, will mean that the bearing has been rotating in the hub. Check also for the same faults on the stub axle. Do not regard the bright ring on the upright at the base of the axle as a sign of bearing wear—it is normal wear caused by the seal lip. If there is no sign of a ridge at the edge of the polished area, this means that serious wear has not occurred. Apply some bearing fit compound to any slightly worn areas before re-assembly.

Check the working surfaces of the bearing tracks and the balls or rollers, for any marks or pitting. Lubricate the bearings with a few drops of light oil and hold the inner track while running the outer track under pressure across the palm of your hand to feel for any "clicking" or roughness. If anything of this nature is found, the bearing should be renewed.

Always replace bearings as a set complete with the grease seal. Bearing sets for most popular cars are obtainable from accessory shops and most motor factors. In all cases, the "high side" of a taper-roller outer track, or the lipped side of a ball race, should face inwards to the hub. Some races will be marked "thrust" on the edge of the track and it is this side which must face inwards.

Replacing non-adjustable bearings

Thoroughly pack the one-piece, non-adjustable type bearings with grease. A good method is to place a blob of grease in the palm of your hand and scoop and press it in whilst rotating the bearing. Keep pressing in the grease until it has oozed through all the way round. When packing hubs with grease, it is normal practice to leave a substantial air passage through the hub body. If this is not done and the hub is filled completely with grease, a hydraulic action takes place when the wheel is in motion at speed and the grease can be pumped out, to the detriment of the seal and the bearings.

Place the hub upright in a vice and place the outer bearing level in the top of the hub. You can use an old outer track as a drift to tap the bearing down carefully and evenly into the bore. Make sure the bearing is properly bedded in against the shoulder. It will suddenly change note as you tap it down and make contact. Place a generous blob of grease inside the hub and push in the distance piece. Always fit the distance piece, if supplied, with the new bearing kit. The distance piece may be tapered towards the front. Some are thin, crushable types and these should always be renewed to avoid the possibility of replacing a damaged part.

Smear the seal with grease on the lip and the outer edge. Place the seal squarely in the hub bore and tap it down evenly. A good method is to use a small square of clean hardwood covering the seal to avoid damage or, alternatively, a large socket or an old outer track which fits against the edge of the seal. It should be tapped in gently to avoid damage and to ensure that the seal fits flush and square in the bore.

Replacing adjustable bearings

Follow the same procedure for adjustable bearings. These are normally of two-piece construction, so the hub and the bearings can be packed with grease after the outer tracks have been fitted. Never mix the inner and outer parts of the bearings as they are factory-matched.

Before refitting the hub to the axle, especially if a new seal has been fitted, clean any rust from the upright at the base with some 400 grade wet and dry paper. But do not rub along the line of the axle. Use a few drops of paraffin as a lubricant, to ensure that the seal will have a smooth surface

17 Lubricate the bearing with a few drops of light oil, then run the bearing cage on your hand to feel for any "clicking"

18 Use a block of hardwood as a drift to replace the two outer tracks. The block should be the same diameter as the tracks

19 Before re-fitting the hub to the stub axle, thoroughly clean any rust from the axle shoulder with wet-and-dry paper

20 Grease the stub axle with high-melting point lubricant. Make sure no dust or grit settles in the grease as the hub is fitted

21 Tighten the securing nut, replace the drum and then adjust the end-float. On the Imp this must be done by the 'rocking' method

to run against. Clean the axle thoroughly and then carefully smear it with grease.

Adjusting end-float

Re-fit the brake disc to the hub (where applicable) then replace the hub on the axle, reversing removal procedure. Non-adjustable bearing hubs will have a specific torque figure recommended by the manufacturer. The tightness of the nut and the thickness of the thrust washer determines the end-float of the bearings to a specific limit, which can vary between very slight pre-load (no end-float), to 0.05 mm clearance. The correct figure must be adhered to in order to achieve the proper setting. Manufacturers usually advise that the nut should then be rotated to the nearest split-pin hole alignment after the nut has been tightened to the correct figure.

The adjustment procedure of adjustable bearings varies according to the vehicle, but generally the end-float, which can be measured with feeler gauges between the inner track of the outer bearing and the thrust washer, is between 0.025 and 0.15 mm. The ideal is about 0.025 mm, but the limits are given as it is not always possible to get an ideal figure at the nearest convenient point at which a split-pin can be inserted.

The centre nut should always be tightened up to bed-in the bearings before checking, usually between 0.7 and 4 kg/m (5 and 30lb/ft), at the same time revolving the hub. Spinning will also tell you when the bearings are tightening by the noticeable slowing of the hub. This is a good guide to tightness if you do not have a torque wrench. Slacken off the nut about half a turn or sufficient until you can feel a slight amount of play.

The easiest method of setting the clearance using a feeler gauge is to insert a 0.05 mm blade between the thrust washer and the inner track of the outer bearing cage. This feeler is thick enough to be able to push it to and fro to judge a firm fit. Nip up the nut by hand until this is

achieved. You will now need to check whether a split-pin can be fitted through the slots in the castellated nut into a hole in line, or very nearly in line, with the slot. If the nut has a castellated cover arrangement, the cover should be tried on several positions to find the point where a set of slots is aligned, or nearly aligned, with the split-pin hole. If the thread is fitted with an adjusting nut and a locknut, the adjusting nut is simply held with one spanner as the top nut is tightened down.

After the new split-pin has been pushed into the hole, before bending the tails over to secure the nut, check with the feeler gauge to ensure that the smallest gap within the limits specified by the manufacturer has been obtained.

If a feeler blade cannot be pushed down in between the thrust washer and the bearing, as will be the case with splined centre-lock hubs, check the end-float by rocking the wheel. There should be a small amount of movement at the hub. If the amount appears to be excessive, try to find a point where you can align the nut with another split-pin hole. This is a tricky adjustment, but bear in mind that on no account should the bearings be set in such a way that there is no play at all.

The golden rule for adjustable bearings is that there should be some play in the wheel to guard against expansion damage which could arise from the natural heating of the hub at speed.

Once you are satisfied that the bearings are correctly set, a smear of grease inside the grease cap is all that is needed before lightly tapping it home. Replace the brake drum or caliper and disc pads, making sure that they are tightened to the correct torque as given in your manual or by a main dealer. Reconnect any brake pipes as necessary and bleed the brakes (see pages 87 to 90).

Replace the road wheel—correct torque settings are important here—remove the stands and lower the car to the ground. Finally, take the car for a road test, then re-check the bearing adjustments.

Electrics made easy

Many car owners are nervous of their car's electrical system. The wiring, fuses and circuits can certainly cause confusion. But if the subject is approached logically, bearing in mind a few basic principles, a car's electrics become less of the daunting mystery that many people imagine them to be.

Electricity is the flow of electrons along a cable or wire. Electrons are part of the atomic structure of materials and are far too small to be seen. The fact that electricity cannot be seen in action is one of the main reasons why many people find it hard to understand.

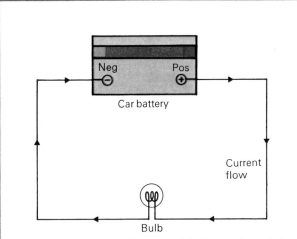

1 A simple circuit. Current flows out of the battery through the positive terminal, runs into the bulb and returns to the battery

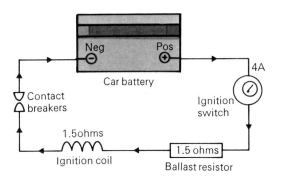

2 The ignition circuit is an example of wiring in series. This means that all components receive the same amount of current

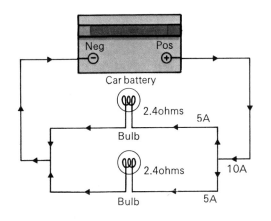

3 Car lights are always wired in parallel circuits. The supply of current is split into two, so the supply in each branch is halved

Trevor Lawrence

Electron flow

Electrons require three things before they can flow—a suitable conductor, a circuit and something to push them around the circuit.

Conductors are materials that allow electricity to flow through them. The best conductors are copper and aluminium, but most metals can be used as conductors. A material that will not allow electricity to flow through it is called an insulator. Rubber, PVC and porcelain are examples of insulators in common use. All cables that carry electricity are wrapped in an insulating sheath, to prevent the electricity flowing into another conductor.

If a conductor or wire has a large diameter, many more electrons will be able to flow through it than if it has a small diameter. Consequently wires and cable are available in different thicknesses, so that the right size cable can be used to match the flow of electrons or electrical current. If too small a cable is used for a given current flow, there will be excessive restriction or resistance to the flow of electricity and the cable will overheat.

The second requirement for electron flow is that the conductors should form a circuit (fig. 1). Electricity cannot flow along a wire unless the wire then returns to the source of power, because the same electrons flow round the circuit over and over again. This is why a battery always has two terminals or connections, one marked positive or +, the other negative or —. It is assumed that the electricity flows out from the positive terminal, through the circuit and then flows back into the negative terminal of the battery.

The battery provides the third requirement for electrical flow. It pushes the electrons round the circuit. The battery can be thought of as a store of electricity that works in the same way as a cold water tank in a house. The water pressure in the tank forces the water through the pipes, much as the battery pushes the electricity round the circuit.

The pressure of water in the pipe is equivalent to the voltage in the electrical circuit (usually 12v or 6v at the battery). When a water tap is turned on water flows through the pipes. The rate of water flow will vary according to the size of the pipes. In the same way, the current, the amount of electricity flowing along a cable, will vary according to the size of the cable. The extent to which a cable restricts the flow of electricity is called its resistance. Resistance is also casued by components in the circuit. All electrical components, such as light bulbs, heaters and motors, resist the current to some extent.

Faults in a circuit

Most circuits in the car's electrical system are reliable, but faults can occur. One fault that can be dangerous is the short-circuit. A short-circuit means that the circuit by-passes the component it should be supplying and the electricity

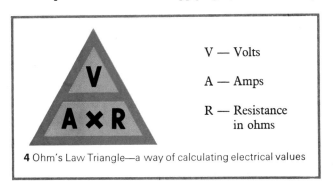

V — Volts

A — Amps

R — Resistance in ohms

4 Ohm's Law Triangle—a way of calculating electrical values

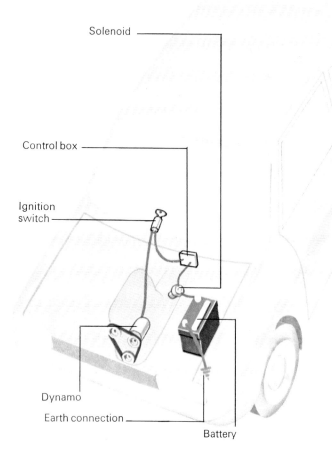

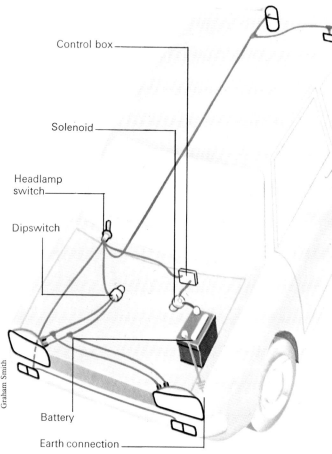

5 The charging circuit (above) and headlamp circuit (below). The dynamo and lights are earthed to the body to complete the circuit

flows straight back into the battery. A short-circuit can result from frayed insulation, when the plastic or rubber covering of the wires wears away until the conductors touch. Short-circuits are dangerous because the current flowing through the wires can cause them to overheat, which may result in a fire in the electrical system.

For this reason most circuits are protected by a fuse. A fuse is a short strip of wire and has a low resistance. If a short-circuit occurs the circuit will lose the resistance of the components that have been by-passed, so the flow of current through the fuse will rise. The fuse will then heat up rapidly, melt and break the circuit, thus preventing the flow of current altogether.

Electrical measurement

It is helpful to know how current, voltage and resistance are measured and the relationship between them, because these values often have to be taken into account when extra electrical components are fitted to the car.

Current is the basic unit of electricity and is measured in Amperes (amps). An amp is equivalent to 6.28 billion billion electrons passing a point in the circuit in one second.

Voltage is measured in volts and can be measured between two points in a circuit. The negative terminal of a car battery is usually assumed to be at zero volts, so it can be said that the positive terminal is at 12 volts.

Resistance is measured in ohms. As a general rule, one volt will cause one amp of current to flow through a resistance of one ohm.

This relationship can be expressed by the formula Volts = Amps x Ohms which is called "Ohm's Law". A useful way of calculating any of these quantities is the Ohm's Law Triangle (fig. 4). The calculation is made simply by covering up the factor required, then working out the remaining sum.

For example, if a new headlamp is being wired up it is important that the cable is of the right thickness. If it is too thin its resistance will be high and it might therefore heat up dangerously. The resistance of the bulb can be calculated by the triangle. If the bulb is operating on a 12 volt system and has a resistance of 2.4 ohms, the current consumption can be calculated by dividing the volts by the ohms:

$$\text{Current consumption of bulb} = \frac{12}{2.4} = 5\text{amps}$$

The wire carrying power to the bulb must therefore be able to cope with 5 amps without overheating.

To take another example, if an ignition coil is being changed it may be necessary to know the resistance of the coil primary winding so that a suitable replacement can be fitted. If it is known that the coil has a current consumption of 3 amps at 12 volts, it is clear from the triangle that the voltage must be divided by the current to find the resistance: $\frac{12}{3} = 4\text{ohms}$, therefore a coil with a primary resistance of 4 ohms would be suitable.

Electrical power

Power is the rate at which a piece of electrical equipment consumes (or generates in the case of a dynamo or alternator) electrical energy. Power is measured in watts and can be calculated by multiplying the volts by the amps.

This formula—Watts = Volts x Amps—can be used for calculating the power of a certain component, or more usefully for calculating the current consumption of an electrical component when its rating in watts is known.

The calculation is also useful for assessing cable, switch and fuse sizes when fitting electrical accessories to the car, or checking existing circuits. For example, if a rear screen heater is being fitted and is rated at 42 watts, it is relatively easy to calculate its current consumption. Using the above formula the calculation is amps = $\dfrac{\text{watts}}{\text{volts}}$ which, in this case is $\dfrac{42}{12}$ = 3.5amps. The fuse wires and switches controlling the heater must therefore be selected with this quite critical figure in mind.

Car electrical circuits

There are two types of circuit in common use in the motor car—series and parallel circuits.

A series circuit is one in which the electrical components are wired together in a line, starting at the positive battery terminal and finishing at the negative. In this type of circuit there is only one route for the current, so the amps flowing through all the components in the circuit must be the same. An example of this is the primary ignition circuit (fig. 2), where the resistances add together to give a total of 3 ohms. The current flow around the circuit can therefore be calculated as 4 amps, when the contact breakers are closed.

In a parallel circuit more than one electrical component is connected across the same electrical supply or connections. Fig. 3 gives an example of such a circuit. Both headlamps are effectively connected across the battery and therefore both have 12 volts fed to them. Because the headlamp bulbs have the same resistance, the same current will flow through them, in this case 5 amps. This means the total current drawn from the battery is 10 amps.

Therefore, with series circuits the current is the same through all the components and with parallel circuits the current in each parallel branch adds up to give the total current consumption of the electrical circuit.

Parallel circuits are often used with lighting systems. Their great advantage is that if one bulb breaks, current will still reach the others. If the bulbs were wired in series, the failure of one bulb would break the entire circuit.

The electrical circuits in a car are divided up into groups (figs. 5 and 6).

All the circuits are shown connected to the battery. The charging circuit is shown separately as it supplies electrical energy to the battery and the other circuits when the engine is running. The charging system is normally

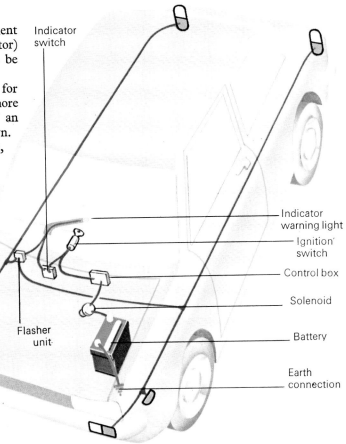

Indicator switch

Flasher unit

Indicator warning light
Ignition switch
Control box
Solenoid
Battery
Earth connection

6 Typical indicator (above) and ignition wiring (below). The spark plugs are earthed, through the engine, to the car's bodywork

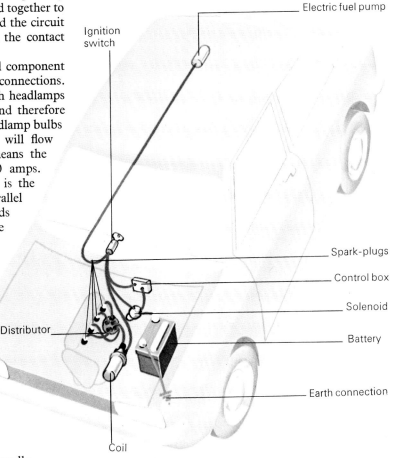

Ignition switch

Distributor

Coil

Electric fuel pump
Spark-plugs
Control box
Solenoid
Battery
Earth connection

capable of supplying the charging current for the battery plus the current consumption of the other electrical circuits when the engine is running at speed.

The charging circuit

The charging circuit consists of an electrical generator, which can be either an alternator or a dynamo, together with its associated control equipment.

The output of the generator depends on its speed which, as it is normally driven by the fan belt, depends in turn on the engine revs. The control equipment or voltage regulator ensures that once sufficient speed is reached by the car the voltage output of the generator remains steady at approximately 14 volts.

The charging current, or amps, produced by the generator will depend upon the electrical load applied. A typical maximum output for a modern car alternator is about 40amps. Failure of the charging system results in the other car circuits being solely dependent on the battery, which will eventually become discharged and incapable of operating the circuits.

The lighting circuit

All the lighting equipment and associated circuits are independent of the ignition switch and include the side-lights, tail lights, headlamps and the number plate light.

All lights on a car are wired in parallel so that failure of one lamp will not affect the others. To prevent total loss of lights, lighting circuits are not fitted with a main fuse. If fuses are used in lighting circuits, each part of the circuit is fused separately.

The ignition circuit

The ignition circuit supplies the high voltage required to operate the spark plugs, which ignite the fuel in the engine. The main components are the ignition switch, ignition coil, distributor and spark plugs. The distributor has low voltage and high voltage sections, the low voltage part being the contact breakers which switch the ignition coil to produce the high voltage (HT). The HT part of the distributor, which consists of the rotor arm and distributor cap, then distributes the HT current to the appropriate spark plug in the correct firing sequence.

The starter circuit

The starter solenoid (see page 39), the starter switch (normally part of the ignition switch) and the starter motor are all linked in the starter circuit. The function of the motor is to crank the engine at sufficient speed to start it. Some starter motors are of the pre-engaged type, instead of the inertia drive type, in which case there is no separate solenoid as it is part of the starter motor (see page 39).

The solenoid acts as a relay to switch on the heavy current required by the starter motor. Because the starter motor draws a large current, initially about 300 amps, the cables are of a heavy gauge and any small resistance in the circuit will result in sluggish operation or failure of the starter motor to crank the engine.

Accessory circuits

Accessory circuits control all the minor electrical components which include windscreen wipers, horns, instrument gauges, heated rear screens, heater blowers, indicators and hazard warning lights. These circuits are normally fused either in groups or singly and when there is a fault on one or more of the accessories the fuse should be investigated first having consulted your handbook. It should be clear from the group of accessories that has failed which particular fuse is at fault.

Wiring systems

A circuit must be continuous from one battery terminal to the other. Consequently there must be a feed cable to each electrical component and a return cable from the component to the battery.

In practice, however, the steel car body is used as the return cable and this method of wiring is known as the "earth return" system. Instead of a wire returning the current to the battery, the circuit is simply connected to the car body. One battery terminal is also wired in this way. Most cars are wired "negative earth" which means that the negative terminal of the battery and the negative end of the circuit are both connected to the bodywork. Some cars are wired "positive earth", with the positive terminal connected to the body and the current flowing to the component through the car body and back to the negative terminal via the car's wiring.

This system has the advantage of nearly halving the number of cables required, which reduces manufacturing costs and saves space. This method cannot, however, be used on glass-fibre bodied vehicles.

The cables used for wiring vehicles come in various thicknesses and have appropriate current ratings. The correct size of cable for a given circuit is selected by the car manufacturer and it is important that if circuits or accessories are added the correct size cable is used. A cable which is too small will overheat and a cable that is too large is a waste of material and takes up more space.

When a large number of wires need to be run to roughly the same point in the car they are carried in a loom. A loom is the complete set of cables bound in a thin plastic sheath with the appropriate connectors at either end.

Wiring in looms makes initial assembly easier, keeps the cables tidy and prevents snagging, but makes tracing cables and repair difficult. To make it easy to identify cables in order to connect them to the appropriate component a colour code is adopted but unfortunately it is not standardized and different manufacturers use different codes. The colour coding adopted by different manufacturers is outlined on page 130.

Vehicle manufacturers are trying to reduce the amount of wiring required and recent developments include a wiring loom tape, which is a flat tape having the wires embedded in it and parallel to each other. The tape can be glued or clipped to body panels and gives a neat wiring system which can be easily traced.

This type of loom, called Fabrostrip, ·has another significant advantage—it is relatively cheap to produce. Car manufacturers are always looking for ways of cutting production costs, in order to keep down the price of the finished car. Unlike almost all other car components, the conventional loom is still largely handmade by highly skilled workers, which is an expensive process. The Fabrostrip looms, though, lend themselves to automatic-production and are consequently cheaper.

In Britain, they were first introduced on the BL Austin Allegro and are likely to gradually replace the conventional loom in many mass-produced cars.

The use of printed circuits is another example of a technical advance being used to cut costs. These are often used in instrument circuits and they simplify the wiring behind the dashboard. A printed circuit is a thin strip of copper mounted on a plastic board. These can be made in huge quantities at comparatively low cost.

Light failures

Symptoms	Possible causes	Remedies
One light fails	Faulty bulb	Replace bulb
	Faulty earth	Clean bulb holder Clean earth contact points and check and renew earth
	Faulty wiring	Repair or replace wiring
Two lights fail	Faulty fuse	Replace fuse
	Faulty junction box	Repair or replace junction box
Three lights fail	Faulty fuse plus any of above causes	Replace fuse then treat as "one light fails"
All four lights fail	Faulty fuse	Replace fuse
	Faulty supply or supply wiring	Check and repair supply or wiring
	Faulty switch	Replace switch

George Wright

1 Any defect in the sidelight and headlight system of your car is not only dangerous but is also illegal

It is illegal to have even one sidelight not working. Most faults are easy to cure once you have located them. There are many reasons for a sidelight failure but fault finding can be simplified by a process of elimination.

The wiring systems used for car sidelights are very complex and differ from car to car. The only way that fault finding can be a relatively quick job is to eliminate those parts of the system that do not need checking. The fault finding flow chart, (fig. 2) will help you do this. Refer to the chart to discover the likely fault, then start at the paragraph relevant to the symptoms.

Faulty supply

Figs. 3 to 5 show the three most common sidelight circuits used on modern cars. The sidelights are designed to work independently of the ignition. The supply comes from the battery, via a connector terminal and a junction box, straight to the sidelight switch.

To test the supply, first check the battery terminals and earth strap (see page 38). A further test is to try any battery-operated components. If these particular components can be seen to work then it is obvious that the battery must be supplying a current.

Tracing the wiring from the battery to the fuse is a very difficult job, especially if you do not have the car's circuit diagram. To avoid this work, try the following method. First, disconnect the battery earth terminal strap. Next, use a long piece of thin electrical wire, about 28 gauge, and connect this between the positive terminal on the battery and the live side of the sidelight's fuse. If you do not know the correct fuse to use, you will have to consult the circuit diagram in your owner's manual (see pages 125 to 130) or ask your dealer. There is no practical method of identifying these fuses when the sidelights are not working. If only one sidelight has failed, it may be simply that the bulb has blown. Check this first.

Then carefully re-connect the earth strap terminal to its connection point and switch on the sidelights. If they now work, the fault lies in the circuit and is situated somewhere between the battery and the particular fuse in question.

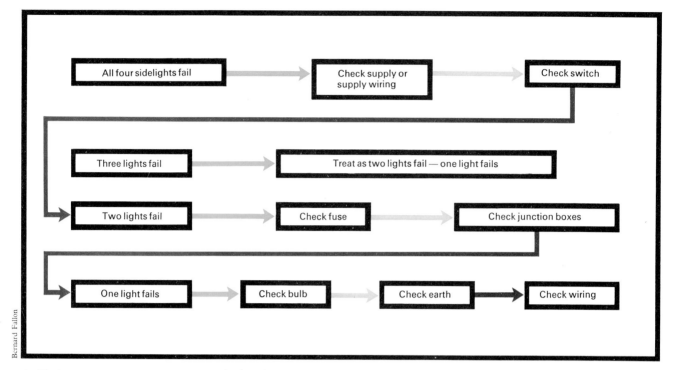

```
All four sidelights fail  →  Check supply or
                             supply wiring      →  Check switch

Three lights fail  →  Treat as two lights fail — one light fails

Two lights fail  →  Check fuse  →  Check junction boxes

One light fails  →  Check bulb  →  Check earth  →  Check wiring
```

→ Most likely   → Possible   → Least likely

2 The fault finding flow chart. Follow the arrows to find which is the most likely, possible and least likely cause of the fault

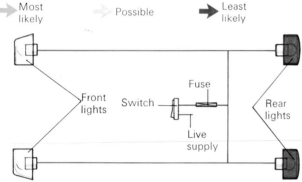

3 This is the simplest wiring circuit for sidelights, where all four sidelights will not operate if the fuse has blown or broken

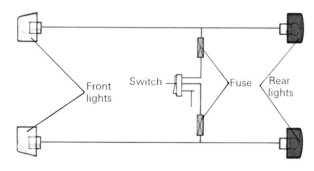

4 This circuit has two fuses, each protecting a pair of lights. If a fuse blows, only the lights on one side of the car will work

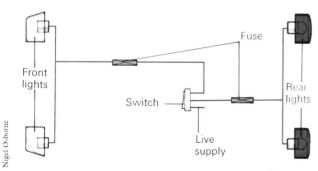

5 This is another circuit where two fuses are used. Here either the front or back pair of lights will go out if the fuse fails

Faults between battery and fuse

Although the supply effectively goes straight from the battery to the live side of the fuse, in practice it often does this via many junction boxes and connector terminals. These junction boxes and connector terminals are used only as straight connectors joining sections of wiring and have no active effect on the supply current. The trouble that can arise is usually simply a problem of bad connections, possibly causing short circuits. The cure is to repair the connections and replace any damaged wiring. Unfortunately, this is not an easy job. It can only be done using a circuit diagram and a great deal of patient searching. Pages 125 to 130 describe how to understand and use circuit diagrams. Faulty wires should be replaced by wires of the same thickness and colour (see page 107).

Faulty switch

Two types of sidelight switch are commonly used. One, fitted mainly to older cars, is a separate switch mounted on the fascia. The second and later type is part of a multi-function cluster which is usually a stalk-actuated switch mounted on the side of the steering column surround on the more modern type of car.

The separate sidelight switch is the easiest to work on having basically just an on/off function. One movement turns on the sidelights, a second activates the headlights. To check these switches, remove the unit from the fascia by unscrewing the bezel or unclipping the unit and bridge the terminals with a screwdriver (fig. 6). If the sidelights now work the switch is faulty. Obtain a new unit. Disconnect the wires from the faulty unit. Take note of their connecting order and connect them to the new unit. Finally, screw the new unit back in place.

The multi-function cluster switch is more difficult to check. It is largely a matter of dismantling the switch and finding the correct terminals by trial and error. Pages 110 to 112 explain how to dismantle the switch and the basic method for finding and testing a particular function of the switch. They also describe how to remove the switch and replace it with a new unit.

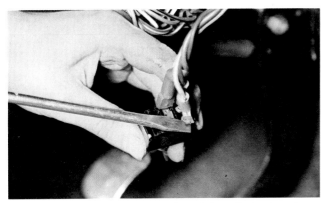

6 To check the light switch, remove the unit from the fascia and bridge the sidelight terminals on the switch with a screwdriver

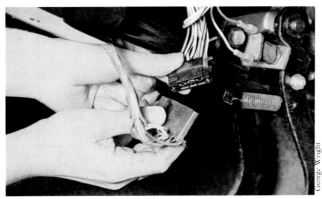

7 Junction boxes are usually hidden from sight but can be eased into view and then pulled apart to inspect the connections

Faulty fuses

Figs. 3 to 5 show three typical sidelight wiring arrangements. In one system all four sidelights are protected by the same fuse. In the other systems, either the front and back pairs or the left and right hand pairs of lights share a single fuse each. Your owner's handbook will tell you which component is supplied by each fuse.

If you find that by replacing the original sidelight fuse with a new one that the lights do now work, leave them on for several minutes. If they continue to work, a blown fuse is most likely the sole cause of their failure. If, however, they stop working after a short time, the fuse will most probably have blown again because of another type of fault further along the circuit.

Faulty junction box

Car electrical circuits usually contain a rarely noticed component called the junction box or connector (fig. 7). This junction box is used for one of two reasons. It is either used to conveniently break a large section of wiring into smaller, more workable sections, or it converts a single wire into two or more wires. Junction boxes are usually situated behind the fascia panels or in the engine compartment. They are rarely secured in place by screws or clips. Usually, the tension of the wires they connect holds them secure and in position.

Basically, a junction box is composed of two interlocking sections (fig. 8). The terminals for the input wires are contained in one section and the output terminals are in the other section. When you wish to separate the two sections of wiring, you simply unplug one half of the junction box from the other. The terminals are sealed into cylindrical holes. The wires enter this cylinder and are held in place by a spade connector. On one half of the junction box the cylinder remains a metal-lined hole, on the other half the end of the cylinder forms a metal plug. Each plug on one half of the box connects to a corresponding hole on the other half.

When the box is used to convert one wire to several wires, the single wire is connected to the first cylinder. A metal bridge then connects this cylinder to the next and so on for the number of cylinders required. The output wires are then connected individually to the corresponding cylinders in the other half of the box.

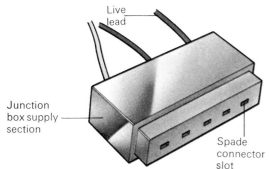

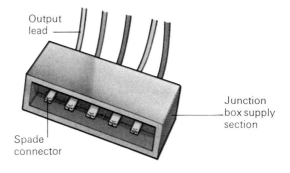

8 This type of junction box converts three wires into five wires. Most boxes have a notch to ensure they are joined the right way

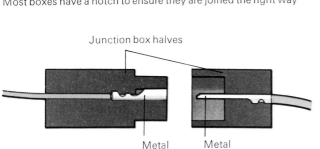

9 This cross-section of a junction box shows the metal cylinder part of the connector (left) and the metal plug (right)

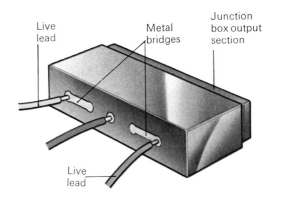

10 When the box is used to convert one wire into two, a metal bridge connects two cylinders on the input side of the connector

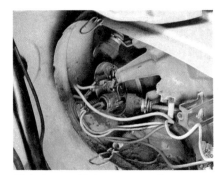

11 A cluster of lights can sometimes appear to be difficult to check owing to their complicated wiring layout

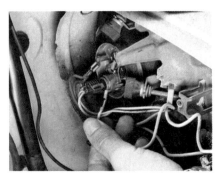

12 If the sidelight is not working, remove the sidelight live supply wire from the spade connector at the back of the cluster

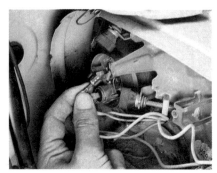

13 Then fix the indicator live wire to the sidelight bulb. If the sidelight then flashes, the fault is in its live supply

There are three types of fault that can occur with a junction box:
1. The box halves may have become separated.
2. The wires may have slipped out of their cylinders.
3. A metal bridge may have fused or broken.

Repairing junction boxes
Only the first problem with junction boxes can be easily cured. If the box halves have simply become separated, clip them together again.

If the wires have slipped out of their cylinders, it is not usually possible to re-fit them. This is because they are a compression fit and it is rarely possible to re-tighten these joints. Fit a new junction box by pressing the spade connectors already on the wires into the corresponding cylinders on the new box.

Similarly, if the metal bridge has fused you will have to replace the junction box completely and then re-fit the wires into the new unit.

Faulty bulbs
Sidelight bulbs on many modern cars are part of a sealed cluster of lights. Depending on the car and type of light fitted, the ease of checking the bulb can vary. There is a simpler method than bulb removal that can be used with some of these lights.

Checking bulbs
Whether the sidelight bulb is an isolated unit or part of a cluster of several bulbs, exposing and removing the bulb is often a tedious job. To avoid doing this unnecessarily the following method can sometimes be used to check the bulb while still in place.

First identify the sidelight bulb. This may be a separate bulb, it may be part of a dual filament bulb, or it may be one bulb in a sealed unit containing several bulbs. No matter what type of bulb it is, it will have a separate terminal and its own supply wire.

To locate the bulb on sealed units containing more than one light or dual filament systems obtain the help of an assistant. The assistant should sit inside the car operating the lights while you check from the outside.

Starting at the rear of the car, check the left indicator, then the right, followed by the brake lights and, finally,

14 The sidelight unit is usually held in place by screws, but in some cases the radiator grille will have to be removed

15 Some radiator grille fixing screws are hidden beneath the bonnet. This has to be lifted before the screws can be removed

16 The grille can then be lifted off. Some light units are held by further screws but this type comes free with the grille

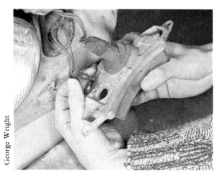

17 The light unit can then be pulled away from the bodywork. The sidelight bulb and holder can then be removed from the back

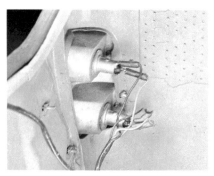

18 This particular rear light cluster, on a Ford Cortina Mk II, is reached from inside the boot after removing the spare wheel

19 The sidelight bulb can be inspected by carefully pulling out its holder, which is a spring fit into the cluster panel

20 Check the inside of the bulb holder and the metal surface of the bulb for any corrosion, which will affect the earthing

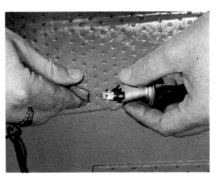

21 The surfaces of the spade connectors at the back of the bulb holders must also be checked, as these are prone to corrosion

22 Run a wire from the bulb to an earthing point. Switch on. If the bulb lights, the cluster panel is badly earthed

the sidelights. If the indicator and brake lights work, simple elimination confirms that the remaining lights or filaments are the sidelights.

Next, locate the rear of the light units and find the supply wires and terminals. If a sidelight does not work, switch on the indicator bulb nearest to it. Then swap the indicator and sidelight supply wires. If the sidelight now flashes, the bulb is sound. If not the bulb is faulty.

Repeat this test for the front sidelights.

If the wire to the indicator will not reach the sidelight terminal, cut a length of 28 gauge electrical wire and join the indicator supply to the terminal.

If the bulb flashes now it is not faulty and neither is the earth. You will now have to try the other tests in the fault flow chart. If it does not flash, you will have to examine the bulb and its earthing.

Replacing bulbs

It is not possible to repair a bulb; you will have to replace any that are faulty. In certain cases, where the bulb is part of a sealed unit, you will have to replace the whole unit. Basically, this is usually a case of unscrewing the transparent bulb cover to expose the bulb or unit, then lifting or twisting them out. Replacements can generally be purchased from local accessory shops. Before actually replacing the bulb or unit test the earthing points. A faulty earth will prevent the bulb from lighting.

Faulty earthing

Car bulbs will not work unless they are properly earthed. This is usually done by the stem of the bulb making earth contact with the metal framework surrounding it. Remove the bulb and check both the bulb stem and the metal bulb holder for corrosion or damage. Clean any corrosion with an emery cloth. Then try the bulb in position again.

On glass-fibre-bodied cars the bulb bracket will not be in contact with metal to act as an earth. For this reason there is a separate wire leading from the bulb to a good earthing point. If you have a glass-fibre-bodied car inspect this earth wire and the connections at both ends. These should be sound and free from corrosion. If they are not, renew the connections or remove the faulty wiring and replace it with a new section.

Faulty wiring

There is a considerable amount of wiring connecting the sidelight bulbs to the fuse or fuses via the switch. This wiring enters and leaves the wiring loom at the appropriate places. A break in, or damage to, any of this wiring may lead to a short circuit. This will blow any fuses and will continue to blow any replacement fuses until the wiring is replaced in the manner described below.

To check this wiring you will need the circuit diagram for your car. By following the colour codes for each wire, using the circuit diagram will help you locate where each wire enters and leaves the wiring loom. The best method is to check each section of wiring separately using any junction boxes or connectors as natural breaks. For this you will need a circuit tester.

Start at the bulb end for each section of wiring and gradually work back to the switch, then the fuse. Disconnect the wire from the bulb and find the first suitable break in the wire. Most probably this will be a junction box. Disconnect the wire at this break. If your circuit tester has a long wire connect one end of the wire to be tested to the circuit tester probe and the other end of the wire to be tested to the clip end of the circuit tester. If your circuit tester has only a short length of wire, use the following method. First, take the bulb end of the wire to be tested and connect it to a clean metal part of the car body. Attach the other end of the wire to be tested to the circuit tester probe. Finally, connect the clip end to another clean metal part of the car body.

Whichever method you have used, if the lamp lights the wire is sound. If not, the wire is faulty and needs replacing. If you find and renew a faulty wire but the light still fails to work, repeat the test on each section of wiring in the sidelight circuit as there may be more than one section that is faulty and which needs replacing.

Replacing faulty wiring

To prevent the numerous wires in a car's electrical circuit from forming an unsightly tangle, car manufacturers tie sections of this wiring into bundles and cover them in insulation material. These bundles of wires, called the wiring loom, keep the wires tidy and well protected. When a section of wiring develops a fault, however, the construction of the wiring loom makes wire replacement a long and arduous job. Understanding wiring diagrams is more fully described on pages 125 to 130.

To replace a section of faulty wire in the loom, disconnect the faulty section at both ends. Cut these loose ends as close to the loom as possible and then bind the remainder to the loom with tape. Next cut a new length of wire, with the same colour code and gauge as that being replaced, long enough to follow the path of the faulty wire along the loom. Feed the wire into place and then connect each end of the new wire to the original terminals.

When doing this, do not just twist the ends of the new wire on to or around the old connecting points. Always solder on a connector of the correct type to the end of the new wire, or use a crimping tool. To tidy up the finished replacement, secure the new wire by binding it to the outside of the loom, at intervals, with insulating tape.

The indicators

Symptom	Possible causes	Remedy
All four indicator bulbs not working	No power supply	Check battery connections and state of charge
	Blown or faulty fuse	Replace fuse
	Faulty flasher unit	Replace flasher unit
	Faulty switching unit	Repair switch contacts or replace unit
	Faulty wiring	Replace faulty section of wiring
	All four bulb earths faulty	Make good earth
	All four bulbs blown	Replace bulbs

Flashing indicators are a standard feature on all modern cars, and these have to be in working order for reasons of both safety and legislation.

Modern high-speed driving depends very much on your ability to indicate your intentions quickly, and flashing indicators are now a vital part of a car's equipment. Originally, simple hand signals were used, but these were unsatisfactory because they were hard to see at night and when vision was blocked by part of the car body. This is why electric indicators were introduced.

A knowledge of hand signals still features in the British driving test, and they can be used as a get-you-home measure if your indicators fail, although in theory this practice is illegal. Strictly speaking, you should inspect the indicators before every journey.

Indicator components
Figs. 2-4 show typical indicator wiring systems. Note that the electricity travels from the battery, via a fuse, to a flasher unit. From here, it travels to a switching unit which sends the flashing signal to whichever set of indicator bulbs you have selected. In some systems, a warning bulb is also placed in the circuit to warn the driver that the indicators are in use.

Indicator problems
When the indicators fail to work, the fault may be in any of the components along this system. The fault location chart (fig. 1) shows the best way to find the trouble.

Checking the battery
The simplest check for the battery is to try all the components that run from it. These are the lights, the starter motor, the heater fan, the dashboard lights and any heated rear windscreen. If none of these is working, the battery is flat and will have to be recharged.

Most battery chargers have a meter telling you the rate at which current is flowing into the battery. If this is reading 'nil' the battery is either fully charged or it has buckled plates, is short-circuiting, and cannot accept charge. A short-circuiting battery, which will give off bubbles, will have to be renewed.

If the battery is fully charged, check its connections—in

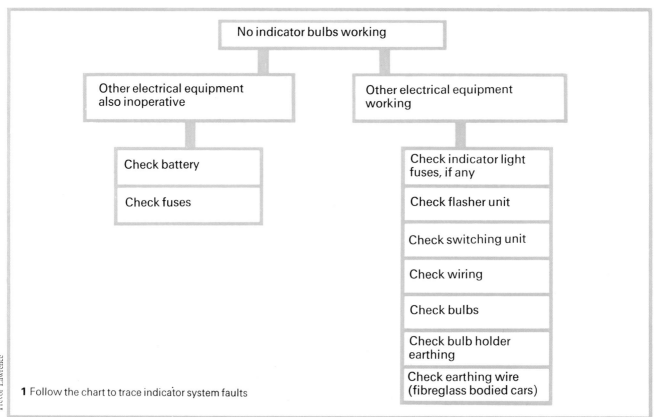

1 Follow the chart to trace indicator system faults

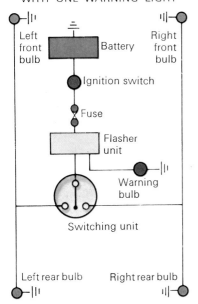

FIRST INDICATOR SYSTEM
WITH ONE WARNING LIGHT

Left front bulb · Battery · Right front bulb · Ignition switch · Fuse · Flasher unit · Warning bulb · Switching unit · Left rear bulb · Right rear bulb

2 Indicator system with one warning light. On this type the warning light will work even if the indicators' wiring is faulty

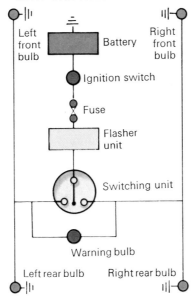

SECOND INDICATOR SYSTEM
WITH ONE WARNING LIGHT

Left front bulb · Battery · Right front bulb · Ignition switch · Fuse · Flasher unit · Switching unit · Warning bulb · Left rear bulb · Right rear bulb

3 Another system with one warning light. On this type the warning light will not work if the indicators' wiring is faulty

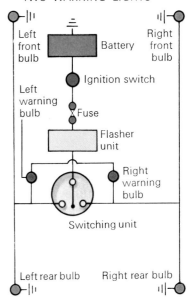

INDICATOR SYSTEM WITH
TWO WARNING LIGHTS

Left front bulb · Battery · Right front bulb · Ignition switch · Left warning bulb · Fuse · Flasher unit · Right warning bulb · Switching unit · Left rear bulb · Right rear bulb

4 Wiring layout with a warning light for each set of bulbs. These lights too rely on being earthed via the bulbs

Trevor Lawrence

particular, the post connections on top of the battery and the braided metal lead to earth (see page 38).

Fuse checks

The fuse lies between the ignition switch and the flasher unit. On most cars it is part of the block of fuses attached to the body of the car in the engine compartment. But occasionally the fuse is in a holder near the flasher unit itself. Once you have found the flasher unit (see Flasher units, below) look to see whether there is a fuse holder in one of the wires leading to it. If so, this is the fuse you want.

Try replacing this fuse with a new one of the same rating. If the indicator lights now operate, and keep operating, your problem is solved.

If you cannot find a fuse alongside the flasher unit, then the fuse you want will be in the main fuse box. This box is usually in the engine compartment, mounted on the bodywork under the windscreen. If you do not have a circuit diagram for your car, either test each fuse using a circuit tester (see page 107), or use the following method. First, find one circuit which works—say the left headlight—and remove each fuse in turn to see if the headlamp goes out. Put each fuse back before trying another. Then, having found the fuse which controls the left headlamp, and knowing that this is a good fuse, try each other fuse in the place of the headlamp fuse. When a fuse is found that does

not light up the headlamp, this—obviously—is the faulty one. So, fit a new fuse in the holder that the 'dud' fuse came from and test as in the previous paragraph.

If you cannot find a faulty fuse, or if fitting a new fuse does not restore the indicators, the trouble must lie elsewhere. Similarly, if the new fuse rapidly burns out, one or more of the other components must be at fault.

Flasher units

Flasher units cannot be repaired, and will have to be replaced if faulty. When replacing a unit, take a note of your car model and year to ensure that the correct replacement is supplied.

The flasher unit is found under the dash of the car, often held by a spring clip (fig. 17). If a dash-mounted radio is fitted, this may have to be removed to reach the unit. Check with your dealer or car main agent if you have trouble finding the flasher unit.

The simplest way of testing the flasher unit is to borrow a replacement unit from a friend with a similar car. If you cannot do this, there is no need to buy another unit to find out if the original unit is faulty. Since the only function of the unit is to make-and-break the electrical circuit, you can simply bridge the terminals with a piece of wire to get a continuous current flowing to the switch. Then, if you operate the switch, the indicator lights should come on

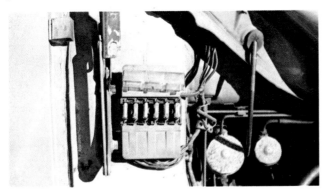

5 Most modern wiring systems use a fuse in the main fuse box to control the indicators. This is usually in the engine compartment

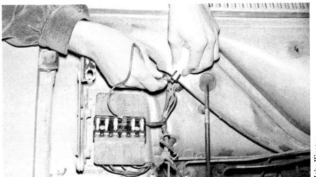

6 Use a test lamp to find the live side of a fuse. The bulb will light up when put between the live side and a good earth point

Jake Wynter

Types of flasher unit

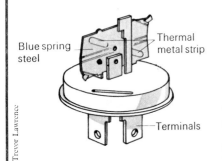

Blue spring steel

Thermal metal strip

Terminals

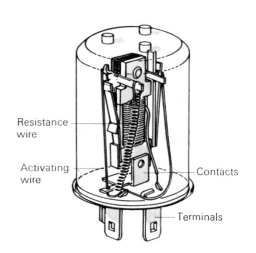

Resistance wire

Activating wire

Contacts

Terminals

7 (left) Thermal leaf type flasher unit

8 (right) Hot wire type flasher unit

Trevor Lawrence

There are two main types of flasher unit, which are not interchangeable. Although these cannot usually be serviced by the owner and should be replaced if they go wrong, it is worth knowing how they work.

The most common type in modern cars uses a simple 'thermal leaf' (fig. 7)—a strip of metal which heats and expands as current flows through it. It is fastened at each end to a leaf of blue spring steel, which suddenly warps when the expanding metal has reached a certain length. This breaks a contact, and current stops flowing through the unit, allowing the metal to cool. The leaf snaps back, the contact is made again and the cycle continues.

This unit has just two external contacts, and is connected directly in the line from the battery, via a fuse, to the indicator switch. A feature of its operation is that current flows through as soon as it is switched on, and stops only when the leaf has heated up and the contact has been broken. This means that the indicator lights come on as soon as the switch is operated.

The other kind of unit has three or more contacts, and is of the 'hot wire' type (fig. 8). It is rather more complicated than the thermal leaf type. As current flows, a wire heats up and lengthens, allowing the main contact to close. When this happens increased current flows through the unit, operating the indicators and energizing a solenoid which closes a second contact to send current to the warning light. As the main contact closes, however, it shorts out the hot wire, which then cools so that the whole cycle can begin again.

With this system, the indicator lights do not come on until the wire has heated up. This means that there is a delay of up to a second between the driver's operating the indicator switch and the lights coming on for the first time—a delay during which the car may have travelled some distance.

With both types, there is generally a characteristic clicking sound as the contacts make and break—a useful audible warning that the indicators are on should they not cancel. There is also a warning light or, sometimes, one for each side of the car. While the main bulbs will still work if the warning light fails, it is an offence in Britain to run a car without a working warning light if indicators are fitted. This is because indicator lights which are wrongly signalling a turn could cause an accident.

continuously on one side or the other. To do this test, turn on the ignition and proceed as follows:

On a two-terminal unit, pull the unit out until you can reach the terminals and connect the bare metal ends of the terminals to each other by using a length of wire, bared at both ends, or a piece of metal. Operate the indicator light switch for either a right-hand or a left-hand turn. If the indicator lights now work, the flasher unit is faulty and should be replaced with a new unit.

On a three-terminal unit, think of the terminals as being three pairs (fig. 9). Connect each pair in turn as described above. If the lights operate when any combination is bridged, again the unit is at fault and should be renewed. If this bridging does not make the indicators come on, the fault lies elsewhere.

Finding the switching unit

On older cars, the switching unit was found only on the dashboard, but current models have it mounted on the steering column. How you get at it depends on where it is.

To expose dash-mounted switching units, first examine the switch from the front and rear. On some units, the locating screws are immediately visible from the front. In this case you can simply undo the screws and lower the

unit. On the other, rear-mounted switching units, you will have to look or feel behind the unit from under the dashboard for the screw heads or the locking nut. Then you undo the screws or remove the nuts and again withdraw the unit and lower it, making sure that you do not accidentally disconnect any of the wiring.

Steering-column-mounted switching units can be reached only after you have removed the steering column surround. To do this, find the countersunk heads of the retaining screws and undo them. The switch unit will now be exposed.

Checking the switching unit

There are two basic types of switching unit, the kind that serves only the indicators, and the combination type which also serves other components. No trouble to tell which type you have: if it is a combination, several other components—horn, headlamps and so on—will probably be out of action too (though it is just conceivable that only the contact serving the actual indicators is faulty).

Combination units cannot be tested or repaired, and if yours is faulty you will have to replace it with a new unit. You could borrow an identical switching unit from the same model car as yours, try it in place of your own and see if the indicators now work. But not many people are willing to let you strip a unit from their car to do this. So if you find your switching unit is of the combination type, check everything else, and fit a new switching unit only as a last resort.

You can, however, test the other sort of switching unit—the kind that serves only the indicators. The surest method is to use an identical switching unit in place of the original, but there is another method.

The switching unit has three terminals, one receiving the flashing impulse from the flasher unit, and one each to carry this signal to indicator bulbs left and right. There is a variety of switching units, and each has its own arrangement of terminals. The best method of testing the unit is to treat the terminals as three pairs (fig. 9), and to use a piece of wire or metal to bridge these pairs as follows:

First, turn on the ignition. Then pick any two of the terminals and bridge them. One of three things will occur: one set of indicators will light, the warning light will also

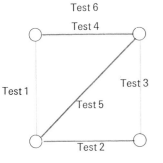
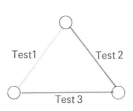

9 Diagrams showing the bridging method suitable for testing three-terminal or four-terminal switching and flasher units

light, or nothing will light at all. If nothing lights, try another combination of terminals, having removed the bridge from the first pair. Repeat for the other combination of terminals.

If the bulbs fail to light during any of these tests, the fault lies outside the switching unit, in one of the other components. If any of the bulbs do light up, the switching unit is at fault.

On older cars, you may be able to open up the switching unit and if it is faulty, try bending the contacts inside to make them press together firmly when switched on. If this does not cure the problem, replace the unit.

Newer cars usually have sealed switching units. These cannot be repaired, and will have to be replaced. Label carefully all the wires as you remove them from the old unit, to help you fit them 'right way round' on the new unit.

Wiring checks

To check the wiring, you will need a length of wire long enough to reach from the fuse box to the rear of the car. The procedure is to connect one end of the wire to a live supply point and bridge in turn each part of the wiring (fig. 10). If

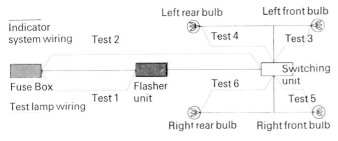

10 This diagram shows the testing order for the wiring of the indicator system. Tests 3 to 6 are unlikely to be needed

11 The switching unit of the Cortina Mk III is below the steering column surround. Remove this by undoing the four retaining screws

12 The two halves of the steering column surround can then be separated and removed, exposing the switching unit

13 This switching unit is of the multi-function type. It is held on to the steering column by a bracket and two bolts. Undo these

14 The switching unit is then freed and can be lowered. Finding which terminals are used for the indicators is largely guesswork

Jake Wynter

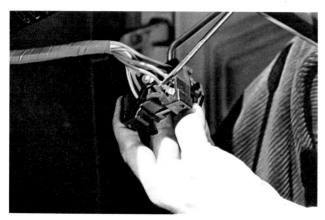

15 Select a set of terminals and carry out the bridging tests. If any other systems operate, you have chosen the wrong terminals

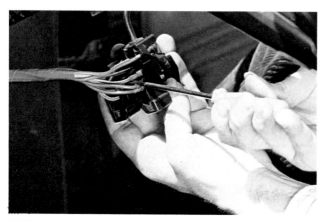

16 If bridging does not operate any of the other systems and the indicators do not work, the fault lies elsewhere

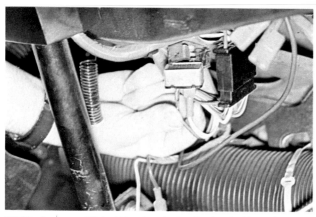

17 The flasher unit is held in a bracket under the dashboard This unit is easy to unclip and lift free for inspection

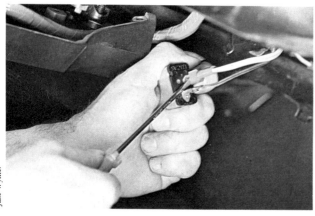

18 Carry out the bridging tests. If the indicators now work, the flashing unit is at fault. If not, the fault lies elsewhere

the temporary bridging wire makes a bulb light up where the permanent wire does not do so, the permanent wire is faulty.

The supply point you choose should be protected by a fuse, so that if your bridging wire laps a serious fault the fuse will blow—and you will not have a burn-out to deal with.

The easiest way to do this is to use the main fuse block. If you do not know which side of the block is the battery side, use a length of wire with a 12-volt bulb. Earth the terminal pin of the bulb by holding it against the bare metal on the engine, hold the wire to the bulb casing, and hold the other end of the wire to each side in turn of an empty fuse holder. With the ignition switched on, the bulb will light up when the wire is touched to the battery side of the fuse holder.

But it is to the other, non-battery, side that you connect the circuit testing wire. Do this and replace the fuse. From here on be careful not to touch the free end of the wire to 'earth', or you will blow the fuse for nothing.

To test a section of the indicator circuit, turn on the ignition and turn on the indicator switch in the desired direction—either left-hand or right-hand, depending on which wire you are checking. Touch the free end of the test wire to the far end (that is, farthest from the battery) of the wire you want to check. The faulty part of the wiring will have been found when the bridging causes the indicators to light.

First touch the free end of the wire to the supply terminal on the flasher unit—that is, the terminal not connected to the switching unit. If the system now works, the fault is in the wiring between the flasher unit and the supply (fuse box).

If that does not work, touch your wire to the central contact on the switching unit. If the lights now work, the fault is in the wiring between the flasher unit and the switching unit.

If the above tests do not find the fault, first test the bulbs and their earthing and, if they are not at fault, the trouble must lie in the wiring between the switching unit and the bulbs. This is very unlikely, for it would mean that four different sets of wiring have all failed at the same time.

To replace a faulty section of wiring, first cut a length of wire longer than you will need. Next, disconnect one end of the faulty wiring and connect one end of the new wire in its place. (Always use insulating sleeves over the connection, and the correct electrical connectors). Then trace the path of the faulty wire, passing the new wire along the same path, to the other end. Finally, disconnect the original wiring from this second end and connect the new wire, now cut to size. Pull out the old wire and discard. This can be a lengthy job, especially if the stretch of wiring follows a complicated path, and you may need a great deal of patience and observation.

Checking bulbs

It is unlikely that all four bulbs will have failed at once, but it is a straightforward job to check them.

To remove the bulbs, first remove the lens. In most cars, long screws are used to secure the lens; undo these and lift the lens clear. The indicators may have a separate lens, or the lens may be shared by the indicators, brake lights, sidelights or even headlamps. Also, the rear ones may be secured from inside the boot. Finding the securing screws should be described in the car handbook; if not, you will have to make a careful search.

Another system of securing the lens involves the lens

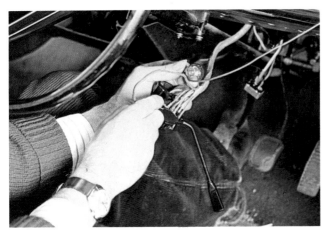

19 Connect a test lamp between the fuse and the flasher unit. If it lights, then this section of the wiring is faulty

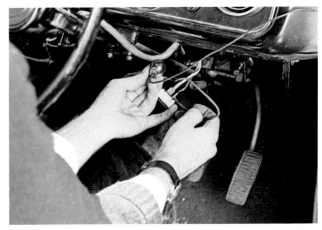

20 If the lamp does not light, connect it between the flasher unit and the switching unit. If it lights, this wiring is faulty

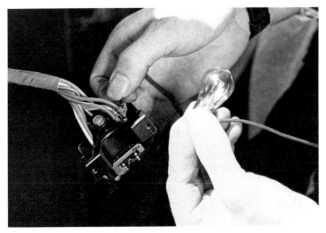

21 If all the other tests do not show a fault, test the wiring between the switching unit and both sets of bulbs

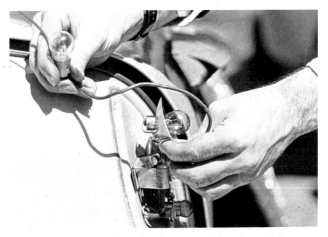

22 The bulbs are sometimes hard to expose. Therefore, while testing them, it is also useful to check their connections

being slotted into a rubber surround. In this case use a small screwdriver to gently prise out the lens, taking care not to shatter it.

Bulbs are normally of the bayonet type. These can be removed by twisting the bulb while pressing it into its holder. All other bulbs are screwed into their holder by a threaded base on the bulb; these you simply unscrew. The bulb can be tested quite easily by touching its base to earth on the engine, and connecting the side terminal on the bulb to the positive terminal on the battery on positive-earth cars, or to the negative terminal on negative-earth cars. If the bulbs do not light, replace them with new bulbs of the same type. If they do light, check their earthing (see below) before refitting them.

Before replacing the lens, use this opportunity to clean it with warm water and detergent. Do not use petrol as this may dissolve the lens material.

Take care in refitting the lens to avoid excess pressure which may crack the plastic. Rubber-mounted lenses will be easier to refit if you use a drop of detergent smeared around the base.

Indicator lights must be both white or both amber to the front, and both red or both amber to the rear. So, if you need a temporary repair, use coloured plastic.

Faulty earth
It is also very unlikely that all four earths on the indicator bulbs have failed. Only if all the bulbs are working and all other tests have failed should you consider the earthing of the bulbs to be at fault.

Two types of earthing are used on car indicators. On

metal bodied cars, the bulb holder is used to earth the bulb. This bulb holder is made of metal and is in contact with the metal car body. Check the contact of the bulb with its holder, and the contact of the holder with the car body. Both should be clean and rust-free. If you are in any doubt, clean all areas of contact with emery paper. If this fails, or if plastic material has been used around the bulb holder, solder a piece of wire to the metal bulb holder, and solder the other end to a clean bare metal part of the car body.

On glass fibre and plastic-bodied cars, a wire is already used from the bulb holder to a bare metal part of the car, or to a good earthing point. Check this wire and both of its connections. If in any doubt over the condition of these wires, remove the old wiring, clean the contact areas with emery cloth, and solder on a new piece of wire. Be careful to fit this new wire where it will cause no obstruction and not suffer from chafing.

Hazard warning systems
If a hazard warning system is fitted, to make all the indicator lights flash at once, it may be operated either by a separate unit which by-passes the indicator switch or by an integral unit which combines both flasher and hazard warning systems.

Although the wiring is somewhat more complicated, you can trace faults in your indicator light system exactly as described above. The only difference may be that, in checking the switching unit, one of your wire bridges may cause all the warning lights to come on at once—indicating a fault in the switching unit itself.

The car horn

Symptom	Possible causes	Remedies
Car horn makes no sound	Faulty fuses	Replace fuses
	Faulty horn	Test horn, replace if necessary
	Faulty relay	Test relay, replace if necessary
	Faulty compressor (air horns only)	Test compressor, replace if necessary
	Faulty piping (air horns only)	Check piping, replace if necessary
	Faulty horn push	Check horn push, replace contacts if necessary
	Faulty wiring	Replace if necessary

The car horn is an audible warning device fitted in the engine compartment of front engined cars or the front luggage compartment of rear engined cars. It is operated by a horn push fitted on the steering wheel or column inside the car. It is the only means the driver has of warning other people of danger in all conditions of weather and light and it is a legal requirement that it works. It must therefore be operational at all times.

There are three main components in the horn circuit—the horn or horns, the horn relay, and the horn push. It is helpful to know the function and operation of each of these components when trying to locate horn faults. Figs. 2 to 4 show typical wiring layouts of the horn circuits used in modern cars.

How the horn works

There are two types of horn. The most common type works entirely by electricity. The second type, fitted on more exotic cars or available as an accessory, also uses compressed air. Both have the same basic operation.

The wholly electrically operated horn works much like a solenoid (fig. 1). It consists of a metal rod, the axis of which passes through a coil. When a current is passed through the coil, it acts like a magnet and pulls the armature, against a spring, towards the coil. The armature has a small projection that separates a pair of contact points as it moves towards the coil. As the points open the circuit is broken. The coil no longer acts as a magnet, and the spring pushes the armature back to its original position. This closes the contacts again and the cycle is repeated so long as the horn push is operated.

Attached to the armature is a diaphragm. Its rapid backward and forward movement creates sound waves and the horn is heard. A second disc (the tone disc) fitted on the end of the armature determines the note of the horn by controlling the extent of oscillation of the diaphragm disc.

The air horn uses compressed air in place of the coil and armature to vibrate the diaphragm. This compressed air is channeled through plastic pipes to a number of horn diaphragms, one for each note produced. Air horns therefore have extra components—a compressed air source and the connecting pipes. This may be either a rechargeable bottle of compressed air, or more commonly an electrically operated air compressor.

Faulty air horns

If your car is fitted with an air horn, consult your dealer, handbook (or the instructions supplied with the air horn if you have fitted it yourself), to see if it has an air bottle. If it has, recharge it and try the horn again. If it still does not work, carry out the tests below. If the horn uses a compressor, test the compressor first. If it is operating normally, again carry out the tests described for a conventional horn.

Finally, check the connecting tubes from the compressor to the horns. Coat them in soapy water and operate the horn. Bubbles or a loud hiss will show any airleaks. If the pipes leak, fit a new piece of tubing of the correct length and diameter.

Testing a compressor

Most compressors supplied for air horns are reliable units and should give little trouble. The most frequent cause of malfunctioning is omitting the relay when fitting the system. Although the horn will still work, an unlimited supply of

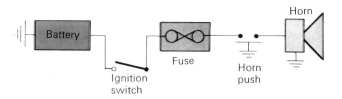

1 A simplified diagram showing the structure of a typical car horn. The power supply is usually more complicated than this

2 The components and switches used in a simple horn system with only one horn. This is the least complicated system in common use

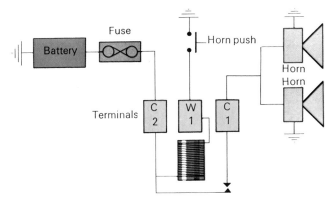

3 A more complex horn system using twin horns. This system has only one fuse and three terminals on the relay

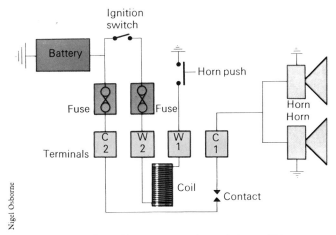

4 Another complicated horn system using twin horns. This system has two fuses and four terminals on the relay

Inspect the unit for physical damage, broken or disconnected contacts, and incorrect wiring (follow the manufacturer's diagram for wiring). If the unit is in good physical condition and has been properly maintained, check the other horn components first. If these are operating correctly, only then suspect the compressor. Although relatively simple in operation, the internal construction of a compressor, especially the type which plays musical notes, is like a wristwatch in having numerous small and finely balanced components. For this reason it is best to either test the unit by substitution or take it to the manufacturer for testing.

Testing the horn
Most car horns are now sealed units and testing them is limited to three checks.

First check the horn mounting brackets. If the horn is not held securely to the car body, operating it causes it to vibrate and this can stop the armature moving freely. The diaphragm will then not vibrate enough to make a sound. If the mounting bracket is loose, tighten it and try the horn again.

Next check the electrical connections to the horn. The wires are usually fitted with bayonet ends that slot onto the horn contacts. If these are not making good contact the horn will not work. If they are making good contact, put a test lamp across them and again try the horn. The bulb will light if the horn is receiving electricity. If the bulb does not light, the fault lies in the supply to the horn (see below).

If the horn is receiving electricity, look for an adjusting screw fitted on the back of the horn. This screw, if fitted, controls the movement of the armature. Too much or too little movement will not produce a note. The adjusting screw alters the gap between the contact breakers—the smaller the gap, the less distance the armature moves before breaking the current and springing back. First turn this screw anti-clockwise several turns, then, if no note is produced on trying the horn, turn it back to its original position and advance it several turns clockwise. If this produces a note, adjust the screw backwards and forwards

current will eventually burn out the compressor. Incorrect lubrication will also set up problems either through lack of oil, too much oil, or oil of the wrong grade. The compressor should be lubricated via the oil holes marked on the unit, with a couple of drops of light grade (3-in-1) household oil every six months.

5 This Cortina 2000, like many cars, has the horns hidden behind the radiator grill. Unscrew and remove the grill to reach them

6 These twin horns are mounted on a single common bracket held by one nut. Check that the securing nut is tight

7 Next, check the wire connections. This system uses spade terminals. Clean the terminals and the connector

8 The leads attached to the horns are the power supply ; the horn is earthed by the bracket. Use a test bulb to check the supply

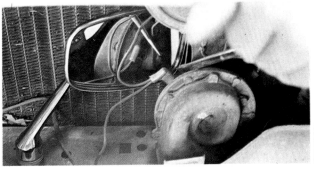

9 Each horn unit has an adjusting screw at the back. A mirror is helpful when looking for this. Adjust the screw and try the horn

until the best note is found. If adjustment does not produce a note, then the horn unit is faulty and will have to be replaced. This is simply a matter of removing the bayonet connections, unbolting the securing bracket, and removing the unit. When fitting a new unit, take care to reconnect the wires in the same order.

Horn pushes, where and why
There are two types of horn circuit, shown in figs. 2 to 4. The horn push has the same basic job in both. The horn components are connected in line, with the horn push last. The horn push consists of a rod with metal brushes on its end. When the rod is pushed the brushes are pressed into contact with a good earth point and the circuit is completed. A spring returns the rod to its normal position away from the earth contact when the horn push is released.

There are two types of horn push; those that are part of a

and-dry paper. If they are too badly damaged a new horn push will have to be fitted.

Next, look at the earthing point where the brushes make contact with the metal surround and if necessary clean the area with wet-and-dry paper. Refitting the horn push is simply a matter of reversing the removal procedures.

With the horn pushes that are part of the steering wheel, remove them as follows. First, disconnect the negative terminal from the battery. Next, remove the steering column shroud, then press the centre emblem button (this is the horn button on some cars), turn it anti-clockwise and lift it clear of the steering wheel. There is a return spring under this button when it is used as the horn push; take care to remove it and keep it safe. Make a mark on the steering wheel hub and on the steering column so that the wheel can be replaced in the same position. Undo the retaining nuts and lift the steering wheel free of the shaft. To reach the

10 The horn push on this Cortina 2000 is located at the side of the steering surround. Unscrew and separate the two halves

11 The horn push is part of a multi-switch, which is held on by two screws. Undo these and remove the switching unit

12 The switch consists of a main terminal block and two removable sets of sockets. Pull out the left set of sockets

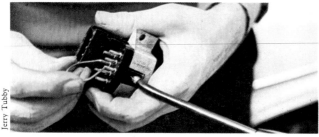
13 The red wire is being used to show the two pins connected internally by the horn push, they are copper coloured

14 Test the horn push by bridging the sockets into which the horn push pins fit. If the horn then sounds, fit a new horn push

switch on the steering column, and those that are a centre button or ring on the steering wheel. The first type are easier to inspect and repair, by removing the steering column shroud. With the other type you need to remove the steering wheel. Once the brushes are accessible repair simply entails cleaning and making sure they make a good contact with earth.

Checking and repairing horn pushes
The horn push that is part of a separate switch on the steering column is the easiest to work on.

First, unscrew and remove the two halves of the steering column shroud. Next, remove the horn switch by unbolting the retaining bracket and lifting the switch away. This may be a combined switch for the horn, indicators and headlamps, but in all cases it lifts clear.

Most horn pushes fitted in this type of system can be removed by pushing them in, turning them and allowing the spring to push them loose. Sometimes a retaining bracket may be fitted to stop the horn push accidentally lifting out. In this case, first unbolt the bracket, then follow the method described.

Inspect the brushes for traces of dirt, rust or damage. Generally the brushes can be cleaned with fine grade wet-

15 The horn relay is used to give a sharp switching action. The area of contact is very small and unlikely to short

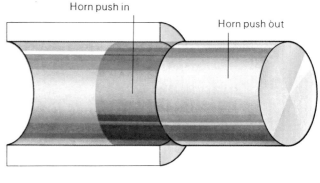
16 The shaded area shows the large area of contact in older horn push systems with the push 'in'. These are likely to short

horn push bearing, you will first need to remove the indicator switch and its wiring, by undoing the retaining screws and bracket.

Finally, undo the retaining screws on the horn push bearing retainer and lift out the bearing. Check it for wear and replace it if there is any doubt about its condition. Clean the horn contacts, which are connected to the indicator switch, with wet-and-dry paper. Refitting is the reverse of removal.

Horn relays, where and why

The car horn needs a high current which could cause arcing across the horn push contacts when they complete the circuit. For this reason many manufacturers include a relay in the circuit. In these circuits, the horn push completes the circuit and the normal lower current is supplied to the horn relay. Inside the horn relay there is an internal switch.

The horn is not directly connected in this circuit, but is separately connected to the battery via the internal switch in the horn relay. When the horn push is operated, it completes the circuit to the relay and the internal switch operates. This connects the horn to the battery, bypassing the horn push, and a high current then passes to the horn. In this way the relay internal switch completes the circuit to the horn and this has a sharper switching action to prevent arcing (see figs. 15 and 16).

There is no universal position for the horn relay. The easiest way to find it is to follow the wiring from the horn. The wires will run straight to the relay. If there is no relay, one of the horn wires will go straight to the fuse box and the other will go to the horn push inside the car.

Testing the relay

There are two types of horn relay, both doing the same job. One type has three terminals and the other type has four terminals. These relays are all sealed units, so only a few tests are possible.

First, use a test lamp to make sure that the relay is receiving electricity (see fig. 18 and 19). Next, test the operation of the relay by bridging the terminals with a wire or screwdriver. The horn should sound instantly when these bridges are made. If it does not, the fault lies outside the relay and the other components should be tested.

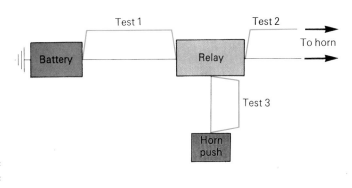

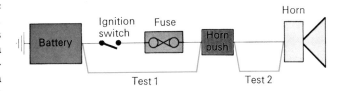

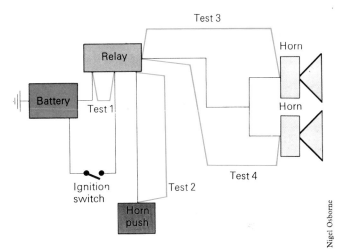

Nigel Osborne

17 The order of work for wiring tests on the various horn systems. If the horn works when any bridge is made, that section is faulty

18 The horn relay is fitted on the side of the engine compartment in this Cortina 2000. It is a four terminal canister type relay

19 Connect a test lamp between the supply terminal and a good earth point. The lamp lights if power is reaching the relay

Jerry Tubby

20 To remove the faulty relay, undo the two mounting screws and lift it out. Then replace it with a new unit

If the relay is faulty, remove it by undoing the retaining screws and disconnecting the wires. Bolt on the new unit in the same place, and correctly refit the wiring as it was on the old unit.

Testing the wiring

If the horn components have all been tested and are in good working condition, you should test the wiring and replace any faulty sections. Refer to the diagram (see fig. 17) for the testing method for the wiring and see page 111 for replacing faulty wiring.

Checking horn circuit fuses

There are several places in the circuit for fuses in the various systems. The simplest system (fig. 2) has one fuse in the main fuse box. The simplest system with a relay (fig. 3) again has one in the main fuse box. The more complicated relay system (fig. 4) has two fuses—one in the fuse box and one near the relay. Trace the fuses by following the wiring from the relay. To locate the particular fuse in the main fuse box used by the horn circuit, follow the method described on page 109 to locate the indicator fuse. Replace any faulty fuses.

The charging system and fanbelt

Symptom	Possible causes	Remedies
Ignition light comes on	Warning light short-circuiting	Trace and repair
	Loose or broken fanbelt	Adjust or replace fanbelt
	Poor generator or control box connections	Trace and repair
	Faulty generator or control box	Trace and repair or replace faulty component

The ignition warning light staying on when the engine is running on tickover, usually indicates that the battery is not being charged. This is something that must not be overlooked and should be corrected immediately.

The electrical charge in the battery is maintained by the car's charging system (see figs. 1 and 2). This normally works efficiently and reliably and needs little servicing. But a serious fault in the system is shown by one immediate symptom—the sudden illumination of the ignition warning light when the engine is running above idling speed. Unless there is a fault in the warning light wiring, this means that no charge is being put back into the battery to compensate for that being taken out.

The fault must be traced and repaired immediately or a 'flat' battery, an overheated engine or a ruined generator may result. There are four likely causes of the ignition light coming on: a short-circuit in the warning light wiring, a loose or broken fanbelt, poor generator (dynamo or alternator) or voltage regulator connections, and/or a defective generator or regulator unit.

Ignition light short-circuiting

If the warning light suddenly goes on, look for a fault in the wiring before checking the charging system. The light should come on when the ignition is switched on to signal that the circuit is energized. When the engine is started and the revolutions rise, it should go out, showing that the battery is being re-charged. On older cars fitted with dynamo type generators it is quite usual for the light to glow but this should happen only when the engine is idling.

The warning light is usually fitted into the rear of the instrument panel on the dashboard. A single wire runs from the bulb-holder to a source on the voltage regulator unit.

Though short-circuit faults are not common, a quick visual check of the wiring may save a time-consuming examination of the charging system in the event of a fault. Ensure that a live contact is not touching bare wire anywhere along its route or at the connectors. Look for signs of burnt or split insulation. If necessary, replace the whole length of wire. Use insulating tape as an emergency measure.

Loose or broken fanbelt

The fanbelt (its correct name is the generator drive belt) is a continuous V-section reinforced rubber belt. Its function is to drive the generator and the fan/waterpump assembly. Some cars are fitted with an electrically operated fan and in these cases the belt has no connection to the fan at all.

The fanbelt runs on pulleys of which there are usually three (fig. 3). These are the generator pulley, the waterpump pulley and the crankshaft pulley which drives the belt.

There are two ways in which a faulty fanbelt can affect the charging system and cause the ignition light to come on. First, due to excessive wear, insufficient tension or grease,

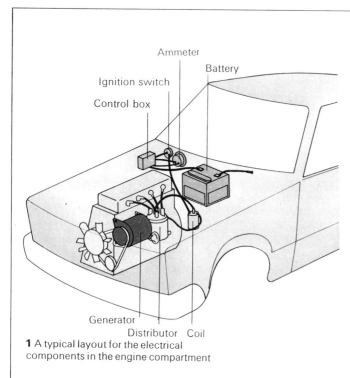

1 A typical layout for the electrical components in the engine compartment

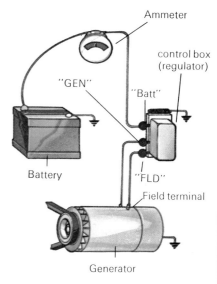

2 A simplified illustration of the charging system. Check all these connections

3 A typical fanbelt and pulley arrangement

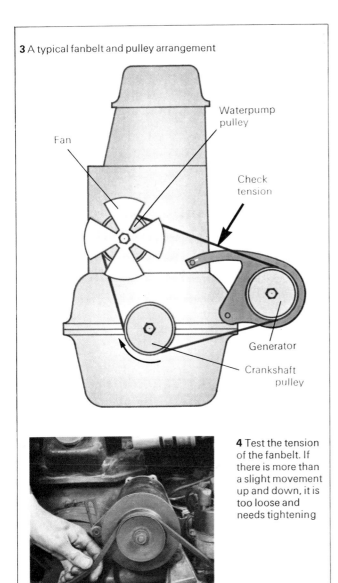

Fan

Waterpump pulley

Check tension

Generator

Crankshaft pulley

4 Test the tension of the fanbelt. If there is more than a slight movement up and down, it is too loose and needs tightening

the belt may slip on the pulleys instead of driving them round. Second, the belt may break in which case the generator will not produce a charge at all. A slipping belt causes the generator to turn at too slow a speed to charge the battery. Sometimes a slipping belt can be detected by listening for a screeching sound when the engine is revved.

Check the tension of the belt by holding it between finger and thumb in the middle of its longest run between pulleys (fig. 4). Push and pull the belt with an in-and-out movement. Play should not exceed 2 cm ($\frac{3}{4}$in.) for dynamo belts or about 1 cm ($\frac{1}{2}$in.) on alternator systems.

Adjusting the fanbelt

The generator hinges on two brackets usually mounted on the side of the engine. A slotted adjuster bar is bolted to the generator below the mounting brackets.

To adjust the fanbelt, slacken the mounting bolts and the bolt which secures the generator to the adjuster bar. The whole generator should then be free to swing on its mountings. Ensure that the fanbelt has not slipped off any of the pulleys. Pull the generator away from the engine to tighten the belt, towards the engine to slacken it. You may need a lever (a length of wood will do) between the generator and the engine block to apply the right amount of

tension while you re-tighten the bolts. But if you do this never lever against the central section of an alternator as it is easily damaged. Apply pressure only to the part of the casing joined to the mounting bracket.

On some cars, notably the VW Beetle, the procedure for adjusting the fanbelt is completely different. The generator is mounted in a fixed position and is not moved to adjust the belt. However, the generator pulley is split into two halves and the distance across its V-section can be changed be taking out or inserting shims between the pulley halves. The complete pulley assembly is held to the generator by a large central nut. The system works by making the belt ride higher up the pulley sides when shims are removed, so increasing the tension (figs. 5 and 6). The opposite happens when shims are added.

To adjust a slack belt on a split pulley, first remove the central nut. The outer half of the pulley will then come away revealing the spacing shims. Remove as many shims as needed to take up the slack in the belt. Replace the pulley-half, taking care not to trap the belt. When the central nut has been fully re-tightened, check the belt tension. Special belts are sometimes used for this system.

5 Adjust the fanbelt on tha rear-engined Volkswagen by removing the central nut and prising off the outer pulley

6 With the outer pulley off, remove as many shims as necessary to take up the slack in the fanbelt when the pulley is replaced

Never adjust any fanbelt with less play than recommended otherwise the strain on the waterpump and the generator will damage their bearings.

Cleaning the fanbelt and pulleys

If the fanbelt appears to be adjusted correctly but the ignition light remains on, then it may be slipping due to oil or grease on the belt or pulleys. Swing the generator down to minimum adjustment. The belt can then be slipped off the pulleys quite easily. Remove the belt completely and examine it for signs of oil, grease or any damage (fig. 7).

Wipe the belt thoroughly with a clean cloth to remove all trace of grease. Then rub the belt with a stick of chalk, which will help give it more grip when it is replaced. Clean the pulleys carefully with a rag soaked with a little petrol.

Replacing the fanbelt

If there is still too much play in the belt even after it has been adjusted to the limit then it must be replaced.

Replacing the fanbelt is simply a matter of passing the new belt over the fan and pulleys. However, some cars, particularly transverse engined models, have a cowling round the fan. This makes threading the belt over the fan tips and between the cowling difficult. Look for a small recess in the edge of the cowling provided especially to make the operation easier (fig. 8).

Electrical components—safety precautions

Before carrying out any checks on the electrical circuits make sure that the battery is disconnected. Only re-connect when necessary for checks. Electrical components are

7 Check fanbelt for wear, cracks and abrasion. This one needs replacing

8 On most cars with transverse engines, the belt can be fed into the fan cowling to the pulley through a small recess

easily damaged, so to cut down the risk of having to replace expensive components through accidents, great care must be taken. Alternators are particularly suspectible to accidental damage and there are some things you must not do. Never disconnect either of the battery terminals while the engine is running, do not allow any of the alternator leads to touch earth, and never run the unit with the main output lead disconnected.

Faulty generator or control box connections

Loose or faulty connections on the generator or voltage regulator are frequently the cause of the charging failure signalled by the ignition warning light.

A dynamo has two terminals at one end of the casing (fig. 9). One of these terminals is noticeably smaller than the other. The smaller one is the F terminal and the larger one the D terminal ('G' or 'GEN' on American cars). Check that there is a good connection between the wires and the terminal posts. Trace both wires back to the control box. This is usually prominently located on the side of the

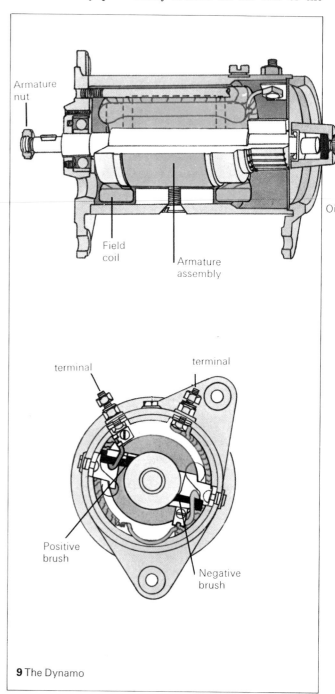

9 The Dynamo

engine compartment and contains the voltage regulator, the current regulator and the cut-out switch (fig. 13). Look for faulty insulation and breaks in the wires. Repair or replace any defective sections of wire. The wire from the F terminal leads to the voltage regulator and the wire from the D terminal goes to the cut-out switch. Examine the connections here and clean and restore them if necessary. There are usually five terminals on the control box, some of which have multiple connectors, so check all these at the same time. Particularly important is the earth lead marked E; trace this from its connector on the box to its source (often a point nearby on the bodywork). Ensure that the earthing point is clean and that a good contact is being made.

On alternator systems a plug-in plastic multiple-connector carries all the electrical leads to a point on the alternator casing (fig. 14). Pull out the plug and check that none of the connector tags is dirty or bent over. Replace the plug and make sure that it is pushed firmly into place. There is no control box to monitor the output of an alter-nator. Components inside the alternator itself regulate the system. One exception is the voltage regulator, which is usually built into the alternator but on some cars is found as a separate component outside the alternator. Make a thorough check of all the leads and connectors to see if there are any broken or loose wires.

Internal generator faults

If all the above checks have been made but the ignition warning light still comes on then it is likely that the problem is an internal fault in the generator.

Generators rely on carbon brushes to pick up and feed out generated current. When a charging failure occurs it is most commonly worn-out brushes that cause the problem.

The brushes are held in position and tensioned by springs. As the brushes wear down and become shorter the spring tension on them becomes weaker. If they are allowed to wear below a minimum length they will not perform properly. This results in a much reduced output charge from the generator.

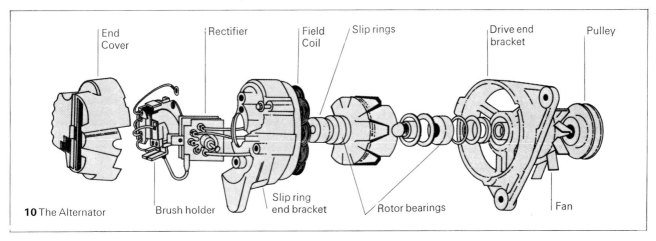

10 The Alternator

End Cover — Rectifier — Field Coil — Slip rings — Drive end bracket — Pulley — Brush holder — Slip ring end bracket — Rotor bearings — Fan

11 Locate the generator and clean the terminals and wires to ensure good electrical contact

12 The dynamo on an early Leyland Mini has two connections 'F' is connected to the control box and 'D' to the cutout switch

13 The control box is readily recognised, although it may be fitted in different places

14 The alternator in a recent Mini. The multi pin plug connections should be clean and undamaged

Dynamo brushes can be changed and other faults, such as commutator wear, can be dealt with fairly easily. Alternators however, are extremely difficult to test and repair without specialized knowledge and expensive equipment. Even a slight mistake made while testing an alternator can cause serious damage to the sensitive and delicate components within it. The brushes can be changed without too much difficulty, but apart from this there is little else you can do in the event of a fault. It is far better to take the alternator to a specialist for any tests or repairs.

Changing alternator brushes

All alternators work on the same principle and basically contain the same components. However, design differences between types means that there are several ways of changing the brushes according to the type.

Check first with your car dealer or electrical specialist to find out if the brushes can be changed without dismantling the alternator. Find out also any maximum wear measurements on the brushes and whether the brushes have to be renewed as a complete brush/holder replacement unit.

If your alternator does not have to be dismantled to change the brushes, the job is simple.

The brush-holder unit is located on the outside of the end cover and contains two rectangular carbon brushes (figs. 18 and 19). Undo the retaining screws and remove the connecting wires (usually spade connectors or screw tabs). If the brush and holder is a sealed unit look for a wear limit line on the brush. This appears as the brush wears down and emerges from the holder. If the wear lines are apparent refit a whole new unit.

The brushes can sometimes be removed from the holder. Undo the holder retaining screws on the end cover and disconnect the brushes from their wires. The brushes can then be pulled out of the holder complete with their springs and measured against manufacturer's specifications. Insert the new brushes, reconnect the wires and screw the assembly back onto the end cover.

If the alternator (fig. 15) must be dismantled to check or replace the brushes, first remove the end cover. This is held in place by two or three set screws. The rectifier pack will then be visible (fig. 16). Remove the wires from the rectifier, making a note of their positions and colours. The wires are usually attached by screw tabs. Undo the retaining nuts which hold the brush-box assembly in place and withdraw it from the alternator (fig. 17).

The brush holder is screwed in place on the brush box. It may be of the sealed unit type. If so, simply disconnect the wires and transfer the replacement unit. Alternatively

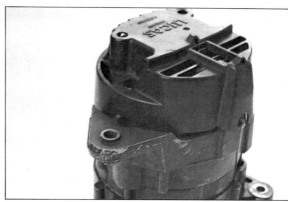

15 Use a nut spanner or small socket to remove the two bolts holding the end cover on an alternator with internally mounted brushes

the brush holder and the brushes may be separate components. Undo the holder screws and disconnect the wires and fit a replacement as described above.

The condition of the brush bearing surfaces on the slip rings is important too and these should be freed of all carbon deposits before refitting the brushes. Where the slip ring contact faces are 'end on' beneath the brush housing the contact areas may be cleaned by using fine glass paper in a circular motion. If your alternator has brushes that bear on the slip ring sides (predominantly on external control box alternator types) the slip ring contact faces are best cleaned by securely wrapping the glasspaper round a screwdriver blade, inserting this tool through the end plate access slots and pressing it against the slip ring sides, then rotating the alternator pulley. In either case you should ensure that both slip ring contact faces are cleaned.

Note: take great care not to leave the glasspaper inside the alternator when extracting the screwdriver, otherwise the unit will have to be dismantled.

Finally, reassemble the alternator and fit it back on the engine.

Faults in dynamo systems

Fault finding and repairs on dynamo system components are relatively straightforward. Before you begin to dismantle anything a few simple checks can help isolate the cause of the trouble.

Testing the dynamo

Output from the dynamo can be tested with a voltmeter. Connect a length of wire across the F and D terminals on

18 An alternator with externally mounted brushes. The brushes are very easily replaced

19 The plastic brush retainer is usually held in place by one screw

16 Remove the cover to expose the brush unit. Note the position of wires before going further

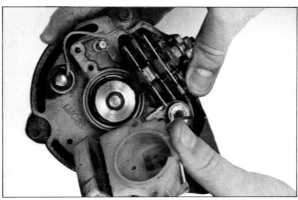

17 Two screws hold the brush unit in place. It is replaced as a unit if wear is evident in the brushes

the dynamo. Connect the voltmeter between the D terminal and an 'earth' on the metal body or engine. Start the engine and increase the revs slowly. Do not speed up the engine to more than a little over twice tick-over speed. The voltmeter needle should show a smooth rise to 12-14 volts (or 6-7 volts, depending on whether the car has a 12 v or 6 v battery) if the dynamo is in good condition. If the reading is low or absent or if the needle fluctuates wildly there is a fault in the dynamo brushes or commutator. Should no response be shown on the voltmeter at all, disconnect the F terminal from the D terminal and lead a wire from F to earth while you carry out exactly the same test as above. Both tests should be tried, as some dynamos have an internal earth while others earth through the voltage regulator points of the control box.

If the dynamo is faulty it must be removed from the engine and dismantled.

Repairing the dynamo

Look for two screws or bolt heads on the end of the dynamo furthest from the pulley (fig. 21). These are the bolts which hold the end-plate in position. Remove these and tap the plate lightly with a mallet to free it. As it comes away the central revolving part of the dynamo—the armature,—will be revealed (fig. 22). Remove this from the dynamo by pulling off the other end-plate. The armature will come away with it.

Examine the carbon brushes. They are held in place by holders mounted on the end-plate and are pushed against the commutator by coiled, clock-type springs (fig. 26). Check that the springs are not broken or weak. If there is

insufficient tension, simply clip new springs in place.

If the brushes have worn shorter than about 6 mm ($\frac{1}{4}$in.) they must be replaced.

Remove the brushes from their terminals by disconnecting the wires. The wires may be attached to the terminal by solder, spade-connectors or screws. Carefully pull the spring arms out of the way and slide the brushes from their holders. Fit new ones by reversing this procedure.

Examine the field coils in the dynamo body. If any wires appear to be broken or badly burnt then the whole dynamo unit must be replaced—this is often cheaper than having the coils repaired. Similarly, examine the armature winding, particularly where the wires are soldered to the commutator segments; and buy a replacement dynamo if it is badly damaged.

The commutator is the bright, segmented copper section of the armature. If it is blackened or greasy the commutator end bush has probably been over lubricated. Good brush contact is impossible in these circumstances and the output charge is severely reduced, so clean the commutator thoroughly with petrol. If it still appears dirty or glazed after cleaning, polish it with fine sandpaper. Do not use emery abrasive as the grit particles are conductive and could cause trouble if they are allowed to become embedded between the commutator segments.

If there is severe wear or pitting on the commutator, it can be skimmed on a lathe provided there is enough metal left to do this. Skimming is a specialist's job and the armature must be taken to an expert.

After skimming or polishing the commutator, or even to compensate for normal wear, the insulation between the

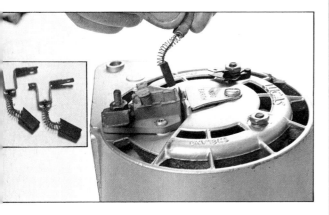

20 Remove the retainer; the brush, spring and terminal come out as one unit and are replaced as a unit

Dismantling the dynamo

21 Unscrew the two through bolts to release the dynamo's end plate

22 Pull the endplate and armature pulley and away from the dynamo housing

23 Clean the commutator gaps of carbon deposit with an old hacksaw blade

24 Undo the two screws to release the brushes from the endplate

25 The brushes can then be pulled clear of their housing and properly examined

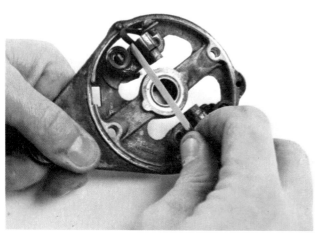

26 The clock springs should be tested for tension, again using an old blade

27 Replace the springs taking care to 'wind' them half a turn for the desired tension

segments must be undercut. If this is not done the run of the brushes over the commutator will be interrupted by the insulation and the charge output reduced. Run a broken hacksaw blade between the segments to cut the insulation down to a depth of about 1 mm below the surface (fig. 24).

When all these components have been checked and repaired the dynamo can be reassembled. When refitting the end plate the brushes must be pulled upwards against their springs to allow the armature to locate in the end-plate. The brushes can be pulled up through the inspection cover. Alternatively if an inspection cover is not fitted, the armature can be replaced and the end plate put back on with

the brushes unsprung. The springs can then be manipulated onto the brushes by using a piece of stiff wire or a thin screwdriver through the ventilation holes.

Finally, remount the dynamo on the engine, adjust the fan belt and reconnect the terminals.

Replacing the control box
The control box is carefully adjusted at the factory and should not be tampered with. To replace it undo the two retaining screws that hold it to the body work. Do not disconnect all the wires immediately. Fit the new box in place, then transfer the wires from the old box one by one.

Understanding a wiring diagram

More car breakdowns result from electrical failure than from any other single cause. It is surprising then that car manufacturers and publishers of workshop manuals do not go to more trouble to explain car circuitry. Many wiring diagrams are badly drawn, too small and often appear to have been included in manuals as an afterthought. The problem is that they often confuse the DIY man more than they help him. This is probably because the amateur is not sure how the diagrams work. Yet wiring diagrams can be useful, and understanding that maze of black lines can boost the car owner's competence to tackle electrical jobs in his car.

There are three main types of wiring diagram in common use. Two of them, pictorial and schematic diagrams, are relatively straightforward. The third, the technical diagram, is often hard to understand. Whichever diagram you are faced with, always bear one point in mind, any diagram simply shows a number of circuits (see page 99), the paths along which electricity travels. If a path is interrupted electricity will not move along *any* part of that circuit.

Pictorial diagrams
Instead of using symbols, pictorial diagrams show each component by a small and simple drawing, intended to make life easier for the amateur. Another advantage of this type is that it indicates the component's location. The result is that the diagram reads like a map of the car—a

1 Identifying symbols can be the most frustrating part of reading a wiring diagram. This table (continued overleaf) shows many that are in common use and others that are less frequently encountered

bird's eye view with all the major components and their wiring in roughly the right place.

This type of diagram often shows the wiring disappearing into a thick black band. These bands represent the wiring looms (see page 127). Many people become confused at this point and cannot find the other end of the wire.

The answer is in fact quite simple. Each wire is marked with either an abbreviation of its colour, for example LG for light green, or a number. The wire is almost always shown as taking a sharp bend to the left or right just before it enters the wiring loom and the direction of the turn shows the way it runs through the loom. So if you are following a wire marked LG that turns to the right, just work round the loom in that direction until you reach another wire marked LG coming out of the loom. This will be the other end of the wire you are following.

Schematic diagrams
Schematic diagrams are not greatly different from the pictorial type. They also usually show the components by means of small drawings, and so are also useful to the DIY mechanic.

The main difference is that the schematic diagrams often distort the actual layout of the car. The main components are often in slightly different positions on the car from those the diagrams would suggest. The purpose of this is to make the wiring clearer. Moving the components out of their actual positions allows the draughtsman to separate groups of wires that might otherwise be easily confused.

This type of diagram also often leaves out the wiring looms and shows the course of each separate wire. This both helps and hinders the amateur electrician. Showing each

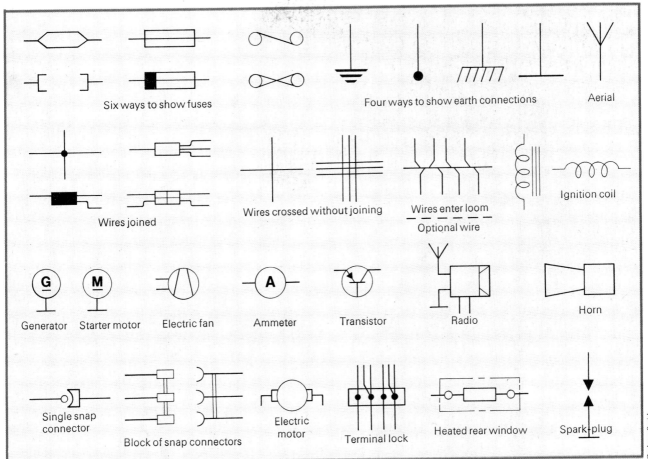

Six ways to show fuses   Four ways to show earth connections   Aerial

Wires joined   Wires crossed without joining   Wires enter loom   Ignition coil

Optional wire

Generator   Starter motor   Electric fan   Ammeter   Transistor   Radio   Horn

Single snap connector   Block of snap connectors   Electric motor   Terminal lock   Heated rear window   Spark plug

Graham Smith

wire may help him to trace the circuit, but the fact that the route of the wire on the diagram is not the same as its actual route on the car can make transferring the knowledge from one to the other rather difficult.

Technical diagrams

Technical diagrams are the most difficult of the three types of wiring diagram. The layout of this type bears little or no relation to the layout of the car itself.

These diagrams are not really much use to the amateur for two reasons. Because the layout of the diagram is nothing like the layout of the car the components often appear in confusing places. One such diagram shows the right hand front indicator on the extreme left hand side of the page. The same diagram shows the engine temperature sensor on the engine block in such a way that most people would expect it to be in the car's boot.

Secondly, most of the components are shown not as pictures but as numbered symbols. Few of the components look anything like the component they are supposed to represent, and the amateur trying to find a particular part tends to waste a great deal of time searching through the diagram's key for something familiar.

This type of diagram will tell you which wire runs where, but will not help in finding either the wire or the component on the car itself.

Quite why diagrams are drawn in this confusing way is something of a mystery. The answer may be that it is far easier for the draughtsman. It may also be that manu-facturers show little enthusiasm for making them easier to understand because they actively wish to discourage the amateur from working on his car's electrics.

Tracing the circuit

It is always wise to find and trace the circuit you are interested in on the diagram first, before you get to grips with the car itself. Trying to follow the diagram when you are sprawled in the car holding together a dismantled dashboard is not the best way of either keeping your temper or ensuring a trouble-free job.

On many diagrams the wires are shown as being extremely close together, and often turn off suddenly at right angles. They are consequently difficult to follow. It is therefore a good idea to mark in the circuit with a pencil, to make the circuit you are following stand out from the rest of the wiring. Another simple but useful rule is to follow each wire with a ruler or straight edge, because the eye can easily wander from one wire to another and you may end up following completely the wrong circuit.

With these basic points in mind, the next job is to find the circuit on the diagram. The best way is to look for a component that you know will be in the circuit. If you want to trace a fault in the lighting circuit, for example, find the position of one of the headlamps on the diagram and trace the wiring from there.

On the technical type of diagram this is not as easy as it sounds, because the headlamps will not be represented by an obvious symbol and they may be literally anywhere on

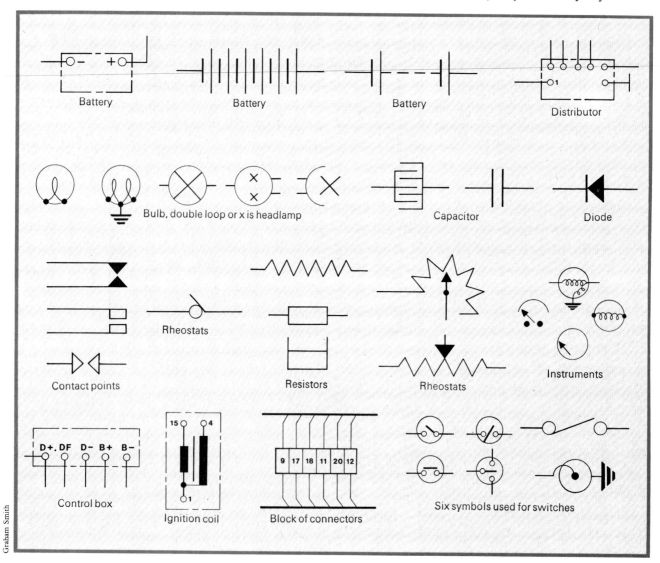

Battery

Battery

Battery

Distributor

Bulb, double loop or x is headlamp

Capacitor

Diode

Rheostats

Resistors

Rheostats

Instruments

Contact points

Control box

D+.DF D− B+ B−

Ignition coil

Block of connectors

Six symbols used for switches

Graham Smith

the diagram. The best way of finding a component on this type of diagram is to look for it on the numbered key. Once you know what number it is, you will simply have to hunt through the diagram until you find that number.

Once you have found a place to start, you can set about tracing the circuit.

Following the wiring through is the stage where many people come unstuck, partly because they become confused by the sheer number of wires on the diagram. The basic principle to remember is that the diagram represents not a chaotic maze of wires, but simply a small number of complete circuits. The six main circuits found in every car are those for the charging circuit, ignition, lights, indicators, accessories and starter motor (see pages 100 to 101). Each of these circuits can be separated from the rest of the wiring in the diagram with patience and a little information.

Tracing any of these circuits is much easier if you know beforehand roughly where the wires will run. Figs. 2 and 3 show simplified diagrams typical of these main circuits. The layout of the circuits can vary, but these diagrams will apply to the great majority of cars.

The symbols on a wiring diagram are another common source of confusion for the DIY electrician. They often differ from diagram to diagram, so examples of common variations are shown in fig. 1.

The battery, at the heart of the electrical system, is often represented by a simple drawing of itself. Alternatively, it may be shown as a series of alternating light and heavy vertical lines. The heavy lines indicate a cell in the battery.

The earthing symbol also often differs. This indicates that a component is wired to the car's body, the body providing the conductor that completes the circuit (see page 102). It is often shown as an arrow head of slightly spaced black lines, but on the diagrams for many European cars it appears as a single horizontal line, with fine vertical lines underneath.

Another way of showing an earth connection, which caused a great deal of confusion, was used on some Volkswagen wiring diagrams. A bold horizontal line ran right across the bottom of the diagram and all earth connections were shown running down to this line. This resulted in many people spending a great deal of time searching for these long wires, which did not of course exist. The bold black line simply represented the car's body, and the lines running to it the connections from the components concerned. In most cases the wires from these components were far shorter than the diagram suggested.

Some components are earthed by their own contact with the bodywork. The metal body of a lamp, for example, in many cases acts as the necessary conductor and there is consequently no wire to the car's body. In some cases this is shown on the diagram by a small circle, though the more common earthing symbols are often used regardless.

Bulbs, when symbols rather than drawings are used, are generally shown as a circle with a fine looped line inside. Headlamp bulbs, having two separate filaments for dip and main beam, are usually represented by a similar line with two loops.

Switches can be shown by a wide range of symbols, but all have one thing in common. The circuit is always shown as being broken in some way.

Fuses, if not clearly marked as such, are generally represented by two small circles joined diagonally by one or possibly two thin lines.

The symbols for points where wires are connected can

2 A normal type of wiring diagram as found in an owner's handbook. This one is for a Ford Fiesta. At first sight it looks confusing because the numbered symbols used do not relate either visually or geographically to the actual appearance and location of the units on the vehicle. However, in fig. 3 (overleaf) we show how easy it can be to interpret this type of diagram. It would be extremely helpful if manufacturers printed their circuits in the colours relevant to the vehicle's actual wiring but, for cost reasons, this is not normally possible.

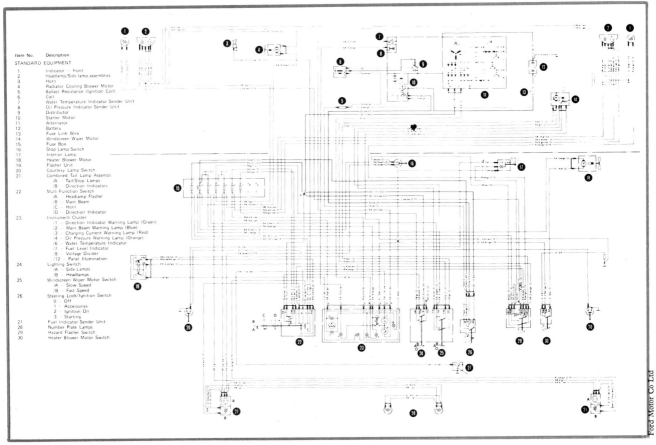

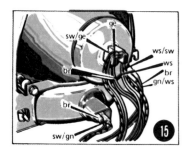

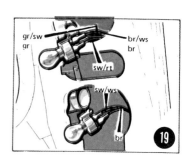

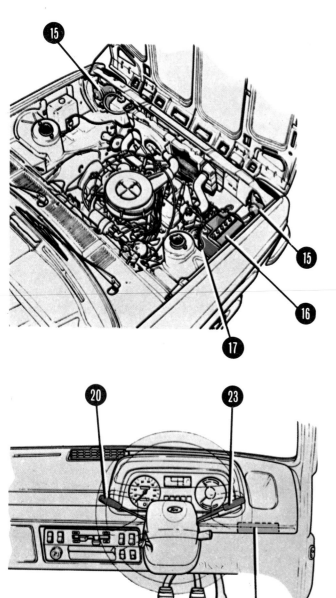

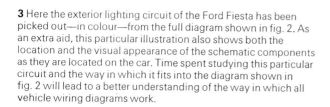

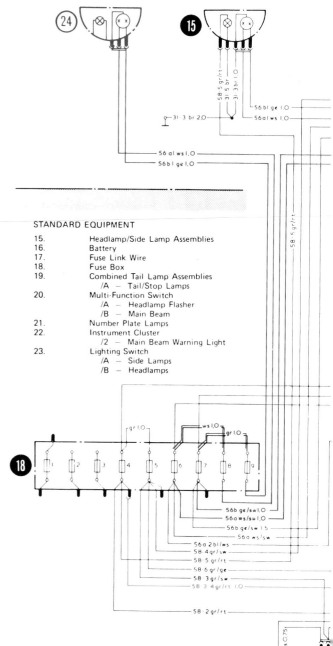

STANDARD EQUIPMENT

15.	Headlamp/Side Lamp Assemblies
16.	Battery
17.	Fuse Link Wire
18.	Fuse Box
19.	Combined Tail Lamp Assemblies
	/A — Tail/Stop Lamps
20.	Multi-Function Switch
	/A — Headlamp Flasher
	/B — Main Beam
21.	Number Plate Lamps
22.	Instrument Cluster
	/2 — Main Beam Warning Light
23.	Lighting Switch
	/A — Side Lamps
	/B — Headlamps

3 Here the exterior lighting circuit of the Ford Fiesta has been picked out—in colour—from the full diagram shown in fig. 2. As an extra aid, this particular illustration also shows both the location and the visual appearance of the schematic components as they are located on the car. Time spent studying this particular circuit and the way in which it fits into the diagram shown in fig. 2 will lead to a better understanding of the way in which all vehicle wiring diagrams work.

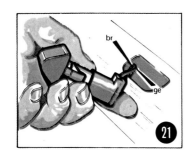
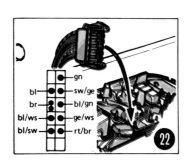
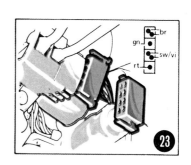

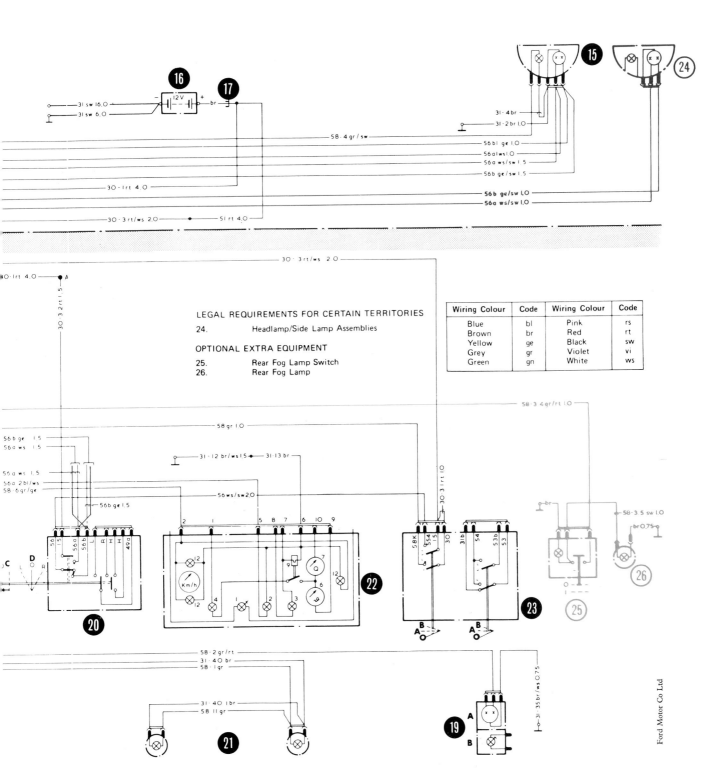

LEGAL REQUIREMENTS FOR CERTAIN TERRITORIES

24.   Headlamp/Side Lamp Assemblies

OPTIONAL EXTRA EQUIPMENT

25.   Rear Fog Lamp Switch
26.   Rear Fog Lamp

Wiring Colour	Code	Wiring Colour	Code
Blue	bl	Pink	rs
Brown	br	Red	rt
Yellow	ge	Black	sw
Grey	gr	Violet	vi
Green	gn	White	ws

Ford Motor Co Ltd

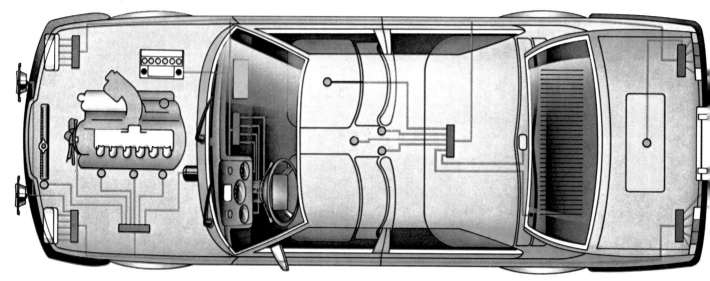

Central vehicle-monitoring system in the dashboard

Data sensor for coolant temperature, oil pressure, oil level, engine temperature, fuel gauge, hand brake, belt latch mechanism, etc.

Subscriber station for switching and monitoring the loads for data feedback.

Multiplex control center LSI switching circuit with control logic for switching and monitoring the loads as well as logic for data processing

4 The wiring harness, or loom, is a source of confusion for many people when they come to work on or read about a car's electrical system. But Bosch, with the 1990s in mind, are developing a means of wiring a car that dispenses with the conventional loom. Their Multiplex system (above) is like the ring-main wiring in a house. A simple cable runs round the car, and current for the electrical components is taken from it. The operation of each component is then monitored by a micro-computer in the dashboard

vary considerably. Snap connectors, which are plastic sleeves with metal sockets that join the wires, are most commonly represented by a simple plain rectangle. A wiring junction, where wires either converge or separate into individual feeds, are often shown by a cross of wires with a dot at the centre.

These must not be confused with wires that cross without joining. Thinking wires join when in fact they do not is a common source of mistakes. Wires crossing are often shown by the lower wire being broken at the point where they cross. Alternatively, the upper wire may be shown as having a loop that takes it over the lower cable.

Colour codes

All wiring diagrams show the colours of the wires, either by abbreviations or numbers. The meaning of the abbreviations or numbers is always shown in a key to the diagram.

Manufacturers wire up their cars to a logical code, so that the wires in each circuit can be readily identified.

Each major circuit is given a base colour. On most British-made cars for example, the ignition circuit has mainly white wiring.

A second or "trace" colour is added to the wires in some sections of the circuit. On British-made cars, the wire from the ignition switch to the solenoid has thin red stripes on the white background, while the cable from the switch to the accessories fuse has a blue trace on the white base.

The trace colour is not added in every case. The general rule in British cars is that the trace is present in the wiring of a fused circuit and the base colour only is used in an unfused circuit.

There are five major colour codes in current use.

Lucas colour code

The Lucas colour code is used on almost all British-made cars. The major exceptions are Ford cars built before 1960 and German-built Fords such as the Capri.

In the Lucas code a different base colour is used for each major circuit. The charging circuit has brown wires and the ignition system is wired in white. The headlamps have a base colour of blue, while the sidelights are red and the indicators green.

French colour code

The code used for French cars differs in that the trace colour is not always a thin line on each wire, but is sometimes a small coloured dot on the connector at the end of the wire.

The base colours differ from the Lucas code on all the major circuits except the sidelights, which are red in both cases. The French charging circuits are black and the headlamp circuit wires are mainly grey, as are the indicators. The ignition circuit is red.

German colour code

The German colour code is different again. The German base colour for the charging circuit is red and that for the ignition circuit is black. The indicator base colour is also black, the headlamps are white and the sidelights grey.

Italian colour code

The Italian base colour for the switch supply circuit is brown. The base colour for the ignition circuit is blue, for the headlamps it is green, and the sidelights circuit wiring is in yellow. The indicator circuit is blue.

Japanese colour code

The Japanese manufacturers are not always consistent. The majority of their cars, however, conform to a code that has white as the base colour for the charging circuit and black for the ignition circuit. The base colour for the headlamp circuit is red. The code for the sidelamp and indicator circuits is yellow.

The doors

Symptom	Possible causes	Remedies
Door swings easily but is difficult to latch	Bad alignment between striker plate and latch	Adjust striker plate
	Faulty latch mechanism	Repair latch
	Worn hinges	Adjust, pack or replace hinges
Door open from outside but not from inside of car	Childproof lock operated	Release lock
	Faulty door linkages	Repair linkages
	Faulty interior handle	Repair interior door handle
Door opens from inside but not from outside	Faulty door linkages	Repair linkages
	Faulty exterior handle	Repair exterior handle
Neither handle operates	Faulty linkages	Repair linkages
	Faulty door lock	Repair or replace lock
Door swings with difficulty	Faulty door hinges	Adjust, pack or replace hinges
Door does not completely close	Faulty latch	Repair latch
	Mis-aligned striker plate	Adjust striker plate
	Damaged hinges	Replace hinges
	Buckled door	Replace door
	Buckled door frame	Straighten frame

There is nothing more irritating to both driver and passenger than a car door that needs violent slamming to close. If the door will not open properly you run the risk of being trapped in the car in the event of an accident. Door problems do not cure themselves, and a slight fault may develop into a more serious condition.

Doors are usually very simple to operate. They do their job so efficiently that it is easy to overlook the need for regular maintenance. It is only when problems occur that people realise that they are complicated units.

Door problems can be confined to seven main areas:
The latch mechanism
Door hinges
The interior door handle
Faulty linkages
The exterior door handle
The locks
The frame

The extent of the problem can vary a great deal. One component may be stiff, loose or seized due to lack of regular servicing. Alternately, all the components in the seven main areas may be badly damaged due to a crash. In either case, fault finding and remedies must be carried out by a process of elimination. You will have to deal with each area separately until you are sure that every individual component is operating correctly.

Faulty latch mechanism

A fault in the latch mechanism is one of the most common problems arising with door mechanisms. It is usually also one of the easiest to deal with. It is important to understand how the latch works before beginning to try and locate and cure the problem.

Door latches are now required by law to be burst-proof.

They must not be able to spring open even in the event of a major crash. To achieve this, the old system, which was similar to house door latches, has been replaced by a slightly more complicated design. There are three main types of latch in use on modern cars. All systems use a striker plate from which the latch cannot escape until the handle is operated.

The striker plate is fitted on the door frame, opposite the external door handle. The latch, or striker, is attached to the side of the door so that it enters the striker plate when the door is closed. The striker plate includes a catch that closes over the striker. This catch retains the striker until the opening mechanism is operated by operating either door handle.

The three types of latch normally differ only by the form the striker takes.

In one system, the striker is a loop-shaped device like a staple. The catch closes over one leg of the staple and this leg has a barb similar to the hasp on a padlock.

The second system uses a thick disc with a slice removed, like a cake with a slice cut out (see fig. 1). The major portion of the thick disc is hidden inside the door mechanism. The cut section sticks out to form two peaks. This disc rotates on a ratchet. When the door is closed, the two segments pivot initially and then spring back to lock on to the striker plate.

The third system uses a single post as a striker. The outer end of this post is shaped like a mushroom. The catch closes over the enlarged head of the post (fig. 1).

The most common problem that occurs with any of these systems is due to a mis-alignment of the striker and catch. This can be caused by one of two things. The striker plate itself may have slipped or the hinges may have become loose or deformed.

If the striker plate has slipped, it can be loosened and

131

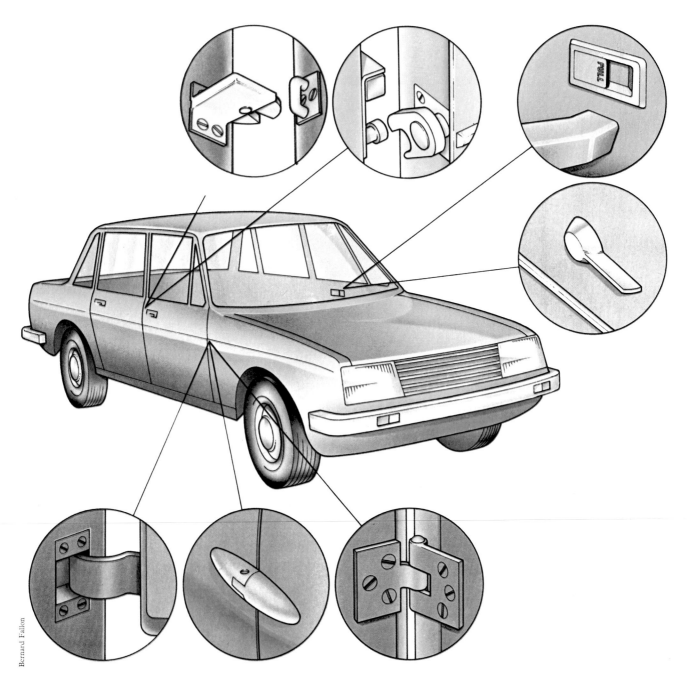

1 A variety of door catches, handles and hinges used by car manufacturers. Only one type of each is used on any particular car

moved to a better position. To do this, mark round its outline with a felt-tip pen. Then slacken the securing screws. You will probably find these very tight, so an impact screwdriver can be very useful here. Undo the screws enough to allow the striker plate to be moved, but not so loose that the plate will not stay in its new position. Close the door and push against the handle. If the door moves in and out and you can hear it knocking, the striker is set too far out. Re-set the striker a little further in and try again. When the striker has been correctly set the door will close with a firm push and it will require quite a hard push to detect any play between the latch and striker. Continue making small adjustments, moving the plate up or down, or in and out, until the door closes properly. Then tighten the securing screws with the impact screwdriver. If you use an ordinary screwdriver, you will probably find that the plate loosens itself within a few days.

To check for bent hinges, close the door as best you can and inspect the fit of the door in the frame. If this is not a good fit, either repair the hinges or fit a new set.

Faulty door hinges

If you suspect the door hinges are faulty, open the door a little, grip it under the lower edge and try to lift it. If it is possible to move the door up and down, even if only by a slight amount, the hinges are worn. Most hinges do wear, so if there is only a slight movement that does not affect the door closing there is no immediate need to do anything. Hinge wear steadily increases, so you will eventually have to do the job.

Damaged hinges must be replaced, but it is sometimes possible to correct or repair worn or bent hinges.

Correcting worn hinges

Car door hinges are constantly in use so wear is inevitable. Not only does the hinge wear, the mounting screws also move within their holes. When this happens, the door will no longer fit properly into the door frame and the fault will have to be rectified for reasons of both safety and comfort.

There are three basic types of door hinge fitted to cars:

2 You must remove the door trim to inspect the linkage system. To do this, first unscrew and take off the window winder handle

3 Next undo and remove the internal door handle. When re-fitting, make sure that it is put back in the same position as before

4 If an armrest is fitted, remove this. It is usually held on by two screws hidden in recesses on the underside at each end

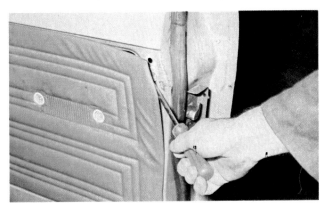

5 Carefully, lever off the trim by using a screwdriver to prise out the retaining pegs. Then peel back any protective film under it

1. The external hinge, now mainly found on older cars only. The hinge mechanism is normally clearly visible from outside the car.
2. The internal leaf hinge. In these hinges, there are two interlocking leaves—one fitted to the door and the other to the frame. They are usually completely hidden when the door is shut.
3. The sliding hinge. A single plate is attached to the door and a curved bar extends from this plate into an opening on the door frame. To prevent the door opening too far, the curved bar has an enlarged end which butts against another plate on the door frame.

The first two types of hinge both pivot about a hinge pin. Inspect the hinge and hinge pin. If the pin has a mushroom-shaped head and a bolt or clip at the bottom, it is possible to remove it. Do this by removing the bolt or clip and lifting out the pin, while an assistant supports the weight of the door. If the pin is not of this type, the manufacturers only supply complete hinge units and you will have to replace the whole hinge (see below).

Packing hinges
Damaged hinges will have to be replaced completely, but it is sometimes possible to correct worn hinges even when they do not have removable pins. This can only be done where internal leaf hinges are fitted. By putting a thin sheet of packing material behind either hinge, you can correct the wear by taking up the slack.

To do this, first decide whether the door needs to tilt up or down. If the door needs to tilt up, work on the lower hinge. Similarly, work on the upper hinge to tilt the door downwards.

The shim can be made from a thin sheet of metal, such as brass, steel or aluminium. Undo the door hinge, then place a piece of cardboard against the hinge and draw round the hinge to give the required shape. You can then use the cardboard template to make a metal shim, complete with the necessary bolt holes.

The thickness of the shim material depends entirely on the amount of hinge wear that has taken place. Try to slightly underestimate the necessary thickness, then build it up by using supplementary shims until the door closes smoothly. When the fit of the door is correct, tighten the securing screws with an impact screwdriver. Some hinges are bolted on which makes them easier to tighten because you can grip the bolt more securely with a socket and avoid any damage through the tool slipping.

Adjustable hinges
On some types of hinge, a plate is secured to the door frame and is cranked at right angles to the door. It is secured to the side of the door frame post parallel to the side of the car.

When these hinges are used, there is a facility for adjusting the upper hinge. It is secured either by bolts or studs screwed into a plate within the door frame post. These bolts or studs are secured by nuts behind the plate. To adjust the hinge, you will have to slacken the bolts or studs and move the plate.

Where bolts are used, open the door to get at them and slacken them with a spanner. It is slightly harder to slacken the stud system. You will first have to remove the door trim, then use a short extension socket or box spanner to slacken the internal nuts behind the studs.

When you have slackened the studs or bolts, ease the hinge plate forward slightly. Then tighten the bolts or studs and try the door. You may have to repeat this procedure several times until you find a correct adjustment. Then tighten the studs or bolts fully and replace the door trim if it was removed.

Stripped hinge mounting screws

There is one other type of hinge wear that can be repaired. This is when the hinge mounting bolts or screws have stripped threads, or when the screw holes themselves have become enlarged.

If the bolts have stripped threads, simply remove them using the method described above, then fit new bolts.

If the mounting screw holes have become enlarged, unscrew the screws and replace them with a slightly larger self-tapping screw as a temporary measure. A more permanent cure can be made by enlarging the screw hole and replacing the screws with a nut and bolt. This is only possible when there is room to place a spanner or socket behind the hinge plate to tighten the nut.

Replacing hinges

A worn or damaged hinge that cannot be repaired by any of the above methods will have to be replaced.

Hinges that are bolted or screwed in place can be replaced by undoing the bolts, removing the hinges and fitting a replacement hinge. Remember to mark around the outline of the hinge to aid accurate placing of the new hinge and have an assistant support the door weight.

Hinges that are welded on will have to be cut off and a new hinge will have to be fitted. Arc welding equipment can be hired, but as the job will probably require a section of the door frame, door, or both to be cut away, it may be more trouble than it is worth.

Faulty internal door handle

Failure of a car door to open or close correctly may be due to a fault in the internal door handle. The most likely faults, and their cures, depend on the type of door handle fitted to the car.

Before starting to dismantle and inspect your door handle, make sure that the problem is not due to accidentally applying a childproof lock. These devices are often fitted to the rear doors and prevent the door from being opened from inside the car. Your car handbook or dealer will tell you if you have childproof locks, and how to engage or release them.

There are three basic designs of internal door handle, but a great many variations of each basic type. Decide

7 When you have exposed the internal linkage system, test its operation by re-fitting and working the internal handle

which basic type of handle is fitted to your car from the descriptions below. Then adapt the dismantling technique to suit your car.

Flush mounted handles

Many modern cars have an internal operating handle which mounts flush with the door. These handles are pulled inwards to open the door. In this case, the handles are not released from the mechanism.

To check the handle, first remove the bezel between the handle unit and the door trim. This is usually a split bezel and the two halves can be carefully levered out using a screwdriver.

Remove the window winder and any other fittings protruding through the trim. Then remove the trim itself.
This is secured by clips. Start along the bottom edge and lever the trim away from the door. It is best to get the lever as close as you can to each clip before levering it away. Continue until all clips are released. In most cases, the trim can now be lifted straight out. In some cars, a wooden capping is used at the sill. On these cars you pull the trim out from the bottom of the door until it is free of the window winder and handle. Then pull the trim down to free its top edge from the capping and take it away.

The apertures in the door, behind the trim, are covered with plastic or wide adhesive tape. Uncover the opening nearest the latch to expose the linkages connecting the door handles to the latch mechanism. Operate the interior handle to see if its motion is being transmitted through the linkage. If it is not, the linkage itself should be checked (see below).

If the handle unit is broken, you will have to replace it with a new one. To do this, you will have to disconnect the linkage. Make sure that the linkage has not already separated from the interior handle, if it has, then this is the reason for it not working.

To disconnect the linkage from the handle, there is no general system and you will have to carefully study the linkage on your car. It is usually a case of either lifting a rod out of a bracket, undoing a locking screw or bolt, or prising off a spring clip.

The interior door handle unit is held in place by two or three retaining screws and the linkage connections. When you have released the linkage, unscrew the unit and simply screw in the new unit. Then re-connect the linkage.

Faulty linkage

Door handles and locks are not a direct connection to the latch. They are connected to the latch by a series of rods and levers forming a linkage system. Although these linkage systems are usually trouble free, there are one or two

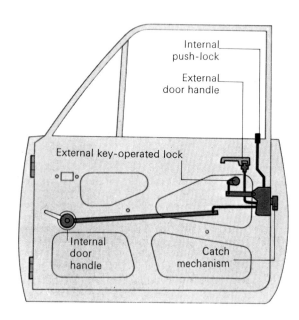

6 A typical door linkage system, connecting the internal handle, external handle, interior lock and exterior lock to the catch

Internal push-lock

External door handle

External key-operated lock

Internal door handle

Catch mechanism

Lynn Williams

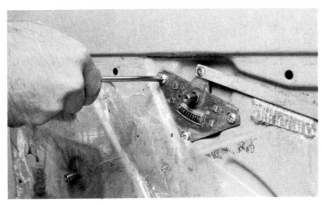

8 To remove the internal linkage system, first undo the retaining screws holding the door handle mechanism in place

9 Remove the clip holding the other end of the linkage to the catch. The internal handle linkage system can then be removed

10 On the Cortina Mk II, the external handle is held on by two screws. The first is easy to reach. Undo and remove it

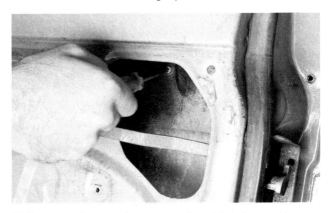

11 To remove the second screw, use a long-bladed screwdriver. The screw is reached through an aperture in the door skin

12 Lift away the handle. There is often a specially-shaped rubber washer between the handle and the door

13 The key-operated lock is a removable barrel, held in place by a circlip. Use circlip pliers to free the lock

14 Then lift out the barrel lock. As it is impractical to try to repair this unit, replacement is necessary

Nelson Hargreaves

things that can go wrong with them.

There are two types of linkage that you will find in the door. These are: circular section rods and flat bars.

With the circular section rods, which are used to stretch across the larger distances, there are two faults which may arise. The rods are connected to the levers (the flat bars) and held in place by retaining clips. These clips may have rusted and dropped off. Alternatively, the rods may have become rusted onto the levers and the resulting seizure may have bent them.

If a lost retaining clip is the problem, clean away any rust and fit a new clip. There are two types of rod/lever connection (see fig. 17). In one system, the rod passes through a hole in the lever, is bent over after passing through the lever and is held in place by the clip.

In the second system, a hole in the rod is pressed on to a stud on the lever and held in place by a washer and clip.

With a seized linkage of the first type, clean the area of linkage and coat with a penetrating oil. Leave this to soak until you can remove the clip and pull the rod out of the lever. Then clean the end of the rod and the hole in the lever with a fine wet-and-dry paper. Finally, re-fit the rod and a new clip. If the rod has bent, try to straighten it. If this is either impossible or unsatisfactory, buy a new rod and fit it. To straighten the rod, disconnect it from both ends and lay it on a large flat surface. Gently tap the bent area with a wooden mallet until it is straight. Then try it in place to see if it now works smoothly.

With a seized linkage of the second type, again clean the area and soak in penetrating oil. If necessary, cut off the clip and gently prise the rod off the stud. Clean the hole in the rod and the stud with fine wet-and-dry. Then re-assemble the linkage.

In both systems, lightly coat the linkage with grease or another anti-seizing compound such as Copaslip. It is a good preventive measure if you lubricate all the linkage now and repeat this every few months.

Finally, re-fit the door trim when you know that the door is opening and closing easily.

Faulty exterior door handles

Any faults that may occur with an exterior door handle

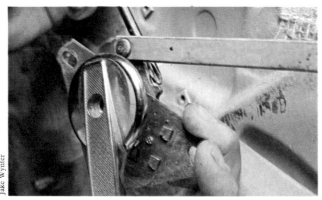

15 The internal door lock on the Cortina Mk II is operated by the handle. It is a "peak" on the mechanism that catches on a ratchet

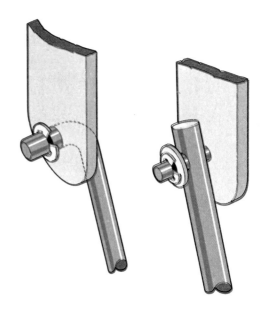

17 Door handle linkage systems consist of rods and flat bars. There are two different types of connecting systems for them

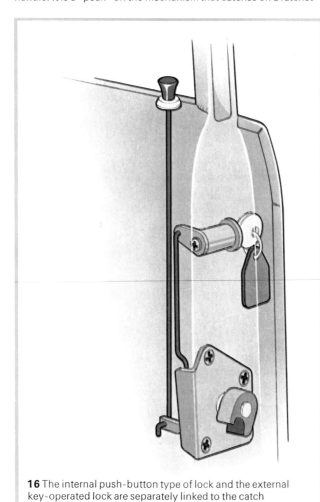

16 The internal push-button type of lock and the external key-operated lock are separately linked to the catch mechanism

adding one more step. The push-button itself is a plastic cover on one linkage. If this breaks off in the lock position, remove the door sill capping to get at it.

The door sill capping is held in place by several securing screws. Undo these screws and lift out the capping. The broken top of the pushbutton can now be reached. The remains of the plastic push-button simply unscrew. Then replace the door sill capping and screw on a new cap or push-button.

Exterior, key-operated locks are connected to the handle and latch by another extension of the linkage system. To remove the lock, you will have to take out the interior door trim as described above. Before actually removing the lock, make sure that the linkage is sound.

The lock is connected to its linkage by a bracket and bolts. To remove the lock, undo the bolts from inside the door panel and lift the lock out. A key-operated lock consists of a barrel surrounding the mechanism. This mechanism consists of a series of tumblers that are moved by the key. Any attempt to dismantle the lock is usually accompanied by these tumblers springing out of the lock and becoming lost. This is not a DIY job. You will have to buy a replacement lock from your dealer and substitute this in the linkage system. In some cases, it is possible to buy a replacement barrel for your lock. This is the cylindrical section of the lock containing the tumblers. It is easiest to take the complete lock to your dealer. If a replacement barrel is available, he will be able to exchange it.

Major door faults
A severely buckled or damaged door will never close securely. Modern car doors are made of a double shell arrangement, that is, they have both an inner and an outer skin. It may not be worthwhile trying to panel beat any bad dents or buckles and the only answer is then to fit a new door. This can either be a factory replacement or bought from a breaker's yard.

To replace a door, follow the instruction given for removing the hinges.

Then, attach the hinges to the new door. It may be necessary to fit the old trim if the door came from a breaker's yard, and to change the door colour.

Finally, complete the repair by following the instructions for adjusting door hinges.

can be treated in the same way described for interior door handles. The major difference lies in the fact that you cannot inspect the actual handle so closely. You will still have to remove the door trim.

Faulty locks
There are two major types of door lock; the interior remote lock and the exterior key-operated lock.

The interior remote lock is either operated by a push-button on the top of the door, below the window, or by an extra movement of the door handle. Interior door handle locks can be treated by the methods described for the normal handle operation.

Interior push-button locks are an extension of the linkage system. Use the methods above for linkage systems,

136

Passing the MoT test

In 1977 in the UK, 5.1 million cars failed the Department of the Environment roadworthiness test, out of a total tested number of $14\frac{1}{2}$ million. This represents an alarming 36% failure rate. If your car fails it can be expensive, but this can often be avoided if you know the points which will be subject to test. The Department of Transport is now separate from the Department of the Environment but, to complicate matters further, the test is still known as the 'MoT' after the long defunct Ministry of Transport.

In the UK, cars over three years old must be submitted annually to an MoT test (and even if your car does not need one it should still be kept to test standard). This is carried out at an approved centre – either a council testing station that specializes in such work, or a suitably-qualified commercial garage. If the vehicle under test is passed, a test certificate is issued to show that the car complies with the regulations. Similar tests exist in most other western countries and most States in Australia.

In Britain it is illegal to use a car on public roads if it does not have a valid test certificate. There are only three possible exceptions to this. You may drive the car without a test certificate when you are, by prior appointment, delivering it for or taking it away from a test. You may drive it to or from a place where defects cited on a test certificate are to be remedied, but again you must make a previous appointment with the repairer. Finally, the vehicle may be taken to a place where it is to be broken up—but in this case it must be towed and cannot be driven under its own power.

Driving a car known to be defective, or without a valid test certificate, can also invalidate your insurance cover. You cannot apply to re-tax a car without a current certificate and, in law, the test certificate covers a car only at the actual time of testing. This means that you can still be prosecuted for driving a defective car on the road, despite there being a test certificate in force.

The main areas inspected in the British test include the lights, steering and suspension, brakes, tyres and wheels, seat belts, wipers and washers, horn, exhaust and chassis structure. A notification of refusal (failure) may be issued by the examiner if any item within these areas is defective.

The refusal notice will specify the defects, and these may be repaired at the testing station (should they have the facilities), at any other workshop, or by the owner at his own premises.

If you leave your car at the testing station to be repaired and retested, you have to pay only the initial test fee. If the car is taken away and returned within 14 days to the same or another test station for repair and retest, only half the test fee is payable, in addition to the full fee already paid when the car was failed. But if you take the car away and carry out the repairs yourself, or have them done by another garage, you must pay another full fee. This also applies if you return the car for repair and retest after 14 days of the date of failure.

Should you disagree with the reasons given for a notification of refusal, you can appeal to the DoT within 14 days. If your appeal is successful, the fee, or appropriate part of it may be returned. The major problem with an appeal is that you must not have your car retested or repaired until the appeal has been heard, and the vehicle reinspected by DoT officials.

1 This exhaust pipe would not pass the MoT test because it has excess corrosion. In this case the pipe can only be replaced

2 This heavy-duty crossmember, on a Rover 90, has a small amount of corrosion. The examiner would probably require it to be welded

3 The front subframe mounts on some cars, such as this Jaguar, are bonded metal and rubber. Check that they have not separated

4 This subframe from a Leyland Mini was photographed in a scrap yard. Corrosion as bad as this cannot be satisfactorily repaired

5 On cars with leaf-type rear springs, investigate the chassis members carefully for any corrosion near the spring mountings

6 This damper mount would probably be failed as the surrounding metal is split. It could also be failed for its loose locknut

7 Check any subframe mounting points for corrosion. They should not be like this mounting which was photographed in a scrap yard

8 Weak jacking points are a common reason for test failure. The general condition of this car would make any examiner suspicious

In the UK, a pass certificate is labelled VT20. There are two failure certificates: VT21 lists any failures; while VT22, which is printed in red, indicates that a complete test could not be carried out as one or more components were faulty, thereby preventing an adequate road, or rolling-road test. The VT22 is concerned mainly with brake faults. The VT29 form is a customer's copy that outlines all the items that have been tested, and indicates whether the car has passed or failed on individual points.

It is worth bearing in mind that some garages are not above making themselves some extra business by failing vehicles and repairing them when no faults exist. It helps to go to a reputable garage or a council testing station where the test will be completely objective, and it is better still if you can watch the test being carried out. This is important if you are going to repair the car yourself if it fails, as you can be quite certain which parts the tester is failing, and can see how worn the relevant components are.

To avoid wasting time and money it is worth while to examine your car before its test. Below we outline the points on which your car will be examined, and how to check them. In general, the advice applies in Australia, too.

Lighting equipment
All lights must conform to the following legal requirements. They must function correctly and be visible at 200 yards. The lenses must be intact and each lamp securely mounted. It is not permissible for any white light to be shown at the rear of a vehicle, except for reversing lights.

Front sidelights: Vehicles must have two white sidelights, with diffused lenses, mounted at the same height.

Rear sidelights: There must be two sidelights at the same height, both red and with diffused lenses.

Rear stoplights: Two stoplights showing a red light must be mounted at the rear on cars registered after 1971. On pre-1971 cars only one light may be fitted, in the centre of the car rear. In both cases the lights must operate only when the brakes are applied.

Rear reflectors: Two red reflectors must be mounted, one on each side, at any point between 38 cm (15in.) (measured from the lower edge) and 107 cm (3ft 6in.) (measured from the upper edge) from the ground.

Direction indicators: These lights must show amber or white at the front, and amber or red at the rear. They must flash between 60 and 120 times a minute, even with the engine switched off. Any direction tell-tale lights should work.

Registration illumination light: There must be a light capable of illuminating the rear number plate. Cars made on or after October 1st 1979, and first used on or after April 1st 1980 will be required to be fitted with red fog warning lamps.

Headlights: These must always be fitted in pairs, and must be matched in shape, colour and size. They may be white or yellow. When on dipped beam, headlights must be adjusted so that an observer facing the car at a distance of 7.6 m (25ft) and a height of 107 cm (3ft 6in.) would not be dazzled. This makes sure that the headlights do not dazzle other drivers. Headlights do not have to dip to the left, providing they comply with the anti-dazzle requirement.

Where a vehicle has a four-headlight system, the outer pair should give both dip and main beam facility. The inner pair should cut out when dipped beam is employed.

Fog and spotlights: Single auxiliary lamps, whether spot, fog or driving, may be used only in conjunction with headlights, except in fog or falling snow.

Reversing lights: A maximum of two reversing lights of no

more than 24 watts each are allowed. These must either be operated by a remote gearbox switch or a panel switch. If a panel switch is used a fascia warning light must be fitted. The lights must not dazzle at 107 cm (3ft 6in.) height and 7.6 m (25ft) distance.

Examine all lights for damaged lenses and make sure they are secure, then check that each one works and is properly visible.

Any damaged lenses must be replaced, as must missing reflectors or coloured lenses that have faded. Change any burnt or blackened bulbs for items of the correct design and wattage. Tracing electrical problems is covered in detail on pages 99 to 107. Check the lights with the engine both running and switched off. If the lights appear dim even with the engine running, check their earth connection. Should

the indicator timing be beyond the limits, unscrew and replace the flasher unit (pages 108 to 113).

As the headlight beam settings will be checked during the test, ensure that these are roughly correct. Your own setting should be followed up by a professional garage setting.

Windscreen washers
All cars must be fitted with effective windscreen washers. Check that the pump (electrical or mechanical) works correctly and that the water from the jets hits the screen at approximately the centre point on both the driver's and the passenger's sides. Clean out any blocked jets or pipes to ensure sufficient water flow and adjust the jets if necessary. Do not go to the test with an empty washer bottle.

9 The jacking point on this Jaguar is almost hanging free, and has so much corrosion that it would fail a test immediately

10 The corrosion on this jacking point is not so severe. The car might be passed if you use a bottle jack under a chassis member

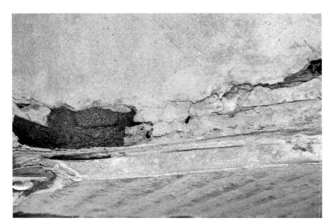

11 Nothing short of complete renewal of the metal would repair this sort of damage, seen in the door sills of a Volkswagen

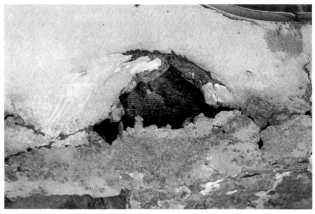

12 If your door sills are as corroded as this, it is not worth having the car tested as it would be failed very quickly

13 The level of rust on this door and sill might not result in the car being failed if the inner sill is still undamaged

14 This elderly Sunbeam shows just how severe corrosion in floor pans can become. Repairs for this damage would be very expensive

If an electrical pump is fitted, check the wiring and switches if the unit fails to work. Also check the supply to the motor and its earth.

Windscreen wipers
The blades and arms of windscreen wipers must be in good condition and must not 'park' incorrectly if they are of the self-parking variety. The wipers should clear a sufficient area on both sides of the screen in two full wipes.

Renew any frayed blade rubbers. If the wipers still fail to clear the screen, renew the arms. These can be obtained at accessory stores.

Horn
Every car must be able to give audible warning of its approach. The horn must make a continuous sound. Units having two or more tones should sound both at once. Horns that play tunes are not allowed on post-1973 cars.

Check that the horn works. If it does not, check the horn unit, the relay, fuse, wiring and horn button as outlined on pages 114 to 117.

Exhaust system
A car should have an exhaust system in good condition, securely mounted, with no leaks and an effective silencer.

On level ground, place one or both ends of the car on axle stands so that you can inspect the exhaust system. Remember the system may be rusty, so guard your eyes. Check that all mount straps and rubbers are in good condition and that they are securely located on the underbody and exhaust.

15 Holes of this size can be repaired, but you should use welded sheet steel, not alloy, and cover an area larger than the hole

16 This MG, seen in a scrap yard, shows how futile it is to repair really severe corrosion damage using alloy sheet and glass fibre

17 Where the car has a separate chassis connected to the body by outriggers, check their condition very carefully for signs of rot

18 Look for any signs of corrosion at the front of the car, near the suspension mounting points or the anti-roll bar brackets

19 If the car has strut-type front suspension, check inside the engine bay to see if the top mounting point is rusting

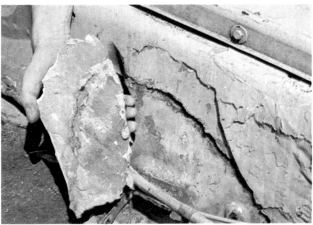

20 This Mercedes shows how not to repair a split inner wing. It has been covered with filler and newspaper which has no strength

Nelson Hargreaves

21 At first sight, this corrosion does not appear too serious, but the car would fail as the suspension bump stop is weakened

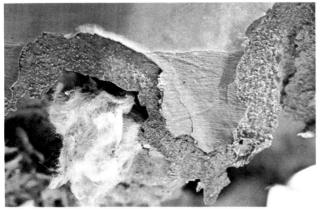

22 This front wing on a scrapped Alfa Romeo shows just how rust can eat away metal. Renewal of the wing is the only answer

Nelson Hargreaves

24 Unless they are extremely rigid, glass-fibre repairs to this sort of damage will not be acceptable to the test examiner

table without the aid of a noise level recording machine and the cause should be rectified by renewing the silencer or pipework, or tightening loose joints, Check that all the nuts and bolts along the exhaust system are tight.

Condition of vehicle structure

The main points a test examiner considers when inspecting the vehicle structure are whether a damaged part or area affects the structural strength of the body, or whether it is unsafe in some other way. This includes rust and collision damage, and general wear.

Inspection

Put the car on axle stands so you can get to the underbody. Test inspectors are no longer allowed to jab at suspect areas with a sharp screwdriver, but they will certainly lever,

23 Ill-fitting, badly rusted wings will immediately make any test examiner suspect the condition of the car's other components

25 Wing damage such as this is dangerous to pedestrians and is illegal. If your wings are like this they should be replaced

Check that nuts and bolts along the system are all tight.

Examine the complete system for corrosion or other damage and tap any suspect areas lightly with a screwdriver handle. Damaged or holed sections should be renewed. Missing tailpipes are not allowed, nor are missing pipe clamps on joints.

Turn the engine on and check for leaks by feeling with your hand for gas blown out (do not actually touch the hot pipework). Small leaks in pipes or boxes, well sealed with exhaust paste and bandaged, will usually pass. Bad leaks, particularly in areas such as silencer seams, expansion boxes or the joint between pipe and silencer, whether sealed or not, will fail.

High silencer noise levels are not allowed. This will be due to defective silencer baffles, holed pipes and boxes or loose connections. Excessive noise will be perfectly detec-

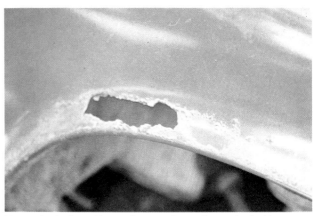

26 Rust in the lips of front wings can be easily repaired with a proprietary filler and will probably not cause a test failure

scrape and push the structure as well as carry out visual inspection.

Starting at the rear, look for any heavy rust scaling or holes in the chassis or subframe members. Pay particular attention to any box members or outriggers, especially in front of the rear wheels (fig. 2). On cars with rear semi-elliptic springs (leaf type) investigate thoroughly the chassis members which hold the rear spring mounts or hangers (fig. 5). Weak jacking points should also be watched for.

Check any points where the suspension is anchored to the body, as well as damper body mounts (fig. 6)—check inside the boot for this too. Boot pans (the floor of the boot) must be sound and rear bulkheads on vehicles with subframes should also be carefully inspected (fig. 7). Note that old underseal often hides chronic rust patches.

Examine both inner and outer sills for rust holes and weak jacking joints.

A couple of small holes in the outer non-load-bearing sills may pass, but not any in the inner, load-bearing structures. Repairs to the inner sills must be effected by welding in new metal. Poor repairs will not pass. Corroded chassis sections may need replacements welded in.

Central floor pans should be rot-free and have no holes. Any repairs must be made by welding new metal—pop-riveted patches will not suffice. Chassis crossmembers and outriggers must be free from decay, as must any seat belt mounts. On some cars it is possible for the entire rear bulkhead behind the back seat to corrode and crack, so remove the seat squab and check.

Moving to the front of the car, look for corrosion around the front suspension mounts and the anti-rollbar mounts (fig. 18). Inspect any subframe or chassis members, and the steering system mounts. It must also be remembered that corrosion is not the only point to look for; you should also check for distortions caused by accident damage.

If the car has strut-type front suspension, look inside the bonnet and see that the inner wing metal, round the top suspension mount, is not corroded or breaking away (fig. 19).

On certain cars, such as the Wolseley 1500/Riley 1.5, the inner wings are prone to corrosion. On these models the inner wings hold the suspension bump stops and in extreme cases these can completely rot away, causing instant failure.

The body
The condition of the body shell externally is not quite so important, in that surface rusting or minor holes in panels do not count. Large holes, badly rotted wings (especially near lamps or mount points), loose or corroded inner wing braces and badly rusted or separated door pillars will not pass, however. Sharp edges will also mean failure.

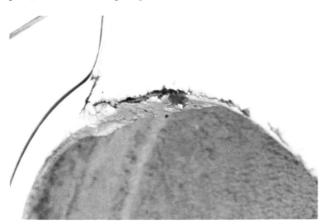

27 If the edge of the wing is rusted, however, and leaves a sharp jagged lip, the examiner will fail the car on safety grounds

The battery box must be intact, and the battery firmly held by clamps. Defective bonnet or boot or door catches will fail, as will rusted or worn door hinges that cause the door to be lifted before it will shut, or prevent it being shut properly.

On cars with replacement fibreglass wings and front ends, a well attached wing (sufficient rivets and bonding) will pass scrutiny. However, fibreglass front ends will not pass unless the engine compartment has been properly reinforced with bracing struts as a protection against crushing in an accident, the original strength having been removed with the metal bodywork.

Test repairs
A test examiner may be satisfied if small holes in open areas of chassis box members or subframes have a plate welded over them. Anything worse, particularly near suspension or body mounts, and the subframe will have to be renewed or a new chassis section welded in. Rotten load-bearing outriggers must be cut out and a new section welded, as must any weak members or jacking points.

Floor pans may be patched using welded sheet steel (not alloy). Small holes in bulkheads may also be cured in the same way, unless they are important to the structural rigidity or have mounting points, in which case the mounting points must be replaced with complete new sections.

Load-bearing sills must be welded in position if renewed—pop rivets will not suffice. Non-load-bearing sills (outers) can be riveted, but it is still best to tack weld them and seal the seams to prevent ingress of water which can cause corrosion. This is covered in a later article.

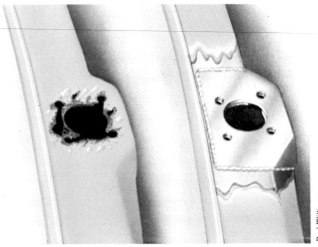

Paul Williams

28 Where the mounting point for MacPherson strut-type suspension is rotten, a flitch plate can be welded in to make a new mount

Defective suspension body mounts must be cured by the complete removal of the component or panel. However, a cheaper and simpler method can be used for such items as Macpherson strut type front suspensions coming through the inner wing. This is to rust-cure the damaged area with a proprietary compound and then bolt a strong 'flitch plate' on and weld it at the edges, the new plate forming the strut mount (fig. 28). These are available from motor factors.

Wing repairs will be accepted only if the work has been done well and the component is secure. In bad cases it is advisavle to cut off the old wing and bolt or weld on a new item. Any newly welded components should maintain the strength of standard ones. Separated or rotten door pillars must also have new sections welded in.

MoT test: transmission, wheels

Many motorists who had their cars tested in the UK in 1977 discovered that the DoT can be strict when checking the steering mechanism, for a total of 46% of all failures did not pass for this reason. The transmission, tyres and wheels will also be examined closely.

The steering mechanism should not be worn and must not suffer from any excess play if it is to pass the MoT test. The DoT do not lay down any actual limits as to the amount of wear and/or play permissible in a car's steering, since this may differ from model to model, and with the inspector concerned.

The inspection will usually begin at the road wheels, and the inspector will work on the principle that all components are suspect until proven otherwise. Initially the weight of the car is supported on blocks to allow the tester to feel for play and to listen for any knocking sounds which indicate worn ball joints or idler gear where applicable.

All ball joints on the steering are rigorously tested by hand and by lever. The dust covers will be examined for harmful splits which allow dirt to enter, and to make sure they are properly attached to the joint.

All securing nuts will be checked to see that they are undamaged and that they are correctly tightened. In some cases, if loose nuts are the only faults found during the test, the examiner may permit them to be tightened during the test, but it is always wise to check them beforehand. Castellated nuts (those with cutouts around them like castle battlements) will be examined to make sure they have split pins of adequate size fitted to prevent them loosening.

On cars with steering boxes, the idler box may be checked using a lever, as play present here does not always show up when the wheels are turned. Tie rods will be inspected for accident damage.

Steering racks and boxes will be examined for leaks, as will any rack gaiters. The mounting points for either steering system will be checked. On steering boxes the securing nuts must be tight, while on steering racks the U bolts must not be loose and any rubber mountings must not be perished. Boxes and racks will be tested for excess wear.

Rack and pinion steering will not be expected to have much play in evidence, whereas some steering boxes are designed to have a certain amount of slack present. A lot depends on the particular model of car being tested, and the inspector should take this into account.

He will closely examine steering boxes with external screw adjustment, or internal shim adjustment, for any undue stiffness in operation when the wheels are turned to full lock. This is because some people overadjust the steering in an attempt to reduce excess play.

On the steering column, a loose pinch bolt (fig. 3) or worn splines on the steering pinion are not acceptable. Where the column is split into two parts, the connecting joint will come under scrutiny. Universal joint types will be checked to make sure the joint is not worn, while the Metalastik rubber-metal-rubber sandwich type will be inspected to make sure the rubber-to-metal surfaces have not parted. Any safety locking wire will be inspected for breaks. If there is no wire present when there should be, the joint will fail.

Finally, play in the steering column top and bottom bearings will be checked. On some cars these are nylon; on others, felt. If there is too much play it will cause the car to fail. The mounts holding the steering column to the fascia will also be checked for tightness.

Worn ball joints must be replaced unless they are of the increasingly rare adjustable variety. Damaged rubber boots must also be replaced, although it is now general policy for the manufacturers to sell only complete units. If the car is fitted with a steering damper, the inspector will examine it carefully for any signs of leakage. Worn steering column bushes can only be replaced.

A less obvious steering check point occurs with cars such as the Mini and the Allegro. The bottom of the steering column mates with a splined stub on the pinion shaft, and in order to locate it safely there is a pinch bolt in the end of the column. From time to time this bolt should be checked since it is possible for it to work loose. Although it is unlikely that the steering would come apart altogether, the risk is not worth the few minutes it takes to test the bolt. A loose bolt could also mean the car will fail.

Examine the steering wheel hub, spokes and rim for fractures or loose spokes. These could cause the car to fail, although cracks in the covering skin of the wheel are allowed.

On vehicles with power assisted steering, the steering operation will be checked with the engine running to see that the hydraulic pump works properly, and that there are no leaks when the fluid is under pressure. The condition of the power unit driving belt, whether it is independent of the crankshaft pulley or incorporated in the main generator drive system, will be inspected. The examiner will be looking for any faults which could cause sudden loss of power assistance which could be very dangerous. Any defects within the power assistance mechanism can only be put right by servicing or replacement, with the exception of the drive belt which can be retensioned.

1 Both ball joints on this Jaguar track rod are badly worn. One has lost the dust cover completely, the other has a split rubber

2 Where a steering box is fitted the track rod is attached to the idler joint. Check that the internal rubber bush has not perished

Nelson Hargreaves

3 Some cars use a universal joint and a splined clamp to connect the steering column to the box. The splines should not be worn

4 This photograph shows the damage that can be caused by foreign matter entering a joint through a split in the protective cover

5 On cars with very high mileage, excessive play in the steering can be caused by worn splines on the steering box rocker shaft

6 On some cars the lower swivel ball joints cannot be replaced as a unit, and the complete lower arm will have to be renewed

Transmission shafts

Cars with combined gearbox-differential units—such as those with front-wheel drive—will have their transmission shafts and couplings inspected. Shafts should be in good condition, the constant velocity joints (at both ends of the shaft where applicable) should be unworn, and any couplings such as universal joints must be in good order. Joint boots should be correctly attached, and have no splits that might let in grit. Cars with independent rear suspension will have their universal joints on the halfshafts inspected in the same way.

Worn constant velocity joints can usually be heard to make rapid knocking noises on full wheel lock, while worn universal joints at the rear can result in a knocking noise as the drive is taken up, and on the overrun. In both cases severe imbalance may also be felt when you are driving at speed. On Chrysler Imps, check that the rubber doughnut coupling on the halfshaft (fig. 9) is in good condition.

Worn or damaged items in this section can be cured only by renewal. Repairs are impractical, unreliable and potentially dangerous.

7 The examiner will check all suspension rubbers to see if they have perished. Again, the complete arm may have to be replaced

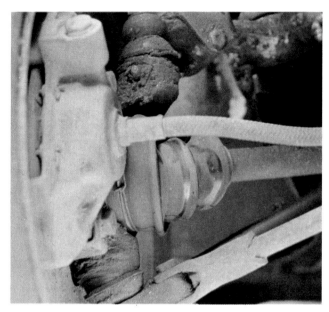

8 Check that the rubber dust covers on constant-velocity joints are intact and listen for any knocking when driving on full lock

9 Some cars, such as the Chrysler Imp, use a rubber doughnut to give a flexible drive coupling. Check these for any signs of wear

10 Leaf springs should be held firmly in place and have no broken blades. The spring clamps should not be broken or missing

11 Check that the U bolts which secure the leaf spring to the axle are correctly tightened and that there are no nuts missing

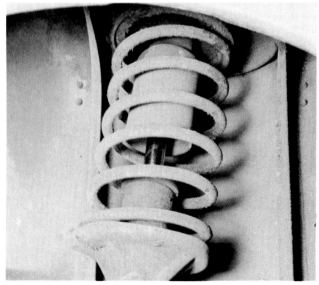

12 Where MacPherson strut front suspension is fitted, check the top bearing for wear, and make sure the rubbers are not perished

13 A certain way to fail the test is to take your car in with any nuts missing from the upper bracket on the MacPherson strut

Nelson Hargreaves

Propshafts

On vehicles with the conventional rear-wheel-drive layout of propshaft and differential, the tester will be looking for worn universal joints and a worn differential nose bearing. Universal joint wear usually causes propshaft whine at speed, and a knocking sound on the overrun or when the drive is taken up. It may also result in vibrations along the floor of the car. An increasing trend among manufacturers is to fit sealed unit universal joints. These can only be replaced not repaired.

Propshaft mounts (where fitted) do not usually come into the test unless their condition is such that the inspector considers them unsafe. The differential and rear axle do not come into the test to any large extent. However, if the unit were making sufficient noise to suggest it might fail within a short time, the inspector might fail the car on safety grounds.

The only cure for worn joints is replacement.

Stub axle assemblies

Little or no play is allowed in trunions, king pins or ball joints. All relevant boots and seals should be undamaged and all securing nuts, split pins and bolts must be tight and in good condition.

Where ball joints are badly worn, replacement is the only remedy. It is becoming more common now for manufacturers to supply only complete assemblies, that is the rod and two joints, rather than separate joints.

Wheel bearings

The front of the car will be jacked up and each wheel rocked, top to bottom, to check for front wheel bearing play. To avoid confusion with stub axle joint play, wheel bearing play is often looked for between the brake caliper and the wheel, where disc brakes are fitted, or the brake backplate and the wheel with drum brakes. Taper-roller wheel bearings can be adjusted for excessive end float, whereas other types have to be renewed if worn. It is unusual for driven wheel bearings to be checked, but if excessive wear is detected they will cause the car to be failed.

If you decide to renew the wheel bearings yourself, it is best to work on one side of the car at a time. If you run into difficulties you can use the other side for reference.

Suspension

All suspension linkage bushes on parts such as track arms, radius rods, wishbones, Panhard rods, anti-roll bars, spring shackles, trunnions and so on, should be in good condition with no appreciable wear. Such bushes are usually made of rubber, synthetic material or metal.

Although coil springs and their seats rarely give rise to problems, they will be inspected for damage and correct location, as will torque tubes and torsion bars, where fitted.

Leaf springs should be held firmly in place and have no broken blades, and no loose or missing spring clamps. The shackles and mounting rubbers must also be in good order.

14 Anti-roll bar rubbers must be in good condition, with no worn or perished components. This rubber would not pass the test

15 Suspension bump stop rubbers must be capable of withstanding any suspension impact. This rubber is completely perished.

16 Check the rubbers on both ends of the dampers. They may be of the flat variety, or eye bushes, and should show no signs of wear

17 The action of the dampers will be checked by bouncing each end of the car. This damper has a bent rod and would not be passed

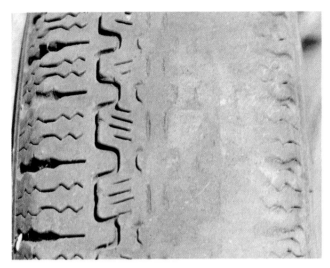

18 Tyres will be closely examined during the inspection. If your tyres are like this it is pointless to submit your car for test

19 Bear in mind that both sides of the tyre will be examined. It is easy to overlook splits like this, but they are very dangerous

On MacPherson strut units, as used on some front suspensions, the top joint bearing must not be worn, and the rubbers must not be perished. All the mounting bolts must be tight.

Anti-roll bar rubbers must be sound—perished rubbers will fail. Bump stop rubbers that cushion the suspension at the greatest extent of its travel must be intact and capable of withstanding any suspension impact.

All parts of the chassis/body structure where suspension units are mounted will be examined for strength. Any corrosion that might reduce the strength of the structure will cause failure.

Shock absorbers/dampers

Each shock absorber will be given a bounce test to see if it works properly. This is carried out by pressing down on each wing of the car in turn, then suddenly releasing the pressure on the downstroke. The body of the car should come to rest after approximately one and a half strokes of the damper. If it does not, the car will usually fail.

The examiner will also check each damper in turn to see whether it has a damaged or badly corroded base, a bent damper rod, perished rubbers or any leaks. The top and bottom mountings will also be checked to make sure they are secure.

On lever arm dampers the lever linkage will be examined to make sure it is not loose, and the pivot bushes will be checked for wear.

MacPherson strut units will be examined for leaks, distorted damper rods, and to see that they work correctly. The damper rod in the top mount (fig. 12) will be checked to see that it fits properly.

Defective dampers must be replaced unless the fault lies in the rubbers, in which case worn eye-bushes or flat mounting rubbers can be replaced. Worn lever arm dampers can be rebuilt, and the internal damper unit in a strut can be replaced, using a suitable kit.

Tyres and wheels

Radial and crossply tyres must not be mixed on the same axle. It is permissible, however, to have crossplies on one axle, and radials on the other. If you do this, the crossplies must always be at the front, and the radials at the rear. Many modern cars, such as the Rover SD1, have been designed around radial tyres and these cars must not be fitted with crossplies.

All the tyres must have a minimum tread depth of at

20 Wheel rims should be in good condition. This wheel would not pass the test as it could cause air leaks and has a jagged edge

least 1 mm in a continuous pattern that covers at least three quarters of the original tread width. It is advisable, although not compulsory, that tyres be replaced before they reach this state, however, as partly bald tyres are susceptible to punctures and can have drastically reduced grip, especially in wet weather.

The inspectors will always examine the sidewalls for cuts and splits and will not pass the vehicle if any are present. Bulges in the sidewall should never be ignored—they usually indicate a serious split in the inner wall of the tyre. Any gouges which expose the ply or cords will also fail the car, as will any perished tyre valves.

When checking your car before taking it for a Roadworthiness test, do not overlook tyres. Always maintain them at the recommended pressures. The inspector may check the condition of the spare wheel and tyre.

Each road wheel must be securely fixed, and there should be no loose or missing nuts or broken studs. In extreme cases, the examiners may check the stud holes in disc wheels for elongation, or the splines on centre-lock wheels for signs of wear. Wheel rims should be in good condition, and any damage likely to cause the wheel to leak air will cause failure. Wire spokes should be straight and firm. Any bent or loose spokes could cause the car to fail.

Damaged wheels must be replaced, as must defective tyres.

MoT test: brakes, road testing

Roadworthiness tests, in all countries which have them, demand that a vehicle's braking system should be in full working order at the time of the test and for a reasonable time afterwards. But defective brakes are a common cause of failure: in 1977 in the UK, for example, 56% of the vehicles which failed the MoT test did so because of poor braking.

In Britain the braking system is checked by a thorough visual inspection followed, provided that no faults in the system are observed, by a road test. In most testing stations a rolling road test—compulsory after June 1979—is used. This employs two sets of rollers which are embedded into the floor and the front or rear wheels of the car are driven on to them. As the rollers are turned (they are capable of revolving at either high or low speed), and the car brakes are applied, gauges register the amount of stopping power that they can exert. Rolling roads provide more accurate figures on the efficiency of the braking than ordinary open-road tests.

Disc brakes

Front and rear mounted discs (where fitted) will be given a thorough examination.

No stripping of parts will be undertaken in the MoT test, but the tester will take a look at pad thickness (where possible) to check that the friction material is not too close to, or below, what he thinks is a safe minimum thickness. A check will also be made to ensure that no pad retaining springs, securing pins or split pins are damaged, missing or broken. It is best to check them yourself before the test, and replace if necessary.

The calipers themselves must be securely mounted. Swinging or sliding calipers will be inspected to see that they operate correctly and are not seized or too loose.

Each caliper will be checked for any signs of the pistons having seized in the bores. A search will also be made for hydraulic fluid leaking from the piston seal(s).

As far as is possible (taking accessibility into account), the brake discs will have their surfaces examined for cracks that may lead to failure. 'Tramming' (scoring) of the disc surfaces, where road grit has been thrown up and trapped under the pad faces, is not a fail point unless the tester considers it to have weakened the disc(s) or affected brake efficiency.

Wear of the disc working surfaces does not cause failure unless an excessive amount of metal has been removed. A disc that is too thin will overheat rapidly in operation and may either fracture or affect brake efficiency by overheating the pad surface. The discs may also be inspected for excessive corrosion between the inner edge of the pad contact area and the hub, as it has been known for some discs to shear from their hubs if weakened in this way (fig. 7).

The disc working surfaces are sometimes used as a means of identifying caliper piston seizure. Both faces of each disc should be shiny from pad contact, but in cases of partial seizure one face may be dull or corroded.

If heavy scoring, corrosion or cracking on the braking surface is visible, the disc must be replaced.

Drum brakes

Drum brakes are not stripped to inspect the internal mechanism.

1 A Leyland Mini undergoes a rolling road test which checks the efficiency of the braking system

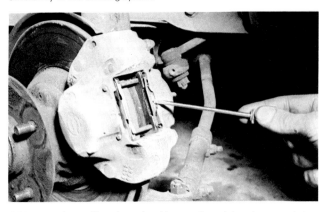

2 The examiner will make a visual inspection of the piston seals in each caliper (indicated by the screwdriver) to check for leaks

3 Ideally, the surface of the brake discs should look like this, with no signs of scoring or cracking that could reduce efficiency

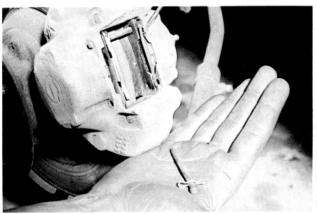

4 These disc brake pads are held in position by two long through-bolts which are in turn prevented from working loose by two clips

Nelson Hargreaves

Excessive travel of the foot pedal or handbrake lever may be taken as an indication that the shoe linings have either worn too far, or that the brakes need adjusting, unless the handbrake actuating mechanism or main brake hydraulics are at fault. On all types of brake the drums should be removed and the linings checked for wear every 5,000 miles.

Drum brakes may be fitted with internal automatic adjusters. If these seize, the brakes can become inefficient. This is a frequent cause of MoT test failure.

Any external brake shoe adjusters will be examined. The tester will require them to work properly. Any rubber dust covers must be fitted, and should not be split.

The drum backplates will be examined for any signs of hydraulic fluid weeping from a wheel cylinder. Sliding type wheel cylinders will be checked to see that they have not seized and that their rubber boots are in good condition.

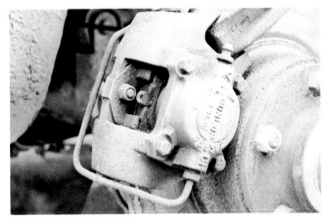

5 An alternative method of securing brake pads is to use a large clamp which is held in position by a single through-bolt

6 The examiner will attempt, where possible, to check the degree of wear in disc pads. Those on the right are dangerously worn

Handbrakes

All parts of the handbrake system should be in good working order. The handbrake should not be difficult to apply, and travel distance to pull the brakes hard on should not be excessive. The normal amount of travel allowed is between three and five clicks on the ratchet, although different design tolerances are taken into account.

The handbrake must be properly secured and its lock/ release mechanism must work properly. Actuating cables must be in good condition, without broken strands and with only minimal corrosion. All cable guides and slings should be serviceable, and any jockey wheels or cable quadrants free to rotate or pivot in operation. Clevis pins should not be badly worn, nor split pins missing. Cable clamps or nuts must be secure.

Any cable adjuster(s) must be in working order, with a reasonable amount of adjustment left. Cable return springs should not be broken, missing or worn. Shoe or pad operating levers must function and their dust shrouds be undamaged. The condition of any cable sheaths and their fixing points is less important unless the brake operation is affected.

Operating rods of any description are expected to be in a reasonable state. On those cars fitted with a compensator tree in the handbrake mechanism (fig. 11), this should not be badly worn, inoperative, or damaged in such a way that its function and the handbrake operation is impaired.

On cars such as Jaguars which have rear disc brakes plus an independent handbrake mechanism, the handbrake pads and their operating linkage will be examined for any wear or defects.

If the handbrake mechanism and its adjustment are in order, but the amount of travel on the handbrake lever seems excessive, it will be presumed that, on drum brake cars, the shoes are worn or badly adjusted. Where disc brakes are fitted, and there is a separate handbrake caliper, the cause could be incorrect adjustment of the caliper.

Adequate handbrake mechanism lubrication is not required by the test, but it is frequently found that incorrectly maintained handbrakes fail on efficiency. Regular lubrication can do much to reduce ratchet and pawl wear.

Older cars with rod brakes, such as early Austin A30s, must have no wear in the rod linkages, and the rods must not be bent.

Brake pipes

All rigid metal brake pipes (bundy tubing) will be examined for leaks and for signs of corrosion that may result in leakage under pressure. Slight surface corrosion is permissible, but a coin edge or screwdriver blade will be used

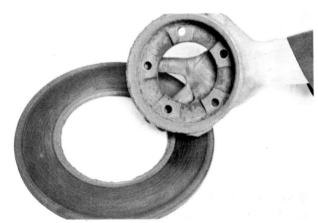

7 Excessive corrosion between the inner edge of the contact area and the hub can cause the disc to shear, with serious results

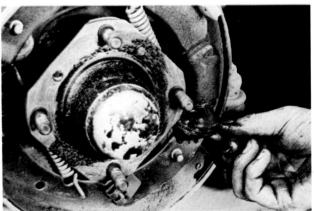

8 Worn rubbers in the wheel cylinders cause hydraulic fluid leaks which can reduce brake efficiency and cause the car to be failed

Girling Ltd

to lightly scrape the pipes to see how deeply the corrosion has penetrated.

There is no official wording in the DoE legislation to state that rigid metal pipes must be clipped to the rear axle on cars with 'live' (or 'beam') axles, but some testers insist that they be secured. The clips should either be made from rubber, or be to a special design available from the car manufacturer. Jubilee clips should not be used, even though some testers may insist on them. The tester will be looking to see whether or not the piping fouls any suspension component, or is in such a position that it may chafe on the axle. To prevent this happening you can either clip the pipe or bend it well away from any other parts. The tester will examine whichever method has been used on your car. If any pipes pass through any chassis section, they must be protected by a grommet.

All brake pipes, including those passing beneath the engine, those underneath the car and any within the engine bay (where they pass to the master cylinder, hydraulic fluid reservoir and the servo if one is fitted) will be inspected. The screw connections at the end of all metal and flexible brake pipes will be checked for signs of fluid leakage. The flexible pipes will be bent by hand to look for any cracking that will show they have perished. Any bulges, which show that the outer hose skin is lifting, will cause failure. Armoured flexible pipes will fail if the metal strands are chafed or broken away, endangering the inner hose at any point.

Brake balance regulators
On cars with a rear brake pressure regulator, this unit will be checked to see that it is secure and has no hydraulic fluid leaks, and that any external mechanisms related to it are in good order.

Brake fluid reservoirs
The hydraulic brake fluid reservoir may be checked to see that the level has not fallen too low, either allowing air into the system or confirming a leak somewhere in the system.

Where the reservoir cap has a rubber seal, the seal may be inspected for signs of distortion caused by fluid contamination. This will warn of likely seal damage elsewhere in the system that may give rise to 'brake pull' or other malfunctions. The tester may also check that the air hole in the reservoir cap is not blocked.

The examiner always checks for a 'spongy' feel to the brake pedal and air bubbles in the fluid reservoir. These mean that the brake hydraulics need bleeding before they will work efficiently. If you have to bleed the brakes, road test the car carefully afterwards.

Servo-assisted brakes
The operation of a brake servo unit may be checked before the road or rolling-road test. With most units, a slight rise of the pedal will be felt as the brakes are applied. The tester may check the servo action by pumping the brakes with the engine switched off until any vacuum has been exhausted, and then, keeping his foot on the pedal, starting the engine. The pedal should rise slightly as the servo vacuum builds up. If it does not, the car will fail.

All brake servo units are expected to give at least two or three assisted pumps before the vacuum runs out, with the engine switched off. Some vehicles, such as Jaguars, are fitted with separate vacuum reservoirs which may take eight or more pumps to exhaust. If the reservoir is corroded the car will be failed. Any frayed or leaking air pipes from the reservoir to the servo will also cause failure.

10 An inefficient handbrake may be caused by stretch in the cables and should be replaced. The new and old cables must match

11 Where the car is fitted with a compensator on the handbrake system, it should not be badly worn, inoperative, or damaged

Girling Ltd

9 Handbrake actuating cables should be in serviceable condition, with no broken or frayed strands. This example would be failed

Nelson Hargreaves

12 Some Jaguars have separate handbrake calipers which act on a second pair of brake pads. The examiner will check for defects

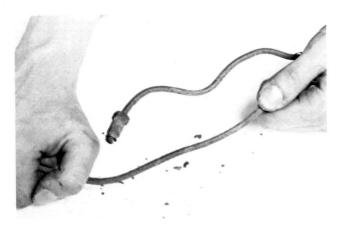

13 Slight surface corrosion on metal brake pipes is permissible, but if corrosion penetrates the surface the car will be failed

14 This brake pressure regulator on a scrapped Leyland Mini is badly corroded, as are the brake pipes. The car would be failed

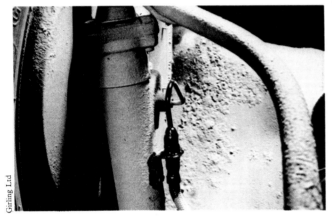

15 This metal pipe has fractured at the union with the flexible hose, causing a serious fluid leak. The car would not pass a test

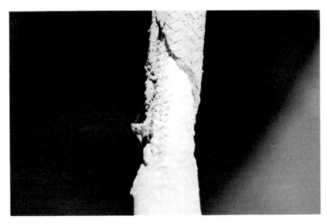

16 Flexible brake hoses will be carefully examined for any signs of perishing. The outer casing on this pipe has completely split

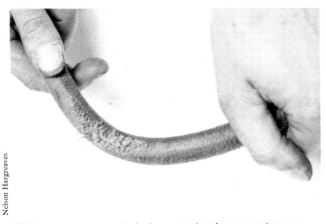

17 This vacuum reservoir air pipe was taken from a car that was refused a test certificate. The pipe is badly frayed and leaks

Seats and seat belts

Before taking any car out for a road test, the UK examiner will make sure that the driver's seat is securely mounted. If the seat is loose or broken it will fail.

Cars registered after January 1 1965 must be fitted with front seat belts of an approved specification set down by the British Standards Institute.

All seat belt anchorages must be properly secured to the vehicle structure. There must be no corrosion within 30 cm (12in.) of the mounting points, which would limit the ability of the belts to stand up to strain caused by the impact of an accident. Only the driver's and front passenger's seat belts are tested, but they will be carefully inspected for any signs of wear or cuts in the fabric. All adjustment mechanisms must work correctly, as must the securing buckles or clips. Any tendency for the buckles to work loose, or fail to stay together when jerked sharply, will cause the car to be failed.

No parts of the seat belt mechanisms or the belts may be missing and nothing in the car may interfere with the belt operation. Inertia reel seat belts will be closely checked to see that the automatic locking balls or pins work properly, and they must also recoil when not in use.

Road and rolling-road testing

The road test or rolling-road test is used to check the efficiency of the brakes as a percentage of the force of gravity (g). Before the test is carried out, the tester will satisfy himself that the vehicle is in a safe enough condition to be tested, and will check the driver's seat mounting and the seat belts.

When a decelerometer is used in the road test, the foot brakes must record 50% efficiency (0.5g) and the handbrake alone 25% (0.25g). When a rolling-road test is carried out the foot brakes must again register 50%, but on low-speed rollers the handbrake need record only 15% (0.15g). Where the system is a split (dual) system, the handbrake has to register 16% (the percentage necessary to hold a vehicle on a gradient of 1 in 6.25). If the system is not split then the handbrake has to be 25% efficient. These figures are the same whatever the type of test.

There is no really certain method by which you can check the efficiency of your brakes without a decelerometer. But as a guide you can measure the stopping distance after an emergency brake stop (choose a quiet road or, better still, private land) from a given speed—say 20mph. At this speed the foot brakes should stop the car in 8.5 m (27ft), and the handbrake in 17 m (54ft), with the car carrying a normal load – the driver and a passenger.

Brake balance is an important part of the road test, and any tendency for the car to pull to one side while braking

151

18 There should be no damaged seat belt mechanisms. This buckle casing has been crushed, damaging the locking mechanism

19 This seat belt has been dangerously weakened by being shut in the car door, and is no longer capable of withstanding an impact

will cause failure. On cars fitted with a rear brake pressure regulator, the examiner will be looking for premature rear wheel lock-up which indicates incorrect adjustment or a malfunction in the unit.

Brake pull can be caused by a multitude of different factors, including defects in the suspension or steering as well as in the brake system itself. However, should the vehicle have passed the visual examination, the most common causes are as follows:

1. A sticking disc pad, piston, or wheel cylinders, caused by partial seizure or by seals swollen through hydraulic fluid contamination.

2. Brake shoe linings contaminated by hydraulic fluid leaks from wheel cylinders or oil leaking past worn axle seals into the drum.

3. Lack of shoe adjustment on drum brakes, or the shoes on one side being adjusted tighter than on the others.

4. Air bubbles in the hydraulic fluid of a single brake line (rather than the whole system).

The examiner will search for other defects that cannot be properly checked by a visual inspection, such as a juddering brake pedal. This is caused by distortion of the discs or drums.

The road test also shows up any major misalignment in the steering or suspension geometry. The alignment is not physically tested, and is not actually part of the test, but if any misalignment is sufficient to affect the stability of the car, its steering, or the road-holding when the brakes are applied, then the car may be failed.

The road test may also reveal 'lost motion' or excess play in the steering. This will have been discovered earlier in the test, but serves to confirm the fault where it exists.

The examiner will also want to see that the speedometer is working and that it is reasonably accurate. A wavering needle indicates a worn or dry cable, and may cause failure.

It can be seen that the MoT examination is a very thorough check. It has its limitations, as testers are not permitted to dismantle vehicles to check for wear, but there are signs that it will become tougher still in the future.

Failure to maintain a car regularly and, where necessary, overhaul it will inevitably result in a fail certificate being issued when it is subjected to the MoT test. In the long term it can be far less expensive to repair faults as they arise rather than leave them until the car fails its test on several major, costly, points and needs to have them all repaired at once.

20 Although the damage to this belt does not look too serious, it would not pass the test. Friction burns have weakened it

21 This seat belt has become so frayed that it is unusable. Seat belts need not be worn in the UK, but they must be in good order

Jerry Tubby

Inside the car

Cleaning the interior of the car is often neglected, even by owners who are conscientious about outside cleaning and general servicing. Yet regular care inside the car will ensure that the upholstery does not deteriorate, the carpets remain smart and the overall appearance stays clean and tidy. Not only will the car be more pleasant to travel in: it will almost certainly command a higher price when the time comes to re-sell or part-exchange.

The job is basically simple and straightforward, although it can be time consuming. But like most chores the task will be less daunting if performed in a simple and methodical sequence. Also, little-and-often is a much better mainte-nance policy than a desperate once-a-year spring clean.

Inside cleaning can be done at any time but it is best to avoid doing the job immediately after washing the exterior. Dust raised from the inside may settle on the newly-shining paintwork and make the outside washing pointless. The ideal weather for interior cleaning is a warm dry day. This allows upholstery and carpets that have been washed to dry quickly. It is also a good idea to work in the open air in daylight, rather than in a gloomy murky garage. This will enable you to see exactly what is dirty and what is clean.

Start by planning what needs to be done and in what order and collect the equipment and accessories needed. Remove all the accumulated clutter—sweet papers, old rags, cigarette packets—from the parcel shelf, glove

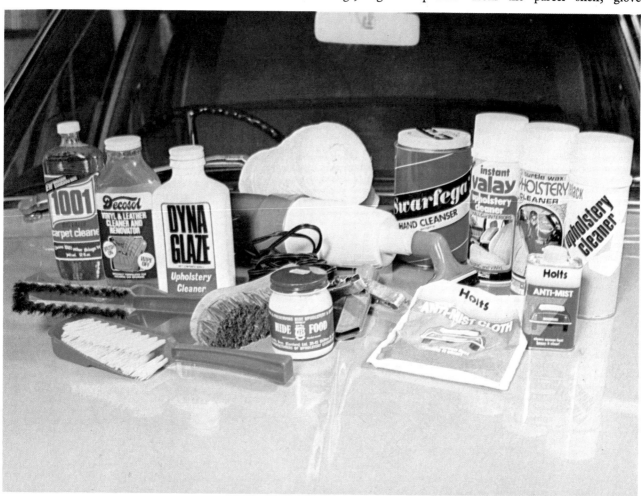

1 Some of the more popular products used for interior cleaning. Upholstery cleaners are available in both aerosol and liquid form

2 The most effective way of removing any dust or dirt from the carpets is to first brush them vigorously with a stiff brush

3 A vacuum cleaner will then remove the dirt quite easily. This DIY car vacuum cleaner runs off the car's 12V battery

4 Most carpets are secured in some way but once the retaining studs, screws or hooks are undone the carpet will simply lift out

compartment, and under the seats. Empty the ashtrays. Now the car should be ready for you to begin your cleaning programme in earnest.

Carpets

Where to start cleaning inside a car is not crucial, but if there is a considerable amount of dust or dirt on the carpets it is sensible to deal with these first. There are several ways to clean car carpets. They can either be left in place, brushed with a stiff brush, then vacuum-cleaned. Or, preferably, they can be taken out, the dust beaten out of them and then shampooed as well.

The conventional upright household vacuum cleaner can be used once the carpets have been removed, but if you decide to leave the carpets in the car, either a compact vacuum cleaner or the type with a long, flexible hose and narrow nozzle will be needed to get into the many confined spaces inside. If you intend using any type of mains-powered vacuum cleaner it will obviously be necessary to park the car near an electricity supply, or use a long extension lead. An alternative is the small cleaner specially made for car cleaning, running from the vehicle's 12V battery (fig. 3). The disadvantage of this type is its low power and limited efficiency.

Carpets may be loose fitted, and removing them is simply a matter of lifting them out. Usually, however, they are secured in some way. A type of press-stud is most common. Other variations are 'Velcro' strips and metal tags or hooks. On a few cars, you will find carpet removal complicated by screwed-on trim, and you may have to unbolt the front seat runners or brackets to remove the central section of floor covering.

Once you have your carpet out, thorough vacuuming is easy. A stiff brushing first will help loosen dirt. If you do not own and cannot borrow a vacuum cleaner you can hang the carpets over a washing line and beat them.

If you have light coloured carpets which are showing dirt marks, wash them with carpet shampoo. Domestic detergent products are perfectly suitable (fig. 5). It is certainly preferable to take the carpets out of the car to do this unless the weather is very hot and you are sure they will dry out quickly. Make sure the carpets are as near 100 per cent dry as possible before putting them back in the car. Leave the car doors and windows open to avoid any build-up of condensation.

While the carpets are out, any necessary repairs to them can be made. For example, fraying edges can be repaired with a self-adhesive upholstery tape. You may well find the sound-absorbing material or felt under the carpets damp and decaying, or perhaps even soaking wet. If so take the felt from the car (fig. 6) and dry it thoroughly. Check the car for water leaks and rust (see page 139). Remember to replace the felt before reinstalling the carpets.

If the felt is in good condition, do not try to glue it down as it will be difficult to remove when wet. Also do not attempt to wash the underfelt as it may well fall apart. It will also be difficult to dry. Should any new carpet or sound absorbent material be necessary, a specialist upholstery firm should be able to provide replacements. Otherwise, straightforward carpet and felt replacements can usually be obtained from a main dealer for your car.

Carpet and felt can be bought pre-tailored to fit the car, or you can buy it by length and do the shaping and fitting yourself. Other forms of sound absorbing material can now be obtained and are often more effective than felt. Your local accessory shop will be able to advise you on these.

5 While the carpets are out of the car, one easy way to improve their appearance is to wash them with a domestic carpet shampoo

6 Many cars have this type of sound-absorbing material under the carpets. Due to water leaks, you may find the felt soaking wet

7 If the material is wet, remove it from the car and allow it to dry thoroughly before you return it to its original position

8 With the carpets and underfelt out of the car, check that the drain-hole grommets are in place. Look also for any signs of rust

Sweep out and clean the floor of the car while the carpets and underfelt are out. Check that all drain-hole grommets are correctly in place (fig. 8) and look for signs of rust. Treat if necessary with a rust converter solution that does not have to be washed off, such as Selleys Rust Converter. Then paint over the area of the repair.

When you reinstall the carpets, be careful to fit the area around the control pedals properly, and make sure all pedals are capable of full, unimpeded movement. Loose or rucked-up carpet here could be dangerous in an emergency.

Rubber mats, either the loose slip ones or the full matting found in some cars instead of carpets, need much less attention than carpets. A wash down with a mild detergent such as washing-up liquid should be sufficient to keep them clean. If this is done with the mats in the car, make sure that no water is trapped under them as this could cause corrosion.

Inside the boot

Next deal with the boot, or the rear luggage space if the car is a hatchback or estate. Remove any mats and plastic coverings and wash them down with detergent. If you find water in the boot or if water gets in while you are cleaning it, pull out the drain plugs or grommets to drain it out.

In a conventional saloon, the rear seat cushion should be easy to remove. In most cases it simply pulls forwards and upwards, though on some models there may be screws. Take the cushion out and brush or vacuum the area underneath (figs. 10 and 11).

The upholstery

How you treat this depends to some extent on what the covering is. Real leather requires 'feeding' with a creamy type of polish to prevent cracking and splitting over a long period. Any type of PVC (including all the imitation leather brands like 'Ambla' and 'Naugahyde') is a much easier proposition.

A foamy detergent solution can be used quite successfully to remove dirt and grime from the seats, but you will need quite a lot of water to wash off the detergent and it is wise to remove the seats from the car to do this. On the other hand, many proprietary upholstery cleaners are available. Some, like Turtle Wax Upholstery Cleaner, lift the dirt with little mess and deposit a coating of silicone. These products can safely be used on leather and cloth seat coverings and they impart a pleasant sheen to the fabric. They are available in aerosol form, or can be applied with a soft brush, scrubbed well in, and wiped off with a cloth.

If your seats have detachable covers you may be able to have them dry-cleaned or even wash them. But take care if they are foam-backed. The foam may disintegrate during the dry-cleaning process.

Door and quarter panels, fascia mouldings and head-linings can normally be treated with the same type of cleaner as the upholstery.

Removing stains

Grease and oil marks are often to be found, particularly on the inside door panels. They can usually be removed by scrubbing with a small hard nailbrush and strong detergent.

Alternatively, a versatile and useful stain remover is Swarfega, more commonly used as a hand-cleaner. This will dissolve any oil-bound contamination, including paints, beach tar, printing and duplicating inks, carbon paper marks and various glues and waxes. The technique is to rub or brush the Swarfega into the stain (fig. 15). Leave it

9 Remove the boot mat and wash it down with detergent. If there is any water in the boot, pull out the grommets to drain it out

10 Sometimes the rear seat cushion is located by screws but in most cases you simply pull it upwards and forwards to remove it

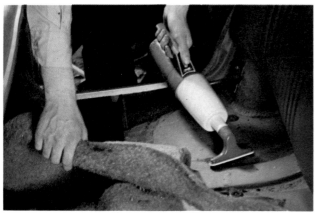

11 You can then clean the area underneath the seat. Make sure the sound absorbent material is in good condition and is not wet

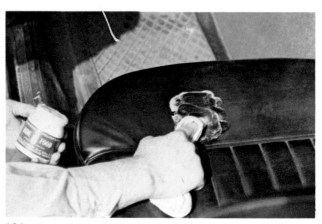

12 Leather seats require 'feeding' with a special creamy polish to prevent them from cracking or splitting over a long period

for several minutes before rinsing it off with water. It is safest to test a small, hidden section of the material in case of damaging side effects.

Headlining

Nicotine stains in the headlining of a smoker's car are hard to shift. Again, scrubbing with a brush and strong detergent is probably the best way to tackle the job. Other more drastic options are to use slightly abrasive household cleaners like Flash.

Paintwork

Exposed paintwork in a car's interior may of course be cleaned and polished in the same way as the exterior bodywork. But heavy wax protection for interior paintwork is somewhat superfluous. A good shine can be achieved with an ordinary domestic general purpose aerosol polish like Pledge or Sheen. The same sprays also produce good results on plastic and wood fascias and sills, instruments, and other interior bright fittings.

Windows

Take care to keep all silicone-rich products like spray polishes away from windows and mirrors. Similarly, do not be tempted to use 'Windolene' type domestic glass polish in your car. Clean the inside of your windows and your interior rear-view mirror with either a purpose-designed glass cleaner like Holts Bright Screen or with methylated spirits.

Be particularly careful with heated rear screens and screen-filament radio aerials. The wires or metallic strips are all too easily damaged by heavy-handed cleaning. Also take care not to score glass with rings.

Seat belts

Seat belts are of course among the most vital fitments in any car. Do not risk weakening the webbing with any of the chemicals employed elsewhere in the car. Manufacturers all stress that nothing stronger than warm, mild soapy suds should be used on seat belts.

Interior chromework

Interior chrome brightwork which is showing signs of deterioration can be treated with chrome cleaners designed for outside use, though this is seldom necessary. Solvol Autosol is a typical example of one of these polishes.

Interior trim

Some cars, Ford Escorts for example, have panels in their passenger compartments made from nothing more than coated cardboard. Where these cardboard surfaces are exposed to a fair amount of scuffing, such as the lower side panels in front of the doors and areas around the parcel tray, they tend to become shabby as the thin coating, usually black, wears away. Paint or dye can be used to recolour the scuffed areas or you can use shoe polish to restore a shine to the affected parts and provide some protection.

Finally, be wary of using volatile solvents such as acetone, lacquer thinners or nail varnish removers anywhere inside your car. Some of the plastic surfaces may be badly damaged by contact with them. Also steer clear of bleaches and reducing agents. If you must use any of these, test a small inconspicuous area of the stained surface first to see if there is any adverse reaction.

The inside of a car is a confined space, so never be tempted to use anything that gives off a poisonous vapour, take care not to score glass with finger rings or a wristwatch.

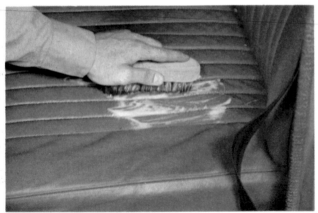

13 Most DIY upholstery cleaners are quick and simple to use. First apply the cleaner to the seat and then scrub it well in

14 When the dirt is loosened, rub off the cleaner with a clean cloth. Leather-look and cloth seats can also be cleaned this way

15 You can usually remove grease and oil marks on the upholstery with a strong detergent. An alternative stain remover is Swarfega

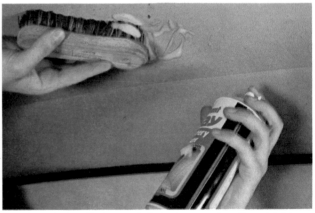

16 Unless the headlining has faded or become heavily stained, you can clean it up by using a proprietary upholstery cleaner

Interior repairs

Many people prefer to have repairs or improvements to their car's interior carried out by a professional coachtrimmer. But many of the techniques for making satisfactory repairs are well within the scope of even the most inexperienced DIY owner.

Kits are available from accessory stores in the UK for mending simple tears in PVC and leather-look seat covers and for repairing fraying edges on carpets. Products like these can be found in Australia and with ingenuity and patience generally will provide a perfectly respectable finish.

Replacing seats

One way to avoid actually repairing a car seat is to replace it with a new or secondhand one. As some car manufacturers do not supply new seats, you may have to obtain a replacement seat from a breaker's yard. It may be possible to substitute seats from another model of car. For example Leyland 1100 seats can be fitted in a Mini. Even if the colour is not right for your car, you can change it simply with an upholstery paint. First wash the seat with turps substitute. Then, to remove any residue of detergent or shampoo, wash it down again, this time with water. Now apply two thin coats of the paint. The result will be a hard-wearing finish which will look good and which will also provide quite a high resistance to cracking (fig. 4).

Removing a seat normally only entails undoing three or four bolts or clips and lifting the seat out. But check that the runners on the floor of the car are the same as for your replacement seat. You may find after close inspection that you have to change the runners over.

Repairing splits and tears

Should a PVC or leather-look seat have a split, tear, or burn, there are several ways of mending it, although none of them may work if the damage is in a stress-bearing part of the seat, such as a seam. If you are confident that you can put it back properly, you can take the seat cover off to make the job easier, but make sure you note any alignment marks on the seat material before you remove the cover. Some seat covers are much harder to remove than others. Fortunately, however, taking off the seat cover to repair a split or tear can in most cases be avoided.

One way to repair a tear in a seat cover is to patch the repair from behind, using a disc made from the same material as the seat itself. A good source for material of the right colour and texture for patching seat covers is underneath the seat itself. Sometimes the manufacturer will leave a generous margin of material around this area so it should be easy to cut off a small piece without disturbing the rest of the cover. But remember that this material will look remarkably new if the material on top of the seat has faded.

1 Removing a car seat is generally straightforward. On this Ford Cortina you simply undo four bolts and the seat will lift out

2 With other cars, like this Saab, you press down a lever under the squab and the seat can be slid right forward and so removed

Barbara Bellingham

3 Although in most cases the runners are an integral part of the seat, some types of runners are mounted separately on the floor

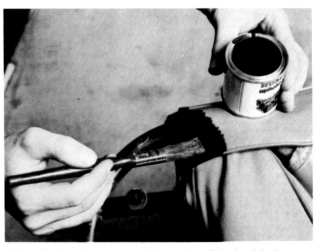

4 If you find a replacement seat in good condition but it is the wrong colour, you can alter it quite simply with upholstery paint

If there is not enough material there, you can try a large department store which carries a range of good quality PVC cloths for the DIY enthusiast: or you could be lucky at one of the smaller shops dealing in manufacturer's remainders. If you do not find what you want, you will have to go to a specialist upholstery firm as it is almost certain that replacement material will not be readily obtainable from the manufacturer.

To repair the tear from the underside, first cut the material to an oval shape, larger than the size of the tear.

Next, manoeuvre the disc into position (fig. 16) and apply a thin coating of the adhesive to the flap and around the edges of the patch. Allow the adhesive to go tacky, then press down on the flap to complete the repair.

If you have left a tear or rip unrepaired for any length of time, the seat material will have shrunk and it will be difficult if not impossible to join the edges together neatly. One method of dealing with this is to stick a repair patch over the top of the tear.

First, you will need a patch of the correct material.

5 If a seat panel is badly damaged you may need to take off the cover to repair it. This seat cover is secured with wire clips

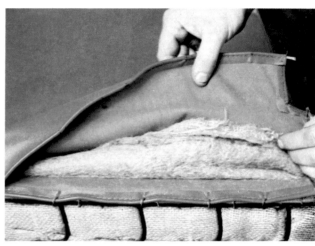

6 Remove all the clips and, noting carefully any alignment marks on the material, pull up the outside back of the seat cover

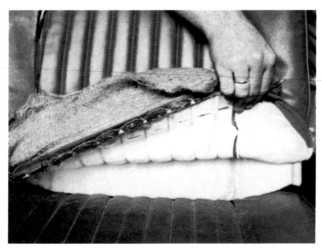

7 Now push the other end of the seat cover through to the front of the seat and pull up the cover so that it comes off inside out

8 A hole or tear like this can be repaired in a variety of ways. One way is to mend the damaged section with a liquid repair kit

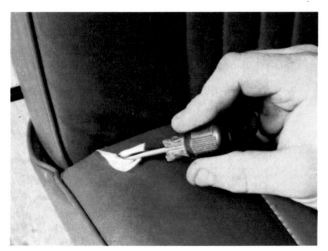

9 First cut the bonding sheet so that it will overlap the hole and then manoeuvre the sheet into position behind the repair

10 Now mix up the repair paste on a piece of card. You may have to mix several colours before an exact colour match is reached

Having marked out the correct position for it, try smoothing out the edges of the underside of the patch with a sharp knife. This will prevent you from snagging and lifting the edge of the repair with your clothes as you move across the seats. Roughen up the area around the tear with emery paper and then apply the adhesive. When it is tacky, firmly press the repair patch into place.

A third way to mend a split or burn mark in a PVC or leather-look seat is to use a liquid repair kit. First place the bonding sheet supplied behind the hole and fill the repair with the pre-mixed paste (fig. 11). Then, having placed the appropriate graining pattern card over the repair paste, complete the process using a hot domestic iron and another, larger piece of card (fig. 14).

Repairing tears or holes in cloth seats can be tricky, but you can try sticking a suitable repair patch to the underside of the tear with a latex-based adhesive. Alternatively, one popular and practical way to deal with shabby seats is to fit loose covers or re-cover them. There are many types of custom-made seat covers available, and fitting a set presents

11 Next fill up the hole with repair paste until it is the same level as the seat. Spread the paste under the edges of the hole

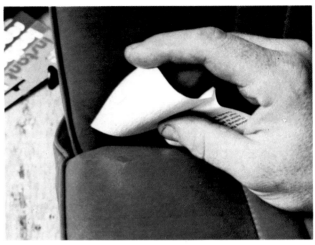

12 Select the graining pattern card to match your upholstery. For unusual grain patterns, you can make up a mould with this kit

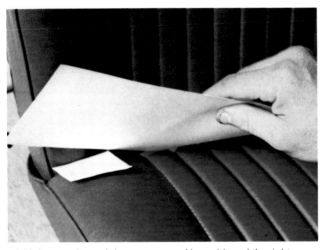

13 Make sure the graining pattern card is positioned the right way up—then place a thin piece of card over the pattern card

14 Complete the curing process by placing a hot domestic iron on the card for one minute. Note that the card is larger than the iron

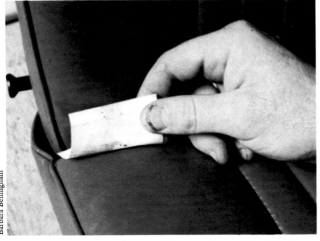

Barbara Bellingham

15 Finally, allow the repair to cool for two minutes, then slowly peel off the graining pattern card and the repair is completed

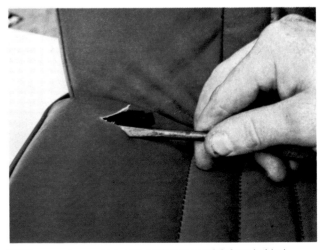

16 One way to mend a tear like this is to patch it from behind. First cut the patch to size and then position it behind the tear

few problems if you are careful. Your local accessory shop will be able to advise you.

Broken seat springs

When a seat sags in the middle, a broken spring or frame is usually the cause. To check this, you will have to take the seat out from the car. If the frame has broken, a piece of rod or piping of the same diameter can be welded in place to join the two halves of the frame together again.

If one of the springs has broken, you can mend it quite simply by using a section of replacement springing (figs. 20 to 23). This springing is cut to length, but allow an extra 25 mm (1in.) or the spring will not support the seat.

In some cases it may be possible to buy replacement springs for a car seat, but you will probably have to go to a coachtrimmer as car manufacturers in general do not supply new springs. Alternatively you could pick up a suitable spring from a breaker's yard—or maybe a tatty seat that has the right springing which can be taken apart and used.

Repairing carpets

Repairs to carpets are generally simple and straightforward. Fraying edges can be covered up with a self-adhesive repair and binding tape. This tape is useful for joining carpets, for edging and for mending small holes but always try to sew on the tape or else it may pull off quite quickly.

Keeping the carpets in place can be a problem, so if you have this trouble, it is a good idea to fit a set of carpet fasteners. A typical example consists of a spike-ring, a plate, and a stud assembly (fig. 27). Generally, it is not a good idea to use Velcro for locating carpets unless it is firmly sewn in place, as it tends to pull away from the carpet.

To fit this type of carpet fastener, lay the carpet down in its normal position. Then lift it up and pop-rivet the stud into position (fig. 24). Mark the top of the stud with wetted chalk and re-lay the carpet, pressing down on the stud. This mark will help locate the spike-ring and plate.

To fit the spike-ring, press it through the top side of the

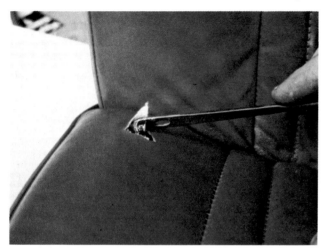

17 Now apply a thin coating of adhesive to the repair, making sure that the edges of the patch and the flap itself are well covered

18 When the adhesive is tacky, press the flap down firmly. This kind of tear is easy to fix but often difficult to mend neatly

19 When a seat sags in the middle, a broken spring is usually the cause. If the frame has broken, it must be welded together again

20 One easy way to mend the seat is to replace the broken spring with this type of springing—available from most coachtrimmers

21 First you need to remove the broken spring. This spring—on a Ford Cortina—is located by small coil springs and metal tabs

carpet and locate it through the plate on the other side of the carpet. Bend over the spike prongs (fig. 26) and finally press the plate over the stud. That part of the carpet will now be held securely in place.

Replacing heel pads

One DIY way of replacing a heel pad on a carpet is to pull off or unstick the old pad and replace it with a new rubber car mat. Alternatively, you can try using a suitable piece of leather for this job. Unlike a rubber mat, leather will not leave any marks on your shoes.

Door panels

If your door panel is split or torn, you can repair it in the same way as a PVC or leather-look seat. In some cases, the door trim is held in place with small plastic clips and it is often difficult to get the trim off without breaking them. There is no real substitute for these clips so you must buy new ones if they break. Occasionally the trim surrounding the clip area will become torn or soggy. A professional upholsterer may use a piece of millboard to support the broken area. An acceptable DIY substitute is to cut up a section of hardboard and use that.

Replacement door panels can sometimes be supplied by your car's manufacturer, but if not you can try a breaker's yard. Again, if you find the right type of trim to match your car but it is the wrong colour, you can paint over it with upholstery paint.

22 Remove the old spring and fit the new one. The replacement spring is designed to slot into the existing alignment holes

23 You may need to tap the side of the spring in order to locate it correctly. Re-fit the coil springs and bend back the metal tabs

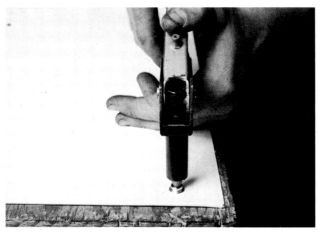

24 One type of carpet fastener consists of a spike-ring, a plate and a stud assembly. First pop-rivet the stud into position

25 Now press the spike-ring through the carpet, having wetted the head of the stud and re-laid the carpet to locate the spike-ring

Barbara Bellingham

26 Next position the plate so that the spike-ring passes through it—then use a hammer to knock back the prongs of the spike-ring

27 Finally, press the plate assembly over the head of the stud and that section of the carpet will now be firmly held in place

Emergency procedures

Ideally, a well-maintained car will never break down, and the procedures outlined in earlier chapters aim to keep things that way. However, it is likely that even the most dedicated do-it-yourself motorist will at some time need to make emergency repairs. This chapter is designed to help if and when a sudden breakdown occurs. It lists useful equipment and spares, and describes the symptoms and remedies of the most common faults. The cleaner jobs are explained first, so that with luck you will be on your way again with maximum speed and minimum inconvenience. If these fail, the dirtier, more thorough procedures are also given, together with references to more detailed information elsewhere in the book. The repairs described in this chapter are strictly 'get-you-home' measures and should be followed up by a later check for safety and reliability.

Tools and equipment
If you carry no tools, spare parts, or other useful bits and pieces in your car a roadside breakdown is a lot more difficult, if not impossible, to cope with. But with a comparatively small and inexpensive survival kit, what would otherwise be an expensive garage job can easily be overcome.

A ball-peen hammer is one which has one end rounded into a ball shape as distinct from the claw end on a carpenter's hammer.

The circuit tester consists of an electrical screwdriver with a small bulb in its transparent handle and a lead from the end of the handle to a crocodile clip. They are not expensive to buy, but you can make one up using an old sidelight bulb holder, two pieces of 28/.012 wire, a crocodile clip, and a probe – a piece of welding rod about 20cm (8in.) is ideal. (See page 40, fig 6).

You may wonder what the socks are for, but if you are wearing clean clothes and have to get your hands dirty to effect a roadside repair, you will find how useful they are. Simply pull them over your sleeves leaving your hands free. When the repair is complete, wipe your hands as clean as you can with paper towels and then strip off the socks.

The length of iron water piping makes a useful lever for L-shaped wheel braces when the nuts have been overtightened, as well as having other uses.

The warning triangle is a valuable safety measure and is, in fact, obligatory in most European countries.

It is wise to carry some spares, especially if you often do long journeys. The basics are mentioned below. When buying a spare fan belt, check carefully that it is the right size for your car, as lengths vary widely.

Essential tools	2-2½m (6-8ft) of 28/.012	Tow rope
0.7kg (1½lb) ball-peen hammer	electrical wire	Jump leads
Pliers with insulated handles	Strong rubber bands	0.75m (2½ft) length of iron
Set of five open ended	Plastic container of water	water piping
spanners	Fine grade glasspaper	**Spare parts**
Medium size screwdriver	Binding wire	Fan belt
Cross-head screwdriver	Roll of kitchen towels	Radiator top hose
Circuit tester	4m (12ft) of string	Bulbs for side, head, stop/tail
Warning triangle	Pair of old socks with the toes	lights
Useful equipment	cut off	Contact breaker points
Torch	Plastic bag	Spark plug
Penknife	Insulating tape	Fuses to cover the basic circuits

Finding the fault

When something goes wrong, the first thing to do is diagnose the fault. The important thing about diagnosis is to remember the symptoms which led up to the failure. If, for example, the engine hiccups, picks up again, and then peters out there is a good chance the cause is fuel starvation. If the engine misfires repeatedly before finally giving up the ghost, the fault is more likely to be ignition.

To locate the culprit scientifically you can do a complete check of the ignition system, and if this does not uncover the fault, do a step-by-step check of the fuel system. But before getting your hands dirty unneccessarily there are a few checks you can make.

Preliminary spot checks

1. Remove the petrol filler cap slowly and listen carefully for the sound of air being drawn into the tank with a hissing noise. This sort of noise would indicate a blocked breather which is causing a vacuum to form in the tank, preventing fuel being drawn out by the pump. The simplest way to clear the breather is to leave the filler cap off and drive on very carefully, expecially on corners, to avoid spillage. If the cap can be left on but allowing air to enter the tank, so much the better, but make sure you don't lose it. Stuffing cloth into the filler hole is not really to be recommended unless it can be secured to the neck of the filler, because there is a possibility of the cloth being sucked into the tank. From the legal point of view, *Construction and Use Regulations* say that the petrol tank may be vented to the atmosphere, so if the breather is blocked, the filler pipe can be said to be acting as a vent.

2. When the engine will not fire and the starter motor turns sluggishly, it may well be that the battery charge is low (see page 55). If the lights dim when the starter turns, first check that the battery connections are clean and tight, including that part of the car where the earth attaches to the car body. If all is well here the fault is almost certainly the battery, so you need either a push start or jump leads to a good battery (see page 49).

3. If the engine spins briskly but won't fire, open the bonnet and look – and sniff – for signs of the carburettor flooding. If it is flooding you will have to get your hands dirty. (See page 61).

4. Make sure all the HT (high tension) leads are clean and firmly attached to plugs, distributor, and coil terminals, and that the terminals themselves are clean. Check also that the low tension leads to the coil, and from the coil to the distributor, are firmly attached to their respective terminals, and that the terminals are clean.

The ignition

Ignition faults are dealt with on pages 118-124, and on page 55, but here are a few emergency measures you can take to get going from a roadside breakdown.

If you find that a cracked distributor cap is causing the high tension current to track to earth, thus preventing plugs sparking, use the point of a knife to score down the line of the crack on the inside of the cap. If you have no knife, a small electrical screwdriver will do. Then score across the crack quite deeply at about 6mm ($\frac{1}{4}$in.) intervals. These score marks will act in much the same way as a fire break. If anyone in the car has some hair spray, you can spray this on to the crack to help seal it. Remove the distributor cap first.

Should your test lamp indicate, when testing the current supply from the ignition switch to the coil (see pages 45-46), that no current is reaching the coil, you will have to bridge from the battery direct to the coil input side marked SW (+ on negative earth cars, or − on positive cars). To do this, attach your emergency length of wire to the live battery terminal and the other end to the input side of the coil. Do this with the other battery terminal disconnected, then reconnect it. The freed end of the ignition switch to coil lead should be taped and secured out of the way.

If you do not have a test light and wish to check that current is reaching the coil from the ignition switch, there is one other way to do it. Remove the low tension lead to the coil input terminal and pull back the plastic insulating sleeve so as to bare the spade connector. Switch on the ignition and touch the connector to a bare metal earthing point. If current is flowing there should be a spark.

Damp is one of the great enemies of good ignition. High tension current will always take the line of least resistance, and if there is any moisture deposited on the high tension leads, distributor cap, spark plugs, or coil, the HT current is likely to 'track' to earth, and so there will be no spark at the plugs to fire the mixture in the combustion chambers. This condition will get worse if the components which make up the ignition system are past their best. The cure is to dry all the leads thoroughly, inside and outside the distributor cap, plugs, and coil with a clean dry cloth. A water-repellent aerosol such as WD40 or Wet Start sprayed over all the parts will also help.

Points

Contact breaker points can also be a source of trouble when the engine will not start. If they are very dirty, burnt, or badly pitted they will be unable to do their job properly. Dirty points can be cleaned by inserting a folded piece of fine grade glasspaper between the two faces, and rubbing to and fro for a minute or two. If you have no glasspaper a nail file is a good substitute. This is only a 'get-you-home' measure when the rest of the ignition system is in reasonable order, and the old points should be exchanged for new ones as soon as possible.

Contact breaker points burn quickly if the condenser has failed, and even if it is possible to clean up their faces they will not last long if the condenser is not protecting them against excessive arcing. A temporary measure is to substitute a radio supressor for the one in the distributor, and there is almost bound to be one on the generator which will do.

An important part of distributor maintenance is to keep the contact breaker points properly gapped and, periodically, to smear the distributor spindle cams with petroleum jelly. If this is not done, the plastic – or fibre – 'heel' of the contact breaker points assembly will wear down quickly by the action of the dry cams rubbing away the 'heel' material. The result of this will be that the gap will become progressively smaller and smaller until the points are scarcely opening at all, and the engine will not start. Re-setting the points is fairly straightforward – normally a matter of loosening the retaining screw and levering the arms holding the points apart with a screwdriver, or pressing them closer together, whichever is required. Properly speaking, the gap should be measured with a feeler gauge, but if you are stuck without one the thickness of a playing card is about right.

The starter motor

The faults which affect the starting system can be a jammed or faulty starter motor, a stuck or faulty solenoid, or loose connections. Putting the car in gear and rocking it strongly may free a jammed starter motor. Failing this, try loosening the starter motor retaining bolts and rocking the motor itself.

One other thing which can cause starter problems is the engine earth strap. If this becomes detached, electrical current has to find some other way to complete the circuit and may try to use a wire such as the choke cable or throttle cable. Neither of these are thick enough to carry the sort of current which flows when the starter motor is energised and, apart from the starter refusing to turn, the cables can become red hot, presenting the hazard of fire under the bonnet. Therefore, check that the earth strap is in place. Other starting system faults are dealt with on page 55.

The cooling system

During very hot weather it is possible for some engines to overheat, especially if you are caught in very slow-moving traffic. To help the cooling system cope with the unusual conditions, turn the heater full on and switch the blower on to its fastest speed. It may be a little uncomfortable but this will probably stop the water from boiling. However, this measure will not work if the overheating is due to loss of water because there will be none to circulate through the heater.

Overheating can also be due to a broken fan belt. Although many cars are nowadays equipped with an electric fan, the belt is necessary to drive the water pump to enable water to circulate satisfactorily. A slipping fan belt will have much the same effect.

If the belt is slipping it should be possible, unless it has become badly worn by the slipping action, to rectify the fault by tightening the belt (see page 119).

You should spot a broken fan belt well before the engine overheats because the ignition warning light will come on brightly at all speeds. The time-honoured way of making a temporary belt is to use a nylon stocking or half a pair of tights. To effect this make-shift cure, tie the stocking round the crankshaft and water pump pulleys just enough to lighten the load. The generator pulley takes quite a lot of power to spin it, but provided the battery is in good condition and fully charged you can drive quite a long way without the need to keep a continuous charge, so long as you do not use lights or electrical accessories.

If you notice the temperature gauge going above its normal warm running position for no apparent reason, stop and investigate. So long as the engine has not overheated already, put a piece of cloth over the filler cap to protect your hand and undo it one quarter of a turn, listening carefully. Beware of steam escaping and burning your arm. You should hear a slight hiss and if you do not it means that the spring is weak or the sealing ring has perished, and the correct pressure is not being maintained in the cooling system. The same test can be made on cars with sealed cooling systems but in this case the cap will be on the expansion tank.

Having checked the filler cap, remove it so you can see the water level. The correct level is normally about 25mm (1in.) down from the base of the filler hole. With a sealed system the level in the expansion tank should be about 65mm ($2\frac{1}{2}$in.) up from the bottom, but there will be a level indicator to show the exact position. This is the level when the engine is cold; when it is hot the level will be higher

1 No one likes to be left stranded by an overheating engine. Overheating can, however, be cured by carrying out a step-by-step fault finding procedure on the vehicle which should lead to your car's cooling system being in good condition (see page 56)

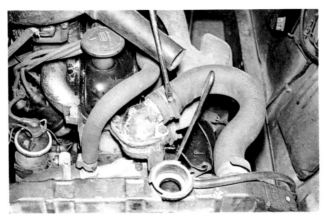

2 The main radiator hose leads from the top of the radiator to the thermostat housing

due to expansion.

If the water level is low you must check for leaks. First look to see if there is any wetness showing and if there is try to find its source. Seepage past hose clips can often be the reason for water loss and the cure is simply a matter of tightening the clips. Seepage past the water pump spindle cannot be cured except by fitting a new pump. A small radiator leak can be cured by using Bars Leaks or Rad Weld. These are preparations which are poured into the radiator and which seek out the leak and block it.

In the event of a top hose splitting, you can make a temporary repair with insulating tape. If you have a piece of foil from a cigarette packet or something similar, position this over the split and bind the hose tightly with the insulating tape. Allow a generous overlap at each end and apply at least two layers of tape.

A thermostat which sticks in the closed position will also cause an engine to overheat since the water circulation will be insufficient to keep the temperature down. A sign of this happening – apart from the reading on the temperature gauge – is a loud thumping noise coming from the radiator. This is caused by a bubble of steam forming in the engine's water jacket and escaping into the radiator through the bottom hose. It is comparatively rare for a thermostat to stick in the closed position but if it does, remove the unit (see page 56) when the engine has cooled down, and drive on without it.

At the roadside it is often easier to release the radiator end of the bottom hose to drain water from the system, rather than the drain plug. Also, it is not always essential to remove the top hose and often the thermostat housing can be left attached.

If you have a leak because of a loose hose clip which cannot be tightened because it is damaged or broken, a temporary repair can be made with binding wire. Put two bands around the hose and twist as tight as you can without breaking the wire.

During summer months, overheating can be caused by the radiator core becoming clogged with dead insects, and dirt, especially if you do a lot of fast long distance driving. The best way to deal with this problem is to get to a garage and use a high-pressure air line to blow the muck out from inside the engine compartment. Failing this, poking the core clear with a piece of wire, also from inside the engine compartment, is laborious but should work. Take care, however, not to damage the core.

An air lock in the cooling system can also be a source of overheating. To cure this, run the engine until it warms up and the thermostat is open – you can check this by feeling the temperature of the top hose. Put the heater controls in

the 'On' position and loosen the clip on the heater return pipe where it joins the water pump or bottom hose. This should be done with the engine stopped to avoid the danger of your fingers being hit by the fan blades. Start the engine again and pull off the heater hose being careful to keep your hand clear of the fan. Should there be any difficulty about this, it is possible to remove the blades on some cars. You cannot take off the fan belt because the water pump will not work. When there is a steady flow of water from the hose, stop the engine and reconnect the hose. Finally, top up the radiator to the correct level.

General tips and make-shift repairs
The following sections contain general advice to bear in mind rather than specific remedies for particular emergencies. Some of the commonest problems are quite easy to overcome with the help of some everyday items and a little ingenuity.

A flat battery
If you have a completely flat battery and another motorist can give you a jump lead start, first of all increase the setting of the throttle stop screw so engine revs will be well above the normal tickover with your foot off the accelerator pedal. This is done so that the generator output will be high enough to keep the cut-out in the control box (see page 120) in the closed position. When the cut-out is closed, current is flowing from the generator into the battery, charging it, as well as supplying power for the ignition. If engine revs are not high enough the cut-out will be open, which means that the battery will be called on to supply the current for the ignition. Since it is flat it will not be able to do so, and the engine will die. After about half an hour's driving, the battery should be sufficiently charged for you to be able to reduce revs to a normal tick-over.

One cause of a poor battery connection of the type which has a 'hooded' terminal (see page 39, fig. 3) is the screw which holds the cap down on the battery points not biting into the post. This can happen if a battery has been taken out and replaced several times. A simple way to get it to hold the cap tightly is to wrap the screw with a piece of cigarette packet foil to act as packing.

The ignition switch
To cure a faulty ignition switch when current is not reaching the coil, make a bridge from the battery to the coil switch terminal with your piece of electrical wire as described on page 39. If current is not reaching the coil, it is quite likely that the ignition switch will not operate the starter motor. If this is the case, either press the solenoid button (see page 51), or by-pass the solenoid as shown on page 52.

Towing
In the unfortunate circumstance of needing to be towed there are certain things to be careful about. First of all the maximum legal length of a tow rope is 4.5 metres (15 ft.). Moreover, the law requires that if the tow rope exceeds 1.5 metres (5ft.) it must be clearly visible. This is usually done by tying a piece of cloth to the middle of the rope.

Next, you must find a suitable part of your car to which to tie the tow rope.

If your car is equipped with a steering column lock, you must turn the ignition to a position which renders the lock inoperative. If you forget, at the first deviation from a straight line the column will lock up with the wheels going to right or left, and it would be very difficult if not impossible to unlock it quickly enough to prevent an accident. You may have to turn the key to the ignition 'On' position, in which case remove the switch (input) lead from the coil and tape it aside so it cannot short to earth.

To tow or be towed well calls for a certain technique. The towing car should always take off from rest very slowly so as to take up slack in the tow rope gently. One should try to keep a constant speed when on the move, and braking or accelerating should be done gradually and as gently as possible. It is a good plan for the towing driver to give an arm signal of his intention to brake before actually doing so, so as to give the towed driver time to react.

The aim of the towed driver should be to attempt to keep the tow rope taut at all times. This will entail using the brakes a good deal even when the towing car is keeping at a constant speed. If the towed driver keeps a watchful eye on traffic conditions ahead he will be able to predict what action the towing driver will take, and will be in a better position to apply the brakes in good time.

Punctures

A puncture is a nuisance at any time but it is particularly irksome when the wheel nuts have been over-tightened in the first place. Various methods of getting extra leverage have been mentioned on page 37, including the iron pipe wheel brace extension which it has been suggested you carry in your basic survival kit. Another way to get added leverage, if you have a couple of flat bars such as tyre levers, is to place one of them across the cranked section of the wheel-brace and to insert the other one at right angles, over the first bar and under the crank of the brace. The iron pipe can be used in place of the second bar.

A scissors-type jack or a 'bottle' jack – the type which is free standing and either winds up on a threaded section or is pumped up hydraulically – can sometimes be used to get the additional pressure needed to loosen the wheel nuts. Most cars have four wheel nuts, and if you get two of them at the nine and three o' clock positions, you can arrange the jack head under the end of an L-shaped wheel brace. Then, holding the brace firmly on the nut, wind up the jack until it is exerting its full pressure under the brace. This may be sufficient to start the nut. Having succeeded with two nuts, roll the car forward until the other two are at nine and three o'clock and repeat the exercise.

A broken throttle spring

This will cause the engine revs to soar and make the accelerator pedal floppy. If you attach one end of a rubber band to the throttle spindle arm and the other end to some part which will allow the band to act as a return spring, you will be able to drive normally. In some cases there may be no convenient part to which to attach the free end of the rubber band, so use a piece of string to tie it to, say, the air cleaner.

Fuses

Should a fuse fail and you have no replacement available, a couple of strands of the electric wire could be used as a substitute. Do not overdo the number of strands you use or this could cause the wiring to become overloaded, heat up, and even catch fire. Remember, too, that a fuse usually blows because of some other fault in the circuit such as a 'short', so if the replacement fails soon after fitting, you should try to trace the fault in the circuit affected.

Windscreen wipers

When a windscreen wiper is fitted to a splined drive spindle, the splines can become damaged if the wiper arm is removed and incorrectly refitted. This can result in relative movement between the mating splines so that in time the drive is lost. Cigarette foil can come to the rescue here if you wrap a strip round the spindle and then fit the arm. Avoid getting the foil pushed down the spindle as this will not give the packing effect required. Another method is to file two grooves in the spindle diametrically opposed to each other and to fit a U-shaped piece of thickish copper wire over the end of the spindle and into the grooves – several strands of electrical wire twisted together will also do. When you press the arm back into place, be sure to position it correctly to give a proper sweep of the screen, because removing it again will be difficult.

Should the wiper blade on the driver's side become damaged and fail to sweep the screen adequately, or comes off the arm altogether and gets lost, replace it with the one on the passenger side.

The exhaust

An exhaust pipe leak can be dangerous because of the carbon monoxide fumes which are poisonous. A leak usually occurs gradually, but it can worsen quite suddenly after a certain point of corrosion has been reached. There are proprietary bandages and pastes on the market to repair such leaks, but if you can get hold of an empty tin you can make a temporary repair. Remove both ends of the tin and slit it down the side – a can opener will do but a pair of tin snips makes the job easy. Wrap the tin tightly round the perforated part of the exhaust pipe and wire it firmly in place. This will not stop the leak entirely but it will minimise the amount of gas escaping.

Exhaust brackets are by no means indestructible and if one breaks you stand the chance of the exhaust pipe dropping off. The only proper remedy is, of course, to replace the bracket, but a temporary measure is to wire it up to one of the broken bracket's securing bolts.

Leaf springs

If the main leaf spring breaks at the centre bolt, the danger is that under the effects of acceleration and braking the rear axle will be able to move. If you are carrying a flat bar or tyre lever, loosen the U-bolts and slide the bar into place, straddling the break, and bolt up as tightly as possible. Use some binding wire to lash the bar to the nest of springs in several places. With this sort of lash-up you must drive with extremely gentle acceleration and braking. If you do not have a flat bar, tighten the U-bolts as much as possible, and lash the piece of iron pipe to the spring nest with binding wire. It must be emphasised that the utmost care must be taken and you should check the splint frequently.

Brakes

When descending a long hill, especially in hot weather, the brakes may suffer what is known as 'vapour lock'. As the brake fluid in the wheel cylinders heats up a point comes a little before it actually boils where the fluid vaporises, and since the vapour is compressible, unlike the fluid, the brake pedal will first become spongy and then go further and further to the floor until eventually there is no braking effect at all. In these circumstances, at the first sign of sponginess you should pull off the road and stop to allow the brakes to cool. This will take some time because of a phenonemon called 'heat soak'. This is caused by the absence of a cooling flow of air which is present when you are on the move, and the fluid will continue to absorb heat from the discs or drums and other associated parts until the metal begins to cool by radiation. When you are satisfied

3 Flexible straps must be replaced before they fail, to avoid placing great train on the remaining exhaust supports

4 To remove a strap, lift the exhaust and prise off the strap using a suitable bar – a large screwdriver will do

5 Fit the new strap to the exhaust first, then lever it over the hook with the bar, as shown here

6 To replace a perished cushion block, undo the bolts which hold it to the fibre strap – penetrating oil will make this easier

7 The nuts are fixed, and cannot be undone. The fibre strap itself may need replacing

8 Car-sickness may be due to a leaky tail-pipe which needs replacement

9 The push-fit extension can improve the car's appearance, as well as being safer

that the metal is cool enough, take the rest of the hill in first or second gear.

Vapour lock is aggravated by the presence of water in the fluid and, over a period of time, this moisture is absorbed through flexible brake hoses. To minimise the chance of vapour lock, brake manufacturers recommend that the fluid should be changed every eighteen months.

The filler cap
Many cars these days are fitted with locking petrol caps and it is not unknown for the lock to go wrong so you cannot remove it when you need petrol. Apart from removing the cap altogether which is difficult, some cars have a short length of flexible pipe connecting the metal pipe from the filler cap to the tank inside the boot. It is held in position by two clips similar to radiator hose clips. If you loosen these and slide the hose up the metal pipe, you will be able to fill the tank from inside the boot.

Winter tips
When a car has to be left out on a frosty night, the door locks may freeze up. There are proprietary lock de-icers, but another way is to heat up the key with a match or cigarette lighter, push it into the lock and wait for a few seconds. The heat of the key will melt the ice and free the lock. The process may have to be repeated two or three times before it works.

Getting a start on an icy slope is usually done by using

sacks under the drive wheels, but the snag is that when you have reached level ground where you do not have the same starting problems, you have to go back to retrieve the sacks. A simple way round this is to tie the sacks to the rear bumper with two lengths of rope so you tow the sacks behind you until it is convenient to stop.

The best way to keep going on snowy or icy roads is to keep in the highest gear possible at all times. This ensures that the drive wheels will have the minimum torque possible for the conditions and will be less likely to spin. You should also avoid accelerating and braking harder than is absolutely necessary.

If the car is trapped by a steep road camber and is getting wheel spin on the snow, disconnect the low tension lead from the ignition switch to the coil at the coil terminal, put the gear lever into first, and try driving out on the starter motor. In this way, the drive wheels will turn very slowly and retain sufficient grip to move the car the few feet necessary to get out of the camber. This method is usually only possible with a battery in very good condition.

The carburettor
If fuel is reaching the carburettor and the ignition system is functioning properly, non-starting or engine failure on the move must be due to deficient carburation.

Carburation problems fall into two categories: too little or too much. As mentioned on page 61, petrol flooding will prevent the engine firing because the mixture can be too rich to burn, or because the spark plugs become wet and cannot start. The first cause will lead to the second.

Carburettor flooding can be due to the needle valve which regulates the flow of fuel from the pump to the float chamber sticking in the open position, or because of an incorrect float level (see page 61). To get at the needle valve the float chamber must first be taken off. In the case of SU carburettors remove the top of the float chamber. The needle valve will be in the body of the carburettor just above the float lever. Unscrew the valve and blow it clean.

Flooding can also be caused by excessive use of the choke and slightly sub-standard ignition combined. In cold weather, if the engine does not fire immediately, do not pump the accelerator pedal wildly in an effort to get a start. This merely squirts excess petrol into the inlet manifold which, combined with a full choke, causes pure petrol to be drawn into the combustion chambers, thus wetting the spark plugs. If non-starting is due to excess fuel, pushing the choke in, pressing the accelerator pedal right to the floor and turning the engine over on the starter for several seconds may get you going. If not the alternatives are either to wait for about half an hour for the plugs to dry out by evaporation, or to take them out and dry them.

Fuel starvation due to petrol not reaching the carburettor is dealt with in this chapter under the heading 'Fuel faults' (page 170). However there is another type of fuel starvation when the carburettor is unable to pass sufficient petrol through its jets to give a correct fuel-to-air mixture. This is due to dirt.

To clear the jets, you will first have to take off the float chamber. In most cases they come off downwards after undoing the retaining screws. With the SU carburettor, however, the float chamber is bolted to the carburettor body and you have to take off the 'lid' after removing three screws.

If the float chamber is empty although petrol is reaching the carburettor, the needle valve has stuck in the closed position. Remove it, clean it with petrol, and make sure it can move freely before putting it back.

If your car is fitted with a fixed jet carburettor such as a Zenith, it is usually possible to remove the brass jets with a screwdriver to clean them. Blow through the jet to get rid of any sediment, or if this is not sufficient poke it clear with a stiff brush bristle. Never use a piece of wire as it may scratch the jet orifice. Whilst cleaning the jets you should also clean the inside of the float chamber.

The Ford carburettor is similar to the Zenith but only its main jet can be removed for cleaning, the others are drillings in the casting. If engine failure is due to dirt, cleaning the main jet will get you home. If you want to do a thorough job later, strip the carburettor, carefully noting where each bit lives, and soak the body in cellulose thinner.

The Zenith CD carburettor, often still known as the Stromberg, has a single jet metered by a tapering needle, and if the float chamber is to be removed without first taking out the needle, great care must be taken to avoid damaging it. The inside of the float chamber can be cleaned out as described above. You will seldom have trouble from jet blockage in this type of carburettor and for all practical purposes this can be ignored.

The SU carburettor is similar to the Zenith CD in the way it meters fuel, but it has a metal piston inside the bottle-shaped top which controls the position of the needle inside the jet, whereas the Zenith has a diaphragm. Also, whereas the Zenith float chamber comes off downwards after undoing six screws, the SU's float chamber is fixed to the carburettor body and access to it is by taking off

10 With the exterior of an SU carburettor clean, the damper rod should be unscrewed and removed. The oil can then be drained

11 Next, remove the screws holding the suction chamber to the main body. There may be two, three or four of these

12 Now lift the chamber straight up and away from the rest of the unit. If it sticks, rotate it slightly in order to free it

13 The piston and spring are now both accessible. Remove them by lifting straight up, taking care not to damage the needle

14 To remove the needle, slacken the small grub screw in the side of the piston. The needle should be examined for signs of wear

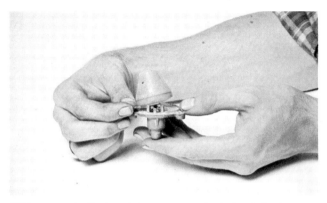

15 To remove the float, so that you can examine it closely for dents or fractures, push out the pin by its non-serrated end

16 Next, you can begin to service the jet linkage. Start by undoing the screw connecting the jet to the choke mechanism

its 'lid'.

The fuel supply from the float chamber to the single SU jet is via a flexible tube, and this can become blocked. To remove this tube detach it from the bottom of the float chamber, taking extreme care. If the float chamber is full and petrol flows out over a hot exhaust manifold, there is danger of fire. Having detached the tube, loosen the jet locknut and draw the jet downwards from its holder. You can then blow the tube clear.

Carburettor flooding can also be caused by the float. In rare cases it may have become punctured, allowing petrol to leak inside. This can be checked by holding the float near your ear and shaking it. If it is punctured you will hear the fuel moving about inside.

A cause of misfiring and stalling can be air leakage past the carburettor flange where it attaches to the inlet manifold, or past the inlet manifold gasket. It may be possible to cure this simply by tightening the relevant nuts but if the gasket has become damaged it will have to be replaced.

If a car with a fixed jet carburettor begins to run bumpily and then stalls, refusing to re-start, the fault could lie in the choke. After a cold start on full choke, it is possible for the choke flap to stick in the closed position so when the engine warms up the mixture is far too rich and it will not run To check this, remove the air cleaner and look into the air intake. When fully open the choke flap should be vertical.

The choke on an SU carburettor operates by pulling the jet downwards which allows more fuel to flow, and if the jet sticks, the mixture will be too rich when the engine warms up. This can be checked visually in the same way.

The Zenith CD has a special enriching valve on the side of the carburettor body and the way to check its action is by observing the position of the choke lever.

HT leads

Another roadside problem which can be circumvented – provided you have the electrical wire and insulating tape suggested earlier – is if a high tension lead needs replacing and you have no HT cable available. Cut off a suitable length of the wire and wrap it thickly with insulating tape

17 All Stromberg carburettors are designed with variable jets. This is the 150CD model

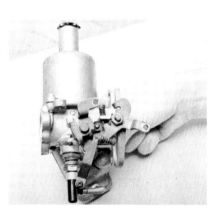

18 SU carburettors are also of the variable jet design. The HS2 model is illustrated

19 The Weber 32 DGV 15B is of the fixed-jet design and is fitted with twin venturi

20 To remove the contacts on a 25D distributor first undo the terminal nut and then, noting their order, slip off the leads

24 Next remove the vacuum advance unit by undoing the two screws which secure the unit to the side of the distributor

21 With the leads and spacers removed the moveable part of the contacts can be lifted off its pivot post for examination

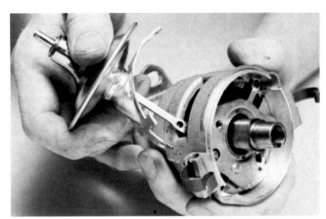

25 Now tilt the distributor downwards so that the vacuum unit actuating lever is disengaged and remove the whole assembly

22 Next, remove the base plate retaining screw so that the fixed part of the contacts can be removed from the distributor

26 The distributor base plate can now be prised out and lifted clear once the two retaining screws have been removed

23 With the points removed, further overhaul of a 45D distributor continues with removing the condenser by undoing its screw

along its entire length and use this as a substitute. If you happen to have a plastic carrier bag, cut off a piece and wrap it around the wire before binding it with insulating tape.

Fuel faults

If the engine hesitates and then dies when you are on the move, there is the possibility of a partial vacuum in the tank preventing the petrol being drawn from it. There is of course, the chance that your fuel gauge is inaccurate and though the dial shows there is petrol in the tank, you have in fact run out. The easiest check for this is to take off the filler cap and to bounce the car vigorously on its suspension whilst listening for the sound of petrol sloshing about in the tank. If you cannot hear the sloshing noise it is likely that you are out of petrol despite what the fuel gauge indicates. Another check is to thread the piece of electrical wire down the filler pipe until you can feel it bottoming. Withdraw it and look for wetness.

If these checks show you do have petrol in the tank you must look for other causes of fuel starvation.

First, detach the fuel pipe where it is attached to the carburettor and then switch on the ignition. On cars which are fitted with electric petrol pumps, fuel should spurt from the detached end immediately – if it does switch off at once.

The majority of cars, however, are equipped with mechanical pumps and this means that the engine will have to be turned over by the starter motor before the pump will work. It is helpful if you have a passenger who can turn the ignition key while you look for the spurt of petrol from the freed end of the supply pipe. On your own it is more difficult. The starter solenoid may have a by-pass plunger (see pages 40-43), in which case you have only to press it to turn the engine over. If there is no plunger, do not attempt to use the screwdriver by-pass method. It is a perfectly reasonable technique for certain purposes but, with petrol vapour in the engine compartment, the sparking which will occur could result in an explosion and fire. In the absence of passenger or by-pass plunger, remove the spark plugs to relieve compression and turn the engine over by pulling on the fan belt.

If no fuel arrives at the freed end of the fuel supply pipe, then you must trace the fault further down the line, starting with the petrol pump.

The petrol pump

When electric pumps refuse to work because the contact points have stuck, a rap on the pump body with the handle of a screwdriver may free them. This, if it works, is only a temporary measure and the points will have to be cleaned or replaced as soon as possible.

With either type of pump, mechanical or electric, if it is not delivering fuel to the carburettor, first detach the supply pipe to the pump. With most cars, the petrol tank is slightly higher than the pump and when the pipe from the tank to the pump is detached, fuel should flow from the freed end. When it does, plug the open end quickly. If it does not flow and you know there is petrol in the tank, either the tank outlet is lower than the pump or there is a blockage. If you have a tyre pump, try blowing through the supply pipe to clear it. In the absence of a tyre pump, blow through it by mouth. This will mean you need a piece of clean rubber tube as so to reach the open end of the supply pipe. Few people carry a spare length of tube, but it may be possible to join the inlet and outlet pipes together – by-passing the pump – and then blow from the carburettor end.

If petrol is reaching the pump from the tank but does not arrive at the carburettor, either the filter is clogged or the pump needs overhaul or replacement. If this is the case you will need professional help.

With electric pumps the current supply may be faulty. To check the electrics, remove the lead to the pump, connect your test lamp between the lead and earth, and switch on the ignition. The bulb should light. If it does not light you must trace the wire back to the ignition switch, looking for shorts, breaks, or loose connections.

With the electric pump, the filter is housed behind the inlet pipe cap which has to be removed to extract the filter. If clean petrol is available, wash the filter gauze clear of dirt; if not, wipe it with a clean non-linting cloth and blow through it. Also remove any dirt from the inlet section.

Mechanical fuel pumps may also suffer from filter clogging. The filter is housed under the domed top of the

pump which must be removed. There are different methods of securing the pump top but it will be easy to see which one is used on yours. Take off the top and you will see the gauze filter. Treat it in the same way as the electrical pump.

You may find it easier to clean the pump if it is first removed from the engine. Assuming both supply and outlet pipes have been detached, take out the two bolts which hold the pump to the crankcase and lift it away from the engine, taking care not to damage the actuating lever. After cleaning the gauze filter, wipe away any sediment from the filter housing body.

The SU mechanical pump has one two-way valve to regulate fuel flow and the AC type two one-way valves, in either case dirt can interfere with the fuel supply. To get at these valves the upper and lower halves of the pump body have to be separated. They are held together (either type of pump) by a series of screws passing through flanges. Some cars are equipped with pumps which cannot be dismantled, except to get at the filter, in which case interior faults cannot be rectified and the pump must be replaced.

Clean all the parts carefully, and while you have the opportunity examine the diaphragm for any sign of damage or porosity. Some AC pumps have the inlet and outlet valves held in place by a retainer plate so that they can be removed for cleaning, whilst others have valves secured by dimps punched into the casting. If you do remove the valves for cleaning, note carefully which way up they are. They are identical except for the way they face, and if you get them the wrong way up the pump will not work. Some petrol pumps, such as those fitted to many Fords, cannot be taken apart like the SU and AC except to get at the filter for cleaning. If there is an internal fault the pump will have to be exchanged.

Assuming the tank to pump section is functioning correctly, the diaphragm is sound, and the pump has been thoroughly cleaned, when reassembled it should work properly. Strictly as a temporary measure, a piece of old inner tube may work satisfactorily as a diaphragm.

27 One of several designs of electric fuel pumps, which need to be removed from the car for servicing. First open the filter housing

28 Remove the cartridge-shaped filter, and clean it and the filter housing thoroughly by brushing them with petrol

Automotive A-Z

The **Automotive A-Z** describes technical terms and phrases found elsewhere in the text which have not already been fully defined. Other technical terms are referred to in the index, which lists the pages on which they are described.

Ball joint

Brake caliper

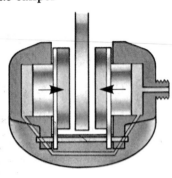

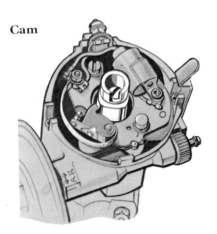

Cam

Accelerator pump A pump in the carburettor which enriches the fuel to air mixture as the throttle pedal is depressed.

Allen key A high tensile steel hexagonal bar with a right angled bend. Either end can be fitted into the hexagonal socket in a screw for removing or tightening the screw. There are different sizes of key to suit different screw sizes.

Alternator A generator, used in most modern cars, which produces alternating current and then converts it to direct current, as distinct from a dynamo which produces direct current. At low engine speeds an alternator has a higher output than a dynamo.

Ammeter An instrument which shows the charge being put into the battery by the generator, or the amount of current being consumed by electrical equipment. A positive (+) reading shows the battery is being charged, a negative (−) reading shows that the battery is discharging.

Anti-roll bar A U-shaped rod which is linked at both ends to the axle or suspension. Its function is to resist body roll by the torsion which is set up in it as the suspension is deflected. See also *Torsion bar*.

Anti-roll rod See *Panhard rod*

Arcing A condition arising when an electrical spark jumps an air gap between two conductors such as the gap between the electrodes of a spark-plug or the points of the contact breaker.

Armature The revolving part of a generator, composed of coils of wire wound round a soft iron core.

Automatic advance The automatic means of varying the number of degrees of engine rotation by which the ignition spark precedes the top dead centre position of a piston on its compression stroke as the engine speeds up or slows down.

Ball joint A joint similar to the human hip, where a ball is able to move in a cup to give multi-directional movement. It is usually to be found on steering and suspension assemblies.

Ball-peen hammer A hammer which has a ball-shaped peen, as opposed to a claw, on the end opposite the striking face.

Ballast resistor A resistor which reduces the voltage from the battery to the ignition coil. Cars fitted with this system have a coil which works on about 8 volts. The resistor drops the battery's 12 volts to the lower figure. During starting, however, the ballast resistor is by-passed and the coil receives the full voltage.

Bell-housing Also known as clutch housing or clutch cover, it is that part of the gearbox which mates with the engine and houses the clutch mechanism.

Bendix drive A system for engaging and disengaging the starter motor. The inertia of a pinion gained by the initial twist of starter shaft throws it into mesh with the flywheel ring gear, thus turning the engine. The shaft is fitted with a coil spring which disengages the pinion when the starter is switched off or when the engine is running.

Bleed nipple A small valve on a wheel brake cylinder or caliper which, when loosened, allows hydraulic fluid to be pumped from the system, either to get rid of air in the system or when changing the fluid. A similar valve will be found on the slave cylinder of a hydraulic clutch system.

Brake caliper An assembly which houses the pistons and brake pads on either side of the brake disc.

Brush A stationary contact which either feeds current to, or draws current from, a commutator in a starter motor, generator, alternator or dynamo.

Bulkhead The part of the car's bodywork which separates the engine compartment from the interior of the car.

Bump start Starting the engine by descending an incline, or having the car pushed, and then engaging gear when on the move, causing the road wheels' motion to turn the engine.

Bundy pipes Pipes, usually of steel, which carry hydraulic fluid to the clutch slave cylinder or the brake flexible hoses from the master cylinder.

Cam The protruding part of a disc or shaft which, by virtue of its eccentricity, imparts movement to another component such as engine valves or contact breaker points.

Capacitor Also known as a condenser or suppressor. An electrical storage device which momentarily stores pulses and then feeds them back into the circuit as in a distributor.

Castellated nut A nut with slots in its crown so it can be locked by a split pin or wire.

Choke A restriction in the carburettor throat to restrict airflow, thus enriching the mixture, during engine starting and warming-up periods. Also used to describe other enriching devices such as those found on SU and Stromberg carburettors.

Circlip A spring steel locating or securing clip in the form of a split ring which fits into a groove in a spindle, or an internal groove in a hollow component.

Condenser See *Capacitor*

Contact brush There are two types. A spring loaded carbon 'pencil' which bears on a brass plate on top of the rotor arm in the distributor, or a fixed metal stud which is contacted by sprung contact on top of the rotor arm.

Compression stroke The second movement of the piston in a four-stroke cycle, when the piston is rising to compress the induced fuel mixture with both inlet and exhaust valves closed.

Conductor Any material or component capable of carrying an electric current.

Crankcase The lower part of the engine which encloses the crankshaft and to which the sump is bolted.

Crankcase breather A device which allows gas pressure in the crankcase to be ventilated. In modern cars the gas is recycled into the air cleaner on the carburettor.

Crankshaft A component in the lower part of the engine incorporating offset journals to convert the reciprocating movement of the pistons into rotary motion to power the transmission.

Crown wheel and pinion Final-drive arrangement in which a large bevel wheel (the crown wheel) engages in a smaller bevel (the pinion) so that the direction of the rotation of the propeller shaft is turned through 90° to drive the road wheels.

Cylinder block Iron or alloy casting in which the cylinders are accommodated.

Cylinder head An iron or alloy casting bolted to the block which accommodates the valves, valve seats, spark-plugs and the combustion chambers.

Damper Also called a shock absorber. A device used in a suspension system to absorb up and down oscillations of the springing caused by road bumps.

Dashboard See *Fascia*

Diaphragm A membrane, usually of reinforced rubber, which separates one side of a chamber from another, as found in petrol pumps and some other components such as Stromberg carburettors.

Differential A gear combination, part of the final drive, which permits the difference in speed of rotation of the inner and outer driven wheels when the car is taking a corner.

Disc brake A braking system where friction pads press against a disc, usually of cast iron.

Dolly A heavy piece of hardened metal with a curved surface. Usually used as an anvil for panel beating,

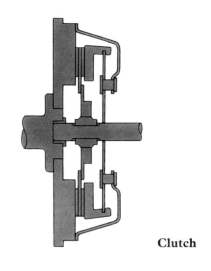

Clutch

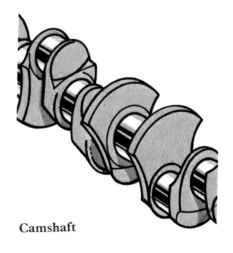

Camshaft

Differential

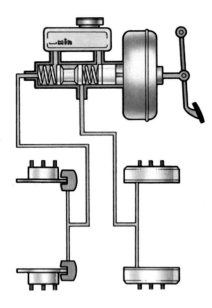

Dual master cylinder

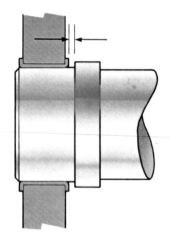

End float

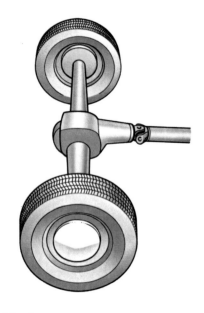

Final drive

being held against one side of a metal panel while it is dressed by a hammer from the other.

Drift A metal rod of steel, brass, or copper used to remove or insert units which are an interference fit in their housings.

Drum brake An internal expanding brake where the friction linings are forced outwards to contact the inside of the revolving drum on the car's wheel.

Dual master cylinder Also called a tandem master cylinder. It has two separate hydraulic elements, one of which works on the front wheels while the other operates the rear brakes or, in some cases, one front wheel and one rear, diagonally opposed.

Dynamo A generator driven by the engine, producing direct current to charge the battery. Excess current is available for other electrical equipment.

Dynamometer See *Rolling road*

Earth The return path for current flowing from the battery to any power-consuming equipment. In most cases this is through the metal structure of the car's body and chassis. This 'earth return system' is so called because the negative terminal of the battery (except on some older cars) is connected to the body.

Electrode A conductor by which current enters or leaves a device. Spark-plugs, for example, have a central and a side earth electrode.

Electronic ignition An ignition system in which a transistorized unit makes and breaks the primary current to the coil. In some systems, the ordinary contact breaker is retained, but merely acts as a switch to interrupt a small non-inductive current in the transistor base circuit. In fully transistorized systems, the current switching is done by a photo-electric cell and an interrupted light source.

End float The amount of possible movement in a rotating direction of any shaft, hub, or other axial component, as limited by its bearings or relating devices. For example, the

end float of a crankshaft is limited by shoulders which bear against the mating surfaces of one or more of the main bearings.

Exhaust manifold Usually a cast iron component which is bolted to the cylinder head and through which exhaust gases flow into the exhaust pipe.

Fascia Also called the dashboard. The panel immediately below the windscreen in which are mounted the dials, switches, and other instruments.

Feeler gauge A strip of hardened steel of precise and uniform thickness used to measure the gap between two adjacent surfaces such as contact breaker points.

Filler A material which, when mixed with an appropriate agent, is used to fill dents and scratches in the car's bodywork.

Final drive The ultimate stage in the transmission of engine power to the driving wheels in which the direction of drive is converted from longitudinal to transverse (except with transverse engines). It incorporates the differential.

Fixed jet carburettor A simple carburettor which has a fixed choke, one or more plain jets and a compensating system, to maintain the correct mixture strength throughout the engine speed range.

Flatting The process of rubbing down bodywork to obtain a uniform surface for painting. The flatted surface also provides a key to improve paint adhesion.

Float chamber The reservoir which supplies fuel to the carburettor. It maintains a constant level through the action of a float which, when the chamber is full, presses against a valve, shutting off the fuel supply from the pump.

Fly-wheel A heavy metal disc attached to the crankshaft which, by virtue of its inertia, stores some of the energy from each power stroke to enable the crankshaft to continue to turn during the non-power part of the combustion cycle. It provides a driving face for the clutch and ring gear in which the starter motor pinion meshes.

Freeplay The movement of any device which takes place before positive action occurs as, for example, the movement of a clutch pedal before disengagement begins.

Gaiter A rubber sleeve which fits over a component to protect it from dirt and water.

Gasket A thin sheet of metal, paper, or fibrous material which is inserted between two mating surfaces. By taking up any irregularities in the two surfaces it prevents the escape of any water, gas, or fuel.

Gasket sealer Also called gasket cement. A paste-like preparation which, when spread on either side of a gasket, assists the sealing effect of the gasket.

Grille An ornamental panel in front of the radiator (or engine in the case of transverse engines) which is perforated to allow the passage of air when the car is on the move.

Halfshaft A shaft which connects each rear wheel of a rear wheel drive car to the differential in the rear axle.

Header tank The upper tank of the radiator which, on non-sealed cooling systems, incorporates the pressurising filler cap. With sealed systems, the header tank has a plug, the pressure cap being on the overflow tank.

High tension Usually described as HT. This is the high voltage current which comes from the secondary winding in the coil and is distributed by the distributor to the spark-plugs.

Hydraulics The action of fluids in motion. With the car, it primarily describes the operation of clutch and brakes by a fluid.

Inertia The reluctance of a moving body to slow down or a stationary body to be set in motion by an external force. A stationary car has inertia as does a rotating fly-wheel.

Impact hammer Also known as a slide hammer. A tool with claws (usually three) at one end to grip a component such as a hub, and a handle at the other. A heavy weight slides along the rod which joins the two ends. As the weight is pushed down the rod, its impact will jar the component loose.

Inlet manifold Similar to an exhaust manifold except that it conducts the air/fuel mixture to the inlet valves in the cylinder head.

Induction The stroke of an internal combustion engine when the piston travels down the cylinder, drawing the air/fuel mixture into the combustion chamber.

Jacking points Specially provided points where the car's jack can be engaged, or points where a nonstandard jack can be applied without danger of distorting the car's bodywork, steering, or suspension.

Jump leads Heavy cables, usually coloured red and black to distinguish positive (red) from negative (black). They feed current from a fully charged battery through a flat one to provide current to start an engine. This is best done when the donor car has its engine running.

Junction box An electrical device used for connecting two sections of wiring. Those which are fused are more often known as fuse boxes.

King pins Hardened steel rods mounted vertically in the steering mechanism about which the stub axle turns.

Lap To use an abrasive paste between two metal surfaces, rubbing one against the other, to achieve a perfect fit. For example, 'grinding-in' valves by using carborundum paste between the valve face and the valve seat, and rotating the valve to and fro.

Lobe The projecting part of an otherwise circular disc (see *Cam*).

Low tension Usually described as LT. Low voltage current supplied by the battery to the ignition coil primary windings.

MacPherson strut A form of independent suspension where the coil springing is arranged concentrically around the hydraulic damper. This is only used on front wheels.

Mandrel A rod which can be used for many different purposes in engineering but, as far as motor cars are concerned, it is normally associated with a tool for centering the clutch driven plate. A whittled down broom-handle may suffice.

Fly wheel

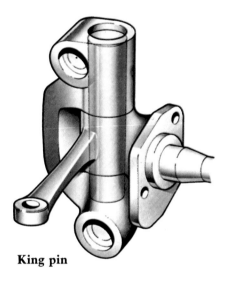

King pin

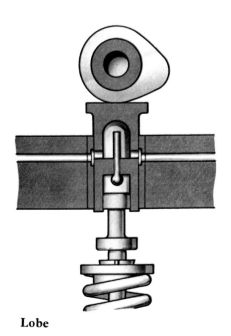

Lobe

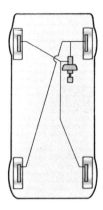

Tandem master cylinder
see *Pressure differential*

Needle valve

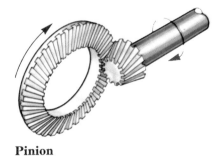

Pinion

Master cylinder The part of a hydraulic system which acts as a pump, forcing fluid through pipes to brake calipers, wheel cylinders, or clutch slave cylinders.

Matrix The part of a radiator which passes water from the header tank to the bottom tank, or moves it through the heating element in the car's internal heater.

Multi-function switch A switch which controls more than one component. Usually mounted on the steering column, a stalk allows the driver to operate the direction indicators, headlamp flasher, main beam and dip, and in some cases the horn.

Needle valve A device which is triggered by the float in the carburettor's float chamber. When the float chamber is full the float rises, like a ball-cock in a cistern, and presses against the needle valve which then cuts off the supply of fuel from the pump.

Oil gallery The part of the lubrication system which conveys oil to parts high up in the engine such as the rocker shaft in an overhead valve unit.

O-ring A ring of rubber or plastic inserted in an aperture to prevent leakage of a fluid.

Panhard rod Also known as an anti-roll rod. A diagonal stay attached to the rear axle on one side and to the chassis on the other to control lateral movement of the body.

Pinch bolt A bolt which bridges a split in a component, such as the small end of a connecting rod. The pressure exerted when the bolt is tightened narrows the split, thus securing the component to a pin or spindle.

Pinion The smaller of two gear wheels which mesh with each other. See *Crown wheel and pinion*.

Power assisted A method of increasing the mechanical advantage of a device. It is applied to brakes where the foot pedal pressure is increased by the vacuum in the inlet manifold acting through a servo device. Also in the steering, where the assistance comes from a pump acting hydraulically.

Printed circuit Made by bonding a thin sheet of copper to a board of insulating material, printing the required circuit on the copper with an acid-resistant fluid, and then etching the unprotected copper away, leaving the printed circuit. Found behind the fascia, it controls many of the car's electrical systems.

Pressure differential warning light A light mounted in the fascia which warns the driver if the pressure on one side of a tandem (dual) braking system drops below that of the other.

Propshaft The propeller shaft. A hollow tube with universal joints at each end – and sometimes another joint in the middle – which joins the gearbox to the differential.

Rack steering A steering mechanism where a pinion on the end of the steering column engages teeth on a rack, the rack itself being extended by track rods to the wheels.

Radius rod A rod attached to the rear axle casing at one end and to the chassis at the other to ensure the correct location of the axle.

Relay An electro-magnetic device for switching current where the manually operated switch is too weak to carry the current required by the consumer unit. The solenoid in the starter motor circuit is a form of relay.

Resistance Electricity is the flow of electrons within a conductor and resistance is the degree of obstruction to the electron flow put up by the conductor. Resistance is measured in *ohms*. If a wire is too small to carry the current required by a consumer unit, its resistance will be high and it will overheat. The filament of a bulb glows white hot because of the resistance it puts up.

Rheostat A variable resistance used to vary the amount of current being fed to a consumer unit. Some fascia lights are controlled by a rheostat so the lights can be varied from bright to dim.

Ring gear A ring of teeth on a fly-wheel in which the starter motor pinion meshes when starting.

Rocker cover Also known as the rocker box. A box which is attached to the top of the cylinder head, housing the rocker arms which operate the valve train.

Rolling road An apparatus to measure the power output of an engine, more correctly known as a dynamometer. It consists of rollers set in a garage floor on which the car's driving wheels can turn. Resistance, usually hydraulic, can be applied to the rollers to simulate road conditions. In the case of brake testing, the rollers are mechanically rotated so the retarding effect of the car's brakes can be measured.

Rotor arm The arm – or in some cases disc – inside a distributor which distributes the HT current to the appropriate spark-plug. This ignites the fuel/air mixture just before the end of the compression stroke.

Self-tapping screw A hardened metal screw which can cut its own thread when screwed into a drilled hole.

Shim A thin metal plate inserted between two faces to maintain a pre-determined clearance. Shims are of varying thickness and more than one may be used to achieve the proper clearance.

Sill The part of a car's bodywork which extends between the front wheel arch and the rear, below the door level. It is usually a box-section.

Shock absorber See '*Damper*'

Slide hammer See *Impact hammer*

Slip ring A component consisting of rotating contacts, similar to a commutator, but used where no commutating of current is required. A slip ring in an alternator collects alternating current via brushes and this is rectified to direct current by diodes. A diode only allows current to flow in one direction, hence the direct current rectification.

Slave cylinder A cylinder which receives hydraulic pressure from the master cylinder and reacts to it. In the case of a clutch, the reaction is to move a plunger which operates mechanically on the clutch fork.

Spacer Similar to a shim, a spacer keeps components a pre-determined distance apart. For example, spacers are fitted between the inner and outer bearings on an axle.

Spigot bearing A bearing, usually of oil impregnated phosphor-bronze, in the end of the crankshaft. The end of the gearbox main shaft fits into it to provide forward end support for the main shaft.

Split pin A pin split along its length and terminating in a small loop, used for locking a castellated nut or similar item in place. The tail of the pin can be opened out so it cannot be shaken free by vibration.

Spring shackle A small plate which is attached to a leaf spring at one end and to the chassis at the other, thus allowing the spring to extend fore and aft under the influence of road shocks due to bumps or potholes.

Stillson Normally referred to as a 'pair of Stillsons' although it is one tool. This is a wrench with adjustable jaws which, when applied to a stubborn nut tightens its serrated jaws as force is applied to the handle. Although the nut – or bolt – can often be freed, the bite of the serrations usually mangles the item to which the wrench is applied.

Stromberg A constant-vacuum carburettor operating through a needle sliding in a jet. As engine speed increases the needle rises to allow more fuel to be drawn in through the intake. The height of the needle varies for different engine speeds ensuring a constant fuel/air ratio. This carburettor is now known as the Zenith CDSET.

Stub axle The short axle found on the front swivel axle or king pin assembly on to which the wheel bearings are located within the wheel hubs.

SU Another form of variable jet or constant-vacuum carburettor. The initials stand for Skinners Union, the small family firm of G.H. and T.C. Skinner who manufactured them.

Tail pipe The part of the exhaust system at the rear end through which the exhaust gases escape. Chromium plated trim can be fitted.

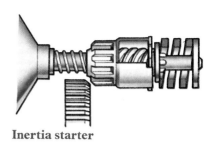

Inertia starter

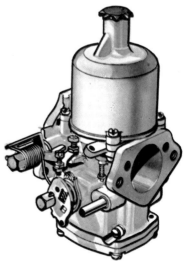

Spacer

SU carburettor

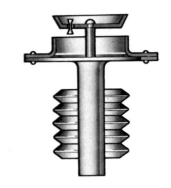

Thermostat

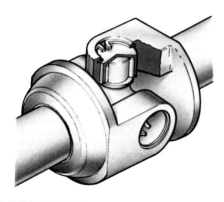

Universal joint

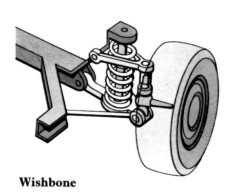

Wishbone

Tandem master cylinder A hydraulic master cylinder which is split into two sections, one serving both front brakes and the other the rear. In some cases the split is diagonal to the offside front brake and to the nearside rear.

Tandem master cylinder See *Dual master cylinder*.

Thermostat A self-actuating device for regulating temperature, as in a car's cooling system.

Thermal metal strip A metal strip usually composed of two metals having different coefficients of expansion. When an electrical current passes through it, it heats up and distorts, returning to its original state as it cools. This type of device is found in many components – the direction flasher unit, for example.

Through bolts Long bolts which pass through the body of a generator or starter motor, holding the end plates in position.

Thrust race A ball bearing inside the clutch housing which bears upon the release mechanism when the clutch pedal is depressed, thus disengaging it. In some cars the thrust race is a carbon disc.

Torque The force exerted by twisting action as with an engine.

Torsion bar Any metal bar or rod which, when twisted, exerts a reactionary force to return to its former state. Some cars have torsion bar suspensions.

Trim A word used loosely to describe exterior bodywork embellishments such as chromium-plated strips, and interior fitments such as door furnishings.

U-bolt Any U-shaped bolt such as those which secure leaf springs to the rear axle, or the inner universal couplings of some front wheel drive cars.

Universal joint A joint consisting of a cruciform member connecting two forks or yokes. This arrangement allows rotary motion to be transmitted when a shaft is out of alignment with another. It is believed to have been invented by Robert Hooke in the mid 17th century. Commonly referred to as a UJ.

Vane An arm on a spindle which is driven by, or drives, a fluid, as in an oil or water pump.

Venturi The intake throat of a carburettor named after an Italian who designed its shape in 1790.

Vice-grip wrench A tool similar to a pair of pliers but having a locking device so that it can be securely clamped on to a component such as a nut, bolt, or stud.

Warning light A light on the fascia to alert the driver to the fact that a function is or is not taking place. The commonest are oil pressure, generator (often called the ignition light), direction indicators, and headlamp main beam. Warning lights may also monitor many other components.

Water jacket The hollow space between the outer wall of the cylinder block and the cylinders, as well as in the cylinder head, through which the coolant is pumped under pressure.

Wet-and-dry paper Carborundum coated paper used for rubbing down paintwork. It comes in different grades of coarseness and can be used dry or with water to act as a lubricant.

Wiring loom Also known as wiring harness. A bundle of wires in the car's wiring system, bound together by some form of outer sheath. There may be one or more for a complete installation.

Wishbones A form of suspension consisting of two forked arms. The inner ends of the wishbones are hinged on the body and the outer ends to the king pins or swivel axle. A coil spring with one end bearing on a transaxle and the other on the lower arm of the wishbone assembly provides the springing. A damper is often fitted inside the coil spring.

Yoke The forked end of a shaft between the arms of which a cruciform trunnion is fitted. The other arms of the cruciform fit between the fork of another shaft so that rotary motion can take place when the shafts are at an angle to one another.

Zenith A carburettor designed by Francois Baverey in 1907 as a fixed jet unit. In an advanced design it is still widely used.

Acknowledgements and where to buy it

We wish to thank the following for their help in supplying materials and/or labour for photography in this book:

Fluid levels, pages 11-17:
R. J. Krafft Auto Services,
253 Gipsy Road,
Crystal Palace,
London SE27

Fibreglassing, pages 28-33:
W. David & Sons Ltd,
Northway House,
High Road,
Whetstone,
London N20 9LR

Gear linkages, pages 80-86:
Quadrant Garages (Osborn) Ltd,
The Quadrant,
Finchley Road,
London NW4

Brakes, pages 87-92:
Central Motors Ltd,
Canterbury Road,
London NW6

Wiring diagrams, pages 125-130:
Citroen Cars Ltd,
Mill Street,
Slough,
Berks

Datsun UK Ltd,
Datsun House,
New Road,
Worthing,
Sussex

Peugeot Automobiles UK Ltd,
Peugeot House,
Western Avenue,
Acton,
London W4 0RS

Robert Bosch Ltd,
Rhodes Way,
Radlett Road,
Watford,
Herts WD2 4LB

Ford Motor Co. Ltd,
Eagle Way,
Warley,
Brentwood,
Essex CM13 5BW

Passing the roadworthiness test, pages 137-152:
Britax Ltd,
Chertsey Road,
Byfleet,
Surrey KT14 7AW

Rustproofing, pages 23-27:
Rustex rustproofing kit from
Sound Service Ltd,
55 West End,
Witney,
Oxon

Rust repairs, pages 28-33:
Jenolite rust killer from
Duckhams Oils,
Summit House,
Glebe Way,
West Wickham,
Kent
and accessory shops, garages and hardware stores

Plastic padding body filler from
Plastic Padding Ltd,
Sands Industrial Estate,
High Wycombe,
Bucks,
and auto accessory shops

Duplicolor aerosol car paint from
Lloyds Industries,
Lloyds House,
Handforth,
Wilmslow,
Cheshire
and auto accessory shops and garages

Fibreglassing, pages 28-33:
Isopon P40 and P38 from
W. David & Sons Ltd,
Northway House,
High Road,
Whetstone,
London N20 9LR
and accessory and hardware stores

Non-driven wheel bearings, pages 93-98:
High melting point grease from
Burmah-Castrol Company,
Burmah House,
Pipers Way,
Swindon,
Wilts
and garages

Bearing fit compound from
Loctite (UK) Ltd,
Watchmead,
Welwyn Garden City,
Herts AL7 1JB
and motor factors

Interior cleaning, pages 153-156:
Hide Food from
Connelly Bros (Curriers) Ltd,
39-43 Charlton Street,
Euston Road,
London NW1 1JE
and some accessory shops

Index

Figures in italics refer to illustrations

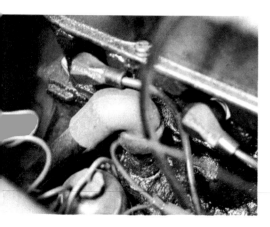

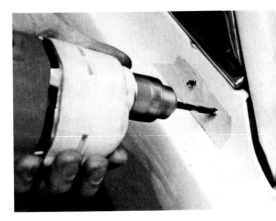

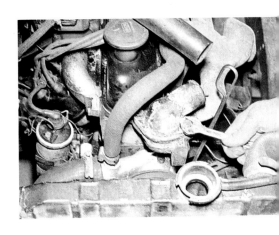

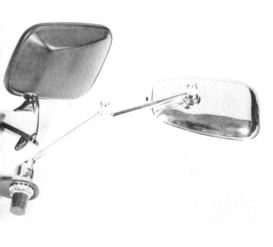